# STAY *Me* WITH

A couple's very public
journey through
HPV cancer

# Mikal Gilmore & Elaine Schock

**COOL**
TITLES

# C🕶L titles

Published by
Cool Titles
439 N. Canon Dr., Suite 200
Beverly Hills, CA 90210
www.cooltitles.com

The Library of Congress Cataloging-in-Publication Data Applied For

Mikal Gilmore, Elaine Schock—
Stay With Me: A Couple's Very Public Journey Through HPV Cancer

p.     cm
ISBN 978-1-935270-48-5
1. Autobiography  2. Entertainment and Performing Arts
3. Cancer and Medical
I. Title
2019

Printed in the United States of America


3  5  7  9  10  8  6  4  2


Book editing and design by White Horse Enterprises, Inc.


For interviews or information regarding special discounts for bulk purchases,
please contact cindy@cooltitles.com

Distributed by Cool Fulfillment: fulfillment@cooltitles.com

*Disclaimer: All lyrics, quotes, article reprints, etcetera are written "as is,"
and no changes have been made to correct grammar or punctuation.

## DEDICATION

For those who have loved and lost someone to cancer.

*May everyone live / And may everyone die*
*Hello, my love / And my love, Goodbye*
—"Here it Is," by Leonard Cohen and Sharon Robinson


*Should my heart not be humble*
*Should my eyes fail to see*
*Should my feet sometimes stumble*
*On the way, stay with me*
—"Stay With Me," by Carolyn Leigh and Jerome Moross

# FOREWORD

MIKAL AND I MET IN late 1977. He had come from Portland to Los Angeles to get away from an awful moment in his history that became the basis for his award-winning 1994 book, *Shot in the Heart*.

For those who do not remember, his brother Gary shot two young men to death in Utah in the summer of 1976. He was sentenced to death, and instead of fighting it, he demanded his own execution. The state was happy to oblige. Relatives and others, including novelist, playwright, film-maker, actor, and political activist Norman Mailer, became identified with the circus that became Gary Gilmore's death march. There was even a love story—a Romeo and Juliet element: Gary had committed the murders in part because his girlfriend, Nicole, had left him. By the time he was on death row the two had reconciled, and reached a suicide pact, though their attempt failed.

The news cycle went into overdrive. No one had been executed in the United States since the Supreme Court suspended the death penalty in 1972 because of the arbitrariness of the law. But a more conservative Court reinstated it in 1976. Gary insisted that Utah be the first state to implement it, and he picked a firing squad to do the job. Gary was convicted of first-degree murder in November and was executed on January 17, 1977.

Mikal did his best to stop his brother's death, but that was impossible. He fought the US Supreme Court and lost. The weight of that decision rested on his shoulders, and it showed. Everyone in America was aware of this battle. They all knew who Gary Gilmore was—and perhaps Mikal Gilmore, as well.

That year, I came back from England after working illegally for three years in the press office of Island Records. I had gone to London on a lark after high school with one hundred dollars in my pocket, and just stayed. London was everything I had read about in magazines. I loved the fashion and music, and, for some crazy reason, I fit in perfectly and got a job in the music business right away. I was seventeen years old. So much for my dream of being a criminal profiler. This was way more fun, and it paid. I didn't have much to lose so I didn't take it seriously when the Home Office—the British office responsible for immigration—started to hound me. Finally, they gave me forty-eight hours to get out of town, or they would take the necessary steps to deport me. Time to head back to my parents' apartment in North Hollywood. To be honest, I was pretty sick of looking over my shoulder for the intimidating home officers. They would just show up at my door. So, I took my overweight cat and obliged. I didn't have any belongings except for a few clothes. It was an easy move and I never looked back.

In California, I got a job as a publicist at a label called Casablanca, whose biggest artist was Donna Summer. Mikal was employed by *Rolling Stone* then, and his first cover story was on Donna. I liked him the moment I saw him waiting for me in the lobby. I even flirted a bit, but he didn't call me. Then I met someone else. Almost directly after that Mikal rang to ask me out.

Timing is everything, and he was late. Not that this mattered much to me, but to be honest, he had a lot of baggage: groupies, stalkers, Mailer's best-selling book about his brother, a TV movie (also about his brother), death threats, and a lot of curious eyes. Still there was something between us that everyone could see. I guess you could call it chemistry.

We became best friends, after he forgave me for marrying someone else. I divorced my first husband and married again, and had three children. During all of this I became a successful publicist in New York, and then Los Angeles, handling some of the biggest artists in the world, including Bob Dylan, Sinead O'Connor, Billy Joel, and Willie Nelson, to name just a few.

Mikal married for a short time, but it was ill-fated and he had no children. He believed he wanted a family but never had one until me. I came fully equipped. Twenty-five years after our first encounter, we became lovers in October, 2001. I remember Mikal had to finish a story on Bob Dylan before he arrived for our first official date. I couldn't believe he couldn't complete the story after. I mean, we had waited all these years. I almost broke it off before it began, and am so glad I didn't. We were married on September 19, 2009.

Almost exactly six years later my husband was diagnosed with HPV-related stage IV cancer of the tongue and throat. We didn't know if he would survive—and there is no stage V. If he did make it, he would require treatment. We were given only a few choices because there was no real research on this type of cancer and recovery. This cancer is transmitted through a sexually transmitted disease, HPV, and it is treated as if the patient was a smoker and had gotten cancer in the same area of the body. It's *not* the same.

We decided to go with the most aggressive and proactive chemotherapy and radiation, because it gave us the best chance. It wasn't easy, as you will read in these pages, but we believe we got through it. I hope it gives you some knowledge.

This is an honest account of living through that experience. We did our best to face each day with grace. We meant it when we said, "Till death us do part," but sometimes, dealing with cancer wasn't the hardest part.

—Elaine Schock

We began this book when I was dying. I didn't anticipate either undertaking. When my doctors told me, in the autumn of 2015, that I had stage 4 HPV-related cancer, I'd begun envisioning what my fading might be like even before I left the hospital parking lot. I thought, "Well, at least I know how all this—this life—ends. There's no more mystery, no more fear of uncertainty." When, an hour later, I told my wife Elaine what the doctor said, she decided differently. She determined to understand everything about my specific malady and, if possible, change my fate. "I want my husband back," she'd said.

I still thought I was looking at the closing of the light, and the closing of the dark as well. There was nothing more to learn. There was just remaining time—a chance to be as good to others as I could manage. I couldn't continue to write. I'd tried, but I was too viciously sick. I planned to tell only a few people beyond our family (my oldest brother, Frank, was missing at the time, and had been for twenty years). I would also inform a couple of friends. My agent. My editors. I did not want to announce it publicly—that is, in our sphere of several thousand Facebook friends.

Again, Elaine felt differently. She urged me to disclose my condition. I was reluctant. I was afraid of sympathy, and I was resistant of the prospect of detailing my decline in the way I had examined the ends of so many artists and public figures I'd studied over the years. Dying itself didn't scare me, but scrutinizing the particulars of cancer might undo me.

When my father was dying of colon cancer in 1962, my mother told my brothers and me not to talk about it with anyone; it just wasn't done in polite society. She also demanded us not to inform my father of what the doctors had found, why he was incapacitated, sleeping constantly but fitfully, spitting a viscous mucus onto newspapers beside his bed that I replaced hourly. He died without knowing he was dying, or what it was that was killing him.

My mother had insisted that it was lung cancer, as the reality of colon cancer seemed sullied to her. Cancer itself was a bad enough stigma. I didn't learn about the true nature of my father's cancer until the early 1990s, when I was researching my family's hidden history for *Shot in the Heart* and obtained his medical records. I was stunned. I was honest on the page when I wrote about it, but that shade of shame, instilled by my mother, still lingered.

Now, knowing I had cancer—a cancer that was likely the result of specific sexual activity—the shame returned. I wanted to go in a concealed way. I soon came to realize, though, that Elaine needed this to be a public conversation. There were no support groups for my kind of cancer, and she was carrying a heavy burden. She needed our friends to help her as she helped me.

So, in October 2015 I announced my diagnosis on Facebook, along with details about the treatment I would undergo, starting in a few days. The response was overwhelming—it was heartening, for both Elaine and me. I still preferred not to post about the daily struggle myself, but Elaine began to write regular missives. They were always met with hundreds of smart, knowing, and helpful responses, though also many scared ones. Our friends were on pins and needles as they followed her accounts. Some people suggested non-medical alternate treatments, but Elaine had no patience for that.

What developed was our public dialogue about the seasons of dying, recovery, and uncertain days ahead. This turned me into a writer again, and it awakened Elaine's innate writing gifts as well. All of this—the medical treatment and our ongoing record of it—depended on her incentive, dependability, and candor. Elaine led the way.

As we went along we realized another cancer was at work, eating away at the American spirit, and we talked sometimes about that, too. Some days and nights it overwhelmed us almost as much as my disease. Then, somebody we both loved very much, David Bowie, died of cancer, and I was asked to write about that. I was still in treatment; I was enfeebled, sleeping fitfully, moving like a 108-pound stick. Elaine worried about what might happen to me physically and mentally if I took on the task. But I took it on.

In some ways cancer has been a blessing to us. We reveal that here. Not everything in these pages is about life and death—there are remarks about events and news, about music and movies, there are jokes, dialogue about family and travel, and there are fears and hopes. Not everything here is about life and death—except it is.

      —Mikal Gilmore

BEFORE

AUGUST
2015

## Mikal Gilmore
### August 27, 2015

Something is going on with me—I can see it in the mirror, and my premonitions tell me that I am in for a reckoning. If so, it is information that I am not yet willing to share. Maybe I never will be. My feeling is such that I have to stay back from it, take time to process. So, I revert to something that has been (next to my wife, Elaine Schock), the greatest joy of my life: music.

Music has kept me company in the hours when nobody else could or would—and not simply because I have worked as a popular music critic and journalist since 1974, when I was twenty-three, but because, long before that, music gave me spirit and spoke for feelings and ideas that I was discovering. It helped shape my aesthetics, my sense of history, and my emotional memories of all sorts: romantic losses, family deaths, social anger and political convictions.

Music—which for me has been the rock 'n' roll and jazz I grew up with, then the blues antecedents I was learning about, and in time symphonies, operas, string quartets, Indian music, and avant-garde. It became a wide and endless set of influences, revelations and stories—not just the story a song was telling, but the story as told or implied by the voice singing it, or, importantly, the story of the artist expressing the music.

Most of those people made the world a better place, even if their own lives were fucked up. Music might be the only thing that redeemed their plight or bad character; it allowed them to enact the deepest truths they could, music for them was something like it was for the listeners; recompense for all the ways life let you down or the ways in which you failed yourself and others. Music has been the world to me, operating on those levels that religion, philosophy, literature and history also performed, except music could embody and deepen all those forms in one deft moment—one turn of a lyric, one breath of a singer or saxophone, one guitar line that was like a Joycean line of thought or an epiphany that didn't end, kept on going until it exhausted the possibilities—then extended that search again the next night.

Fucked up people might be making or listening to all that, and that made for deeper empathy and connections for us all. In the musical church or school, justice and freedom and arguments weren't under the province and rules of authority; instead, they were in the dominion of something far more mysterious: the internal world that knew how to fashion and hear sounds that could embolden at the same moment that it enfranchised communities that authority despised or feared and wanted to contain.

So right now, in this moment, and other moments to come, I am putting aside what I saw in the mirror this morning (a bad intimation of days ahead) to bear witness to and ask questions about music while I still can: Does rock 'n' roll have greatest moments? Pinnacle songs or words or musical blasts that forever metamorphose you, and still save and elevate you years later? Yes, it has a multitude, depending on the years, the context of history, and each listener's pleasures in her or his own myriad instances of critical aesthetic and political knowledge: *This* right here offers the greatest bolt of excitement and enlightenment I've known. Then again, so does *this* one. I was born in time for rock 'n' roll's explosion—I remember Elvis on the Dorsey show—and I'll consider myself a failure if I don't, in some way, die in its thrall.

I've written more than a few times about Bruce Springsteen's music. I tend to spend seasons caught up in batch listening, playing certain albums, tracks, and videos by artists, or from certain movements and times, over and over. Each repeat amounts to a new understanding. One thing, though, hasn't changed for me in recent months, or in the last forty years: the lift and release that comes a couple of minutes into 1975's *Born to Run*'s opening track, "Thunder Road."

In the moments leading up, Springsteen is inveigling a woman, Mary, offering seduction and promise despite her doubts, until she dances across the front porch and makes her way into the front seat of his car, The band has been romantic thus far—Mozart, Roy Orbison, Bob Dylan's "I Want You"— then the drums surge forward big and fast, opening everything into widescreen black & white, and the singer announces his promise and dream: *What else can we do now / Except roll down the window / And let the wind blow / Back your hair / Well the night's busting open / These two lanes will take us anywhere / We got one last chance to make it real / To trade in these wings on some wheels / Climb in back / Heaven's waiting on down the tracks / Oh-oh come take my hand / We're riding out tonight to case the promised land / Oh-oh Thunder Road oh Thunder Road / Lying out there like a killer in the sun / Hey I know it's late we can make it if we run / Oh Thunder Road sit tight take hold / Thunder Road.*

The song "Born to Run" was more structurally brilliant, but "Thunder Road" propels the album's complex collection of short stories and lives, as they move out into a single night, searching for something that might save them or ruin them—and there's only one moment like it in all rock 'n' roll. Its invitation is quite a promise, but it's also—without knowing it—a lie. People die before the night ends. Are Mary and her dreamer on a true road to freedom and discovery?

*Darkness on the Edge of Town*—the next work and the most bitter album in rock 'n' roll's history (and a better album than *Born to Run*)—says that everybody's hurt, wounded, disillusioned, trapped; the singer himself lives in the shadows under a bridge on the outskirts of town, full of hate and defiance. But that original "Thunder Road" moment, the burst of life and power and getaway, isn't a lie in what it promised to listeners, and only a fool would refuse it. Those lines created the feeling of the exhilarating covenant they importuned: roll down the window, let the wind blow back your hair, the night is parting open—in a terrifying way, like a red sea, and the ghosts you leave behind would've kept or killed you with their dead-end histories had you not blown past them.

I've played this moment about a dozen times a day this last month or two, and even Fubar—our youngest and smallest cat, all-black, even with his eyes open—crawls into my arms as I dance and twirl at four A.M., happy in this living, sonic literature, careful never to wake my wife, Elaine Schock, for a moment.

## Mikal Gilmore
### August 28, 2015

It's good to bear witness to life's blessings, big and small. One blessing for me was being in the audience at the taping for *Frank Sinatra's 80th Birthday Tribute*, in December 1995. Bruce Springsteen opened the evening with "Angel Eyes." Later, Bob Dylan performed—at Sinatra's request—"Restless Farewell," with his band and two string quartets. Dylan originally recorded the song for his third album, *The Times They Are a-Changin'*, from 1964. He was about twenty-three when he wrote these lyrics: *Oh ev'ry foe that ever I faced / The cause was there before we came / And ev'ry cause that ever I fought / I fought it full without regret or shame / But the dark does die / As the curtain is drawn and somebody's eyes / Must meet the dawn / And if I see the day / I'd only have to stay / So I'll bid farewell in the night and be gone.*

## Mikal Gilmore
### August 29, 2015

My two favorite moments in the second season of the HBO series *True Detective* were about death. At the beginning of the third episode, Detective Raymond Velcoro (played by Colin Farrell), who had been shot unconscious by riot control rubber bullets at the end of the prior episode, is dreaming of a kind of death as he awakens to Conway Twitty's rendition of "The Rose" playing on a radio. (The song is unforgettably enacted in a blue heaven or blue hell by singer Jake La Botz.)

The other moment came episodes later when David Morse's guru character tells Velcoro, "You must have lived hundreds of lives," and Velcoro replies, "I don't think I can handle another one." When I heard that, I'd never heard another line from a drama resonate more personally—or more comfortingly.

But then there's this, from Billy Joe Shaver's "Live Forever" (co-written by his late son, Eddy Shaver): *When this old world is blown asunder / And all the stars fall from the sky / Remember someone really loves you / You'll live forever you and I / I'm gonna live forever / I'm gonna cross that river / I'm gonna catch tomorrow now.*

The person I most love in this life often says "Because." To me, it's the biggest word there is, because: it's life and life only. Because: it's love and love only. And because: it's death and death only. In the best life, all these becauses make a sequence. It's not an unkind one. It's the best we can hope for. Don't forsake it easily. You're gonna live forever.

## Mikal Gilmore
### August 31, 2015

"You go down the stairs to the dark to find these characters. It's not a place anyone can go, and sometimes it's not a place that you want to go."
—Wes Craven

# SEPTEMBER
# 2015

**Mikal Gilmore**
**September 1, 2015**

The way some people die: *Now there's something coming through the air that softly reminds me / Tonight I'll park out on the hill and wait until they find me / Here slipping through the ether, a voice is coming through / So keep me in your heart tonight and I'll save my love for you. . . There's a prayer coming through the air like a shot straight through my heart / Tearing open the evening sky, tearing me apart / Now I'll ride that signal down the line till I'm home again with you.*
—Bruce Springsteen, "Save My Love"

**Mikal Gilmore**
**September 1, 2015**

*Sleeping Beauty* is Ross Macdonald's most haunting book because it is the story of a man searching desperately to save a lost young woman. The novel resonates on its own, but also because it is in effect an imagined ending to a life of the daughter, Linda, that Macdonald couldn't save. The final few paragraphs are beautiful and indelible—they show a great writer at his best, bringing a complex and frightening tale to an end with astonishing economy and majesty.

I don't know of any novel that slams so hard and gently in its last sentences. This passage, however, isn't that ending; it's a brief exchange between the detective and a woman—a mother whose hell and love can't be relented, because they can't be separated:

"Some German philosopher—I think it was Nietzsche—said that history just goes on repeating itself, the same old story, like a worn-out record endlessly repeating itself. When I first heard that in college, it didn't make sense to me. But now I think he was right. It's the story of my own life."

"Can you tell me what the story is?"

She shook her head. "I don't know what it is. That's the strangest part of it. It seems to be repeating itself, and yet it always takes me by surprise."

"It's true of all of us, Mrs. Sherry. But not all of us have sons."

"I wish I didn't." But then she rebuked her mouth with her stern fingers.

"No, that isn't true. I don't wish Harold dead, or unborn. I know if I didn't have him, I'd be even less of a person than I am."

**Mikal Gilmore**

**September 11, 2015**

My wife, Elaine Schock, is coming home tonight. She has been out on the road with one of her artists. I'm grateful for all kinds of reasons. I miss her.

**Mikal Gilmore**

**September 14, 2015**

Have you ever been sitting outside, reading, listening to music on earphones, mild wind rustling the trees, then you feel a slight movement on the back of your head? That just happened to me. I reached back and brushed what little hair I have left. Settled back calmly to reading. Happened again. Brushed my hair again, this time looking back. Nothing there. Seconds later, again. Could it be a bug? Felt my head, looked around, nothing there. Seconds later, again. This time when I looked around I saw something move. It was a big old bug after all: Elaine Schock. She had been hiding behind my chair, using her fingertips, and she was laughing so hard she was crying. I can't figure out how she got the drop on me. I can't figure out the path she took to get behind me.

**Mikal Gilmore**

**September 15, 2015**

Farm Aid. Elaine Schock will be there, and my heart will be with her.

**Mikal Gilmore**

**September 17, 2015**

"I want you always to remember me. Will you remember that I existed, and that I stood next to you here like this?"

"Always," I said. "I'll always remember . . ."

"Do you really promise never to forget me?" she asked in a near whisper.

"I'll never forget you," I said. "I could never forget you."

—from *Norwegian Wood*, by Haruki Murakami

**Mikal Gilmore**

**September 19, 2015**

Elaine Schock and I have a couple of good reasons to regard our sixth wedding anniversary (today) as our most special one to date. As wedding anniversaries increase, and as each new one is a happy one, then I think the law of this sort of specialness applies. Also, it's our only anniversary that we haven't been together, since Elaine is working at Farm Aid in Chicago today. On the bright side, I get to look after the animals and pet them (I want more) and Elaine is bringing me a very cool Farm Aid shirt. (I've been asking for Willie Nelson's hat, but no news on that yet.) On the brightest side, I get to see my baby tomorrow. She will come back with good stories and a beautiful smile, and I will embrace her with eternal love. Now, more than ever before. Happy anniversary, baby. May yours be the last face I see. Even if a husky is licking it.

## Elaine Schock
### September 20, 2015

A family who sued after a boy's clock was mistaken for a bomb had their suit tossed out of court today. Prejudice runs deep. When a Muslim teen brought a homemade clock to school to show his teacher, school officials thought it was a bomb and hauled the kid away in handcuffs. Neither the school or police believed the clock was a bomb. The kid was arrested because the school thought the clock was some sort of warning. This is from the police chief, so this is horse shit and anyone who paid attention knows it. You have constant slurs against Muslims by the GOP.

Ben Carson said something to the effect of, "We should not elect a President whose religion is Muslim, I guess because they are all evil terrorists." Again, can you imagine if Ben Carson said that about Jews? We would explode, and rightly so. All religions deserve respect in America. The less we give way to this bigotry, the better we will be.

## Elaine Schock
### September 21, 2015

*And I loved deeper and I spoke sweeter / And gave forgiveness I'd been denying / And he said some day I hope you get the chance / To live like you were dying / He said I was finally the husband / That most the time I wasn't / And I became a friend a friend would like to have . . .*
—"Live Like You Were Dying," Tim McGraw

Because.

> **Mikal:** I love the word "because," because it is a little tag Elaine came up with at some point—a code to tell me she was thinking about me in relation to what she posted. Although, she uses it for other things as well. It is her way of saying "This doesn't need extra comment because the truth is self-evident."

**Mikal Gilmore**
**September 30, 2015**

I've written before how much I regularly discover about the depth of family from Elaine Schock and her children, as well as her siblings and their children. Family love, even more than romantic love, reveals an innate need to value the welfare of kindred and progeny above your own. That's not, of course, always a constant possibility—we're all human, we have pains and pride and tempers and other realistic limitations, and we all fall short at times that we wish we didn't. But family is nonetheless the complex, mysterious and imperfect center of all history.

In recent times I've seen the difficult proof of its inward and profound ideal, and that has helped me try to rise to it myself. Thank you, to the role models I live with every day.

OCTOBER
2015

**Mikal Gilmore**

**October 1, 2015**

The forty-fifth school shooting this year—and we still have three months to go. Next year likely will be no less bloody.

**Mikal Gilmore**

**October 5, 2015**

There was a time back in the early 1970s when listening to John Coltrane's *Giant Steps* (from 1960) genuinely salvaged my heart and mind. These days, Elaine Schock does that for me. But when she's asleep, as she is right now, this album—one of the greatest ever made—can still help take care of mind and heart.

Nobody in the history of recorded music ever accomplished so much in a short time as Coltrane, who died at age forty, in July 1967, of liver cancer (some attribute his unexpected death to the results of his earlier heroin and alcohol use). He went through hell and back, saw the unseeable face of God, and left us musical proof.

The Albert Ayler Quartet opened his funeral service, and the Ornette Coleman Quartet concluded it. Miles Davis said: "Coltrane's death shocked everyone, took everyone by surprise." Coltrane was in the process of transfiguring 20th century music when he died. His work will always seem unfinished—nobody has ever picked up from where he left off—and the possibilities of what he might have done, given all he'd already accomplished, remain incalculable. His music is one of the few bodies of art that has persuaded me the human soul might be more than an historical reverie.

**Elaine Schock**

**October 7, 2015**

Obamacare made insurance affordable for those who could not previously afford it. The Supreme Court lets states decide to insure or not insure the poorest, which is so awful, it is not to be believed. If you don't have health insurance and you get cancer or other catastrophic diseases, you will not survive for long.

No one can afford treatment without insurance. For any politician who voted against it, they are indeed signing a death certificate for thousands and thousands without any regard or conscience. I would not want to be those people. And, I would never vote for someone so cavalier with the life and death of their fellow citizens. Because they know better, and frankly so should the people affected by these decisions, because they just left their lives and their families lives in the hands of people who don't give a crap.

**Elaine Schock**
**October 8, 2015**

I propose drug testing on puppies. You know they are just living off the welfare state (you and me), and ingesting anything they can lay their little paws on. Kittens are cool so I'm not going to suggest they are drug tested. I feel this will make me a popular politician. Maybe, run for Speaker? I'm so real and tell it like it is. I can also get a hat with that slogan.

**Mikal Gilmore**
**October 11, 2015**

Life's ideal is to move toward a horizon where vision, knowledge, spirit, love and adventure meet. We see the horizon as often as possible, but we never cross it finally, until we cross it finally. John Coltrane did that, and his mind, discoveries and depths of beauty—a beauty some heard as anger or chaos— can still bring us to the brink of God's touch. He made scripture of music. Others have done that, but Coltrane's scripture was also autobiographical.

**Mikal Gilmore**
**October 11, 2015**

Dear Friends:

I have something I should share with you. Elaine and I have discussed when and how to make this known, and today is that time.

In mid-September I was diagnosed with tongue cancer. Since that diagnosis I have undergone various tests and scans, and Elaine and I have met with numerous doctors and a physician's board. Elaine has been there every inch of the way with me. She has been my strong and tough and devoted advocate, and she is my love. Indeed, I couldn't pray for a better helpmate. I also couldn't possibly do this without her heart and support.

I want you to know that, at present, my spirits are good—in large part, I'm sure, because of the strength Elaine gives me. I'm often a depressive person, but my depression has largely abated since I learned about my condition. I attribute it to the love of a good woman and her family, and to our determination on a course of action. This isn't to say I haven't had a couple of rough days with this, both physically and in other terms. I certainly have, and I know Elaine and my family have. Also, I'm realistic, and I realize that my spirits may sink lower in upcoming weeks and months, but with Elaine's help, I will do the best I can in this regard. More important, this is the sort of crucible that tests one to be as strong and caring as possible to loved ones.

My chemotherapy will begin this week. It will continue for nine weeks, and then will resume for another seven weeks, in conjunction with radiation. Obviously, this will be an arduous process, and I can't predict how active I might be here during these next few months, but I know Elaine will remain active. She will likely be a better source of information than I might be in the season ahead, but I will let her tell you how and when and what she chooses to post. She can share anything she likes. In fact, she will no doubt be a better judge than I am when it comes to divulging news and thoughts.

As I said a moment ago, I can't know how active I will remain here during my treatment, though my intention is to maintain more or less the same pace and level. That is, I intend to keep posting about music and cats and political conditions, and about books and TV shows, when I'm able and moved to. I also plan to continue my writing for publication as much as possible.

I believe we will come through this—not without some difficulty, but I'm quite hopeful. I'm well-informed, but Elaine is even better informed, and her positive and loving attitude is the best therapy of all.

I want you to know that I am immensely grateful for the friendships I share here, and for all the ways you regularly inform and entertain me. Most important, I ask you to be kind to Elaine and our family. They are my soul—they are the ones I will most care about in the seasons ahead. Please be helpful to them in whatever ways you can, and be kind to each other, no matter occasional differences.

With love,
Mikal

**Mikal Gilmore**

**October 11, 2015**

This has been an incredible day here for both Elaine Schock and myself. We're profoundly moved by the gracious words and support so many people have offered, and we will continue to be. Loved ones and friends and community are blessings. Wrap your arms around them all. Thank you, dear friends. We are grateful to you all.

## Mikal Gilmore Transcends the Darkness

by Steve Duin / *The Oregonian* / October 14, 2009

With the hat and guitar, Mikal Gilmore had the '60s look—Dylan's "Nashville Skyline"—down but hardly the sound. It was painful to hear Gilmore on that Aria guitar, his old Milwaukie High School buddy, Steve Mayes, recalls, and it got worse when he opened his mouth.

"He couldn't carry a tune," said Mayes, now a reporter for *The Oregonian*. "It was laughable. He didn't have musical talent . . . but he understood it. He understood how music spoke to people."

Of all the 2009 inductees into the Oregon Music Hall of Fame, Gilmore's work may have the fewest downloads but the biggest impact on iTunes. Visited by the unapologetic voice he brings to the pages of *Rolling Stone*, you are drawn to the music of his subjects—Bob Marley and Jim Morrison, Jerry Garcia and Johnny Cash—in a search for what you missed the first time around.

Gilmore, who lives with twenty-thousand vinyl disks in Los Angeles, still remembers the night he realized where that voice might take him. He'd just returned from the Seattle stop on Dylan's 1974 comeback tour when a local underground paper, the *Portland Scribe*, called. Their music critic had missed the show. Could Gilmore handle the review?

"The act of sitting down that night and writing about it," he said, "is the single act of clarity in my life. I knew what I wanted to do and I've never looked back. The writing was sophomoric at best, but the passion I felt in discovering a calling was instantaneous and quite recognizable, and it has never diminished."

An article on the American pop band, Artful Dodger, introduced Gilmore to *Rolling Stone* in 1976.

Many of his best pieces for the magazine have been collected in two books, *Night Beat* and *Stories Done*. "I tend to take assignments," he said, "that look at people in times that were troubled, yet they managed to overcome their limitations to leave something that mattered and changed the world around them."

It's no mystery that Gilmore can relate. He grew up in the same wretched household that shaped his brother, Gary Gilmore, whose 1977 execution by a Utah firing squad inspired two magnificent books, Norman Mailer's *The Executioner's Song* and Mikal Gilmore's own *Shot in the Heart*.

In that memoir, Gilmore provides an unforgettable portrayal of the violence in that Milwaukie home and the darkness of the neighborhood.

"In Clackamas," he writes, "it was possible for people and their families to live their lives in utter isolation and disinterest. Anything could come from such conditions—transcendence or destruction—but often what came was not for the better. Multnomah may have had a higher crime rate—robberies, drugs and such—but there was a deeper natural meanness to be found in the outlands around Milwaukie."

Gilmore survived thanks to a passion for reading and writing—inspired by his father and an English teacher at Milwaukie High named George Bouthilet—and his love of music. Like his three brothers, he was convinced, he once wrote, that he had survived without children:

"None of us went on to have our own families . . . It's as if what had happened in our family was so awful that it had to end with us, it had to stop, and that to have children was to risk the perpetuation of that ruin."

But when Gilmore finally hits the Roseland Theater Saturday for the Oregon Music Hall of Fame induction ceremony, he will be accompanied by his new wife, Elaine, and the love of her three children.

"I never thought I would have a family again. You don't want what you can't have," he said. "But life is full of surprises. And those surprises can be profound and wondrous."

AFTER

**Mikal Gilmore**
**October 12, 2015**
I said this yesterday, and I happily say it again: Elaine Schock is the best, most determined advocate I could hope for. As I was sleeping this morning she made some calls and got my treatment advanced by a couple of days. I think she could tell I was feeling a little poorly late last night. I couldn't do this without her, even if she won't let me wear a Cthulhu knit cap to my treatments once my hair falls out. (Don't know why.)

> **Mikal Gilmore:** It's only $5.65!
>
> **Elaine Schock:** Way too much money for that hat.
>
> **Mikal Gilmore:** I have so much to lose in that regard.
>
> **Elaine Schock:** It is almost like the doctor saying Mikal can play tennis at the end of his treatments. He doesn't know how to play tennis.
>
> **Elaine Schock:** Right now, I am checking out PICC line fashions. A PICC line is a long thin tube placed in the vein above your elbow so you can receive chemo and other medicine. You gotta be cool no matter what the situation.

**Mikal Gilmore**
**October 13, 2015**
This truism happened across my computer today: "An individual doesn't get cancer; a family does."
—Terry Tempest

**Mikal Gilmore**
**October 13, 2015**
*If Adolf Hitler flew in today/They'd send a limousine anyway.*
—The Clash

**Mikal Gilmore**

**October 13, 2015**

We've been at the pumpkin patch, so we will watch the debate when we get back home. Right now, though, we're at the deli, where the debate is on TV. I've only heard moments of it, but I'm impressed with both Hillary and Bernie.

**Mikal Gilmore**

**October 14, 2015**

When I was a kid, after my father died, I slept for months in a bed that was underneath a ceiling that leaked. This was in Milwaukie, Oregon, outside Portland, so it rained a lot. Never bothered me much. I'd sit up in bed at night, getting rained on, reading so many stories. During that time, I read a lot of Charles Beaumont, and I never forgot his imagination. Beaumont wrote science-fiction and horror stories, sometimes for magazine publication and sometimes for *The Twilight Zone*—television's greatest series.

One of the best, for me certainly the most memorable, of Beaumont's tales was the November 4, 1960 episode of *The Twilight Zone*, "The Howling Man." It's the story of a man who becomes lost in a storm during a walking trip through post–World War I Europe. He stumbles across a castle, the home of an order or monks, and asks for sanctuary from the storm. They deny him—he must leave immediately. He begs again, and this time he hears a strange howling.

After conceding their refusal, the man turns to leave but passes out. He comes to in the castle. He hears the howling once again and searches until he finds a pathetic man locked in a cell. The stranger is there, he says, as the prisoner of a hysterical religious order. Because he once kissed a woman in public the order has imprisoned him, and their leader beats him. The monks discover the two in conversation and take the visitor to the leader of the order. The man tells the leader that unless they set the man free, he will report the order to the police.

Reluctantly, the leader tells him a story: The howling man is the devil himself. He had come to their village after the war to corrupt it. The leader had recognized him and was able to use a god-blessed staff to capture and imprison him. That is why the world is at peace now; the devil may no longer wander it. The man agrees that the leader has convinced him, but the monk isn't so sure.

Once back in the refuge of his room, the man has to decide: Should he free this man? After all, the religious order seems insane—the leader especially. This was one of the darkest, most mesmerizing TV episodes I've ever seen. There are profound questions and intimations here: Does evil exist? Is man imprisoned by it, or does each person carry the devil inside? I was nine the first time I watched it. After *The Twilight Zone* became available on video tape, then in digital form, I watch it every autumn—even if only by myself. It is always creepy and powerful, and its chiaroscuro, Gustave Doré-like staging seems like something the collective unconscious yielded up.

It's almost Halloween. Do you know where your devil is? Can you hear him howling to be set free?

**Mikal Gilmore**
**October 14, 2015**
*To Walk the Night*, by William Sloane, from 1937, has been out of print for years—until just a few days ago:

"*To Walk the Night* is not, as its title might seem to suggest, a mere ghost story. Its central idea is at once less usual and more horrible, but what that central idea is the reader must be allowed to find out for himself. The atmosphere of tense, apparently unreasonable dread and fear has been well worked up, and the climax skillfully developed . . . Though the story might be truthfully described as an extremely tall yarn, the reader, breathlessly turning the pages, forgets his twentieth-century incredulity until the tale is finished."
—L. M. Field, *The New York Times*

"This is a novel that has to be experienced, not described . . . this novel is still as believable now as it must have been back in the 1930s. It is a story that [horror writer] H. P. Lovecraft could have written."
—Robert Weinberg

**Mikal Gilmore**

**October 14, 2015**

Elaine Schock just told me to order a beanie cap. Tessa Schock (Elaine's three children, Samantha, Preston, and Tessa are all from an earlier marriage), do you approve of this one?

**Elaine Schock**

**October 16, 2015**

It has been a week full of ups and downs.

> **Mikal Gilmore:** It will be uppish and downish for a while, and then it will level out. I will make sure that's what happens. You've been through a lot, facing it with amazing strength, courage and heart. You are my blessing every minute of every day. I've never loved you more, but at the same time, this love will only increase.

**Elaine Schock**

**October 18, 2015**

**Mikal Update**

So many very kind and concerned friends have asked how Mikal is doing, that I hope to give weekly updates. This is the first, but I hope that most of the other updates will start with a song title, which will be my way of setting the tone for my words.

Now to the update. The first round of chemo went well. There are the side effects of course, but Mikal is doing pretty good considering. We have many more treatments to go and I don't pretend it is easy, but I am very optimistic and feel the future is so bright. Mikal even bought new shades. He looks good in them, too.

**Mikal Gilmore**

**October 18, 2015**

For Elaine Schock: "Let It Be Me." There is hard-won eternity here, in the voices the Everly Brothers' version of a 1955 French pop composition by Gilbert Bécaud, Manny Curtis, and Pierre Delanoë. The brothers invoke the song's dream and desire—nowhere more affectingly than in a September 1983 performance at London's Royal Albert Hall. The brothers, Don and Phil, had split in acrimony and hadn't spoken for a decade, and the knowledge of a loving bond pulls apart and then is inextricably drawn back together, with sorrow and respect. The knowledge, flashes in the partners' eyes of what they have seen and made. It's a vow as much as my own personal prayer. Let it be me, for as long as we can touch, for without your sweet love, where would life be?

## Mikal Gilmore
### October 19, 2015

"I would say in some ways these have been among the worst weeks of my life," said South Carolina Republican Representative Trey Gowdy. Gowdy chairs the House Oversight Committee that has been relentlessly investigating Hillary Clinton's use of a private e-mail server, and said the words this weekend during a lengthy interview with the political journalism organization *Politico*. "Attacks on your character, attacks on your motives, are one thousand times worse than anything you can do to anybody physically—at least it is for me."

I guess two things don't occur to him. One, he's not the only person hurt by character attacks, and two, he could've avoided this by doing an honest and honorable job.

## Mikal Gilmore
### October 20, 2015

*Looked through the paper / Makes you want to cry / Nobody cares if the people / Live or die / And the dealer wants you thinking / That it's either black or white / Thank God it's not that simple / In my secret life.*
—Leonard Cohen, "In My Secret Life"

## Mikal Gilmore
### October 20, 2015

*Johnny Hartman & John Coltrane* is a treasure trance, like one long heart-thought, perfect for the wee small hours of the morning. The album almost didn't happen—Johnny Hartman, one of the finest saloon-singers popular music ever gave us, didn't see himself as a jazz singer and thought there might be too much contrariety between his and Coltrane's musical views. (Both men worked in Dizzy Gillespie's late-1940s band, though not at the same time. They also reportedly shared a bill at Harlem's Apollo in 1950, but didn't play the stage together.)

We owe deep gratitude to producer Bob Thiele's inspired suasion for making this timeless convocation materialize, at Coltrane's behest. Listen to the quiet majesty of "My One and Only Love": Coltrane plays the whole song through once, like a dream, pauses, then from the shadows comes Hartman, singing devotion that will haunt you. As sublime as Coltrane and Hartman were here—in the best one-off singer and saxophonist pairing I know—they find their communal meaning in the rapport they forged with drummer Elvin Jones, bassist Jimmy Garrison and especially pianist McCoy Tyner. Enough outtakes exist for an additional LP's worth. Someday, God will owe us that revelation.

**Mikal Gilmore**
**October 20, 2015**
Today is the birthday of Elaine's two daughters, Tessa Schock and Samantha Schock. While I am not their biological father, they are two of the greatest loves of my life, and were born exactly ten years apart on the same day. So, happy birthday to my lovely girls. This is always one of my favorite times of the year, as Preston Schock, Elaine's son was born on October 22nd.

**Mikal Gilmore**
**October 20, 2015**
Here's a bad way to wake up: It's about 7:10 A.M. I feel something warm and wet land on my right arm and hear Elaine Schock say, "Ewww!" I open my eyes to see that our cat Fubar just horked near her side of the bed, but got most of it on my bare forearm. Elaine is moving fast, and so am I. Fubar, confused, has been summarily put into the hallway outside the bedroom. The Lord certainly gives us trials. I woke up a couple hours later to find him curled back up next to me, purring like all was well in his world. Which, I pray, it was.

**Elaine Schock**
**October 20, 2015**
Tom Petty. Because.

**Elaine Schock:** I really like Tom Petty. I never actually worked with him, but came close. Years ago I was with ABC Records and Petty was an artist there. When the label was sold to MCA I was one of maybe a handful of people who went over there from ABC. Petty went over, too, but was not happy and refused to record. They formed an offshoot label to resolve the situation, but it took a long time. I was there for the first record he released on Backstreet (or something like that), but everything was pretty separate. I think Paul Wasserman was Petty's publicist at the time. Because of the separateness, I had to sneak Tom Petty records to Mikal. He was at the LA office of *Rolling Stone* then. For some reason they didn't like *Rolling Stone* at MCA, but I did. Mikal was my friend even back then.

**Mikal Gilmore:** Yes, we were friends. She even gave me the complete Buddy Holly box set.

**Elaine Schock:** I did. Mikal was always trying to get me to give him expensive box sets. I gave him an Elvis box set when I was at RCA and he complained because of the weight of it. Could hear him whining all over NYC.

**Mikal Gilmore:** I tried to get the Duke Ellington Centennial box set out of her, too. Tried and tried. Finally broke down and got it myself.

**Elaine Schock:** Mikal Gilmore, well you can't always get what you want unless you buy it yourself.

**Elaine Schock:** And I took him out to dinner at a swell restaurant in NYC. He complained until we got there about this box set being a heavy velvet coffin. Gave him a plastic bag to carry the damn thing in.

**Mikal Gilmore:** One of the most difficult walks of my life. The handles on the cheap shopping bag she gave me broke and I had to lug the velvet coffin across Manhattan, Elaine Schock laughing evilly all the way. She wouldn't let us take a taxi. "It's just another block."

**Elaine Schock:** It was a nice night for a walk. I admit I thought the restaurant was a little closer to my office.

**Mikal Gilmore:** Elaine Schock, was it Red Lobster?

**Elaine Schock:** Red Eye Grill, home of the dancing shrimp.

**Mikal Gilmore:** There's a difference?

**Elaine Schock:** About a hundred dollars.

**Mikal Gilmore:** I realize Red Lobster is pricier, but I thought it would be poor form to bring it up.

## Mikal Gilmore
### October 22, 2015

More on Sloane, written during a night after chemo: Looking for a Halloween read? *To Walk the Night*—a 1937 novel by William Sloane, recently republished—tells a nightlong story to a man mourning the death of a son.

At the story's center is a person who is not a person—no oddity to that fancy in this sort of tale, but great, surprising, and gripping imagination in how Sloane renders it. The reader intuits what is happening all along, but the presentiment won't prepare for how and when the key moments happen, even though the most horrible event is told in the first few pages. When that dread finally arrives in the chronology, near the end, it shocks because of what happens just before—an exchange of words that says everything simply, briefly.

There is something Lovecraftian in the overall aspect and motif of *To Walk the Night*, but as great as Lovecraft was, he never managed this sort of emotion and loss, combined with tension as read in this excerpt:

"I went over and stood with my back to the fire; the heat soaked into my legs and took some of the tiredness out of them. Jerry was standing behind the settle, behind Selena; he took out his package of cigarettes and put one between his lips.

His voice was perfectly casual. 'Gimme a match, will you, honey?' That woman could think, and think fast. Only the smallest trace of some expression went over her face; then she stooped and pulled out from the flames a long twig of mesquite. 'Here," she said, and held it to his cigarette. He drew in a long drag of smoke and looked at her across the flame without saying anything except 'Thanks.' She tossed the twig back into the flames and sat down again. 'We were worried,' I remarked. 'Jerry was positive there wasn't a match in the house, and we used our last up on the mountain. But I see you found one.' Jerry came round the end of the settle and stood at the opposite side of the fireplace, looking down at his wife. 'Yes,' he said, with an unsuccessful attempt at lightness in his tone, 'where did you find the match?' She looked up at him and there was a sort of stillness in her face that I shall never forget. 'Does it matter?' 'No,' he said, 'it doesn't matter at all where you found it. It matters if you found it.' The remark made no sense to me at all, and I still don't understand it, but Selena did.

She stood up. 'You shouldn't have said that.' There was no anger, no sharpness in her tone, only weariness and what sounded to me at the time like despair. Jerry was staring at her; the look on his face was so thinly sharp, so direct, so full of horror that I was instantly aware that this conversation, which was meaningless to me, possessed some sort of positive and dreadful implication for him. 'So,' he said, 'so that's it . . .' He was watching her, I noticed. His eyes never moved from her face.

I saw, too, that he was trembling, that his hands, at his sides, were twitching, and that his lips, which had suddenly become thin and gray, were quivering slightly. He licked them. 'I would have found out sometime,' he said to her at last. She made no reply. 'But sometime is now.' 'Yes,' she said, and her voice was impersonal. Suddenly he was in complete command of himself. 'Do you know what I am thinking?' 'Of course,' she said. 'Am I right?' She nodded her head gravely. 'You know that too.'"

**Mikal Gilmore**

**October 22, 2015**

For Elaine Schock, Van Morrison's version of Ray Charles' song. "What Would I Do." Elaine is my daily and nightly angel. In these hours, in her help and love, I find my eternity in this life. It is all I could want.

> **Elaine Schock:** If it all ended tomorrow, we have lived a very rich life together. But the good news is, we are not through yet.

**Mikal Gilmore**

**October 23, 2015**

[Trump] acknowledged "bad news" in the form of the new Iowa polls, but described himself as "a great Christian," blamed the news media for blowing the polls out of proportion and asserted that the pollsters behind those surveys "do not like me."

**Mikal Gilmore**

**October 24, 2015**

Give it all up to Elaine Schock; she has definitely got herself a difficult patient.

> **Elaine Schock:** Chemo has a vast array of side effects and Mikal is not used to being told what to do about his health. I am stronger and more assertive. He does have cancer, kind of zaps you. Also, I have no choice. There is no giving up in life and death matters. There are so many things that I have had to learn in the moment. I will share my experience because I wish someone had shared theirs. That being said, there is nothing exact about chemo or the combination of drugs and their effect on the body. The only good thing is this may be a long process, but it is temporary. And, I know his tumor has shrunk because that is very noticeable.
>
> Mikal has good doctors, but the side effects of chemo range from chemo brain, which means one can get disoriented,

to the nausea and the drug interaction, to fatigue. These are common side effects and interfere with the quality of life. Being moody and depressed is also common and understandable, which is why I don't kill him. Although this is temporary, the future is then and this is now. That being said, Mikal gets out every day.

**Mikal Gilmore**
**October 24, 2015**

Earlier today, during a long afternoon nap, I dreamed I posted this. So I've decided to make it real: I don't know whether I would've become a writer if my parents had not encouraged me to explore fiction by giving me volumes to read from a very early age—short stories, novels, comic books, plays, it all worked. I wanted to try to figure out how people took ideas, characters and imagination, and wielded them into words and sentences on pages. I never managed the imagination part—I have none—but I kept an interest in the other elements, and in time developed additional ones. Thank you, to my parents. Let's teach each other well.

**Elaine Schock**
**October 25, 2015**

Chemo is a bitch. The side effects can be monstrous. The nausea, from medications taken to combat side effects and chemo brain are hard battles. Mikal is pretty thin now. He has a supermodel frame with the gaunt face to match. There are no great days, but some days are better than others. And, there are times when I think he is just as sick as he can be but there is an upside. We see progress. What was a big tumor on his neck has shrunk considerably. His vocal chords, which were impacted, seem much better now. He gets out every day and I think that is important. I don't know if that will always be the case. Maybe it is too much chemo? Maybe he shouldn't be this sick? I don't know. This isn't an exact science. I look forward to the next doctor visit so we can determine our next steps. Food is tricky, but smoothies seem to work. So if you have a great recipe for smoothies or milk shakes, let me know. We have a long road to go.

**Elaine Schock**

**October 27, 2015**

For me, I don't look back. I have few regrets. I look forward to the future. I only see more successes. And, a long rich life with my husband and kids. Willie has said, delete and fast forward. Well, that is exactly what I will do. There are no guarantees in life but I have been so lucky. And, even though there have been bumps, and even bombs, it always passes. So don't worry about me, I will be fine.

> **Mikal Gilmore:** Elaine Schock is my strength and nerve and determination. She is also the one who invariably kicks my ass when I need it.

> **Elaine Schock:** Mikal is tough, which doesn't make him the best patient, but that's OK. We will get through this. Look, I wouldn't trade my life now for what it used to be for anything. I don't want to look different, don't want to be a younger version of me, and I don't want to have the relationships or work I had back then. I have worked hard to get where I am now. I have a happy marriage, which I didn't always have. And, let me tell you, that is a lot. My children are wonderful and getting their lives together and starting their own families, well most of them. I wish my husband were healthier, but he will be. But if for some reason, we don't have fifty more years, I am still grateful to the years we did have. You do have to go through it all. But as I have always said, I am lucky. Not everyone is, and I know that.

**Mikal Gilmore**

**October 27, 2015**

From enacademic.com: "Regardless of its origins, the [ice cream float] quickly became very popular, to such a degree that it was almost socially obligatory among teens, although many adults did not like it. According to some accounts, it was banned, either entirely or on holy days, by some local governments, giving rise to a substitute treat, the sodaless ice cream sundae. As carbonated drinks were marketed as a miracle cure, they were often considered a substance that required oversight and control like alcohol, another controlled substance that could not be served or purchased on Sundays in many conservative areas."

**Elaine Schock**
**October 29, 2015**

Four people were shot and one stabbed at a party at a Riverside, California shopping center. I just told Mikal this news and he said, "That didn't take long." (This was not long after the Umpqua Community College shootings in Oregon.) I had to explain, this did not just happen today. These were not copy dog shootings. Still, where is a good dog with a gun when you need one?

**Elaine Schock**
**October 31, 2015**
**"The Calm Before the Next Storm?"**

This has been a pretty good week. It started off a little wanky, but gradually got better. We saw the doctor and Mikal is getting treated for anemia and is being hydrated regularly. We are so close to the hospital that he just drives there. This has made him feel much better. He is even eating a little and going out for short trips. I think he looks great, still runway skinny. There is fatigue, but it is better. It has been two weeks since the last chemo treatment and there is a certain amount of recovery before the next one on Friday.

Food cravings are big these days. I didn't know this was a thing with patients receiving chemo, but it seems to be. After work I will hunt down these usually fattening items only to find that Mikal doesn't really like the way they taste. I am not eating what he doesn't. No matter how much I like his leftovers. I don't need to gain his weight. Will power, I got this.

I count down the days and hope the next round is easier, though it probably won't be. But the good news is, in the short term, we learned how to manage chemo better, and in the long term, we are closer to a cure. There has been noticeable progress. Mikal is lucky, he has a great doctor and a dynamic and smart team of nurses. Last but not least, he has a huge number of people who are supporting and thinking of him. The World Series had a moment when they stopped the game and stood up to cancer. They had signs with their loved one's name on it, some who made it and some who didn't. So even though I do not have a sign, I stand up for Mikal.

> **Mikal Gilmore:** We learned valuable things this time, including ways to fight nausea. For me the immediate worst part of this is losing the ability (for a while) to taste things. That inhibits appetite and depresses attitude. I've acquired a couple of tricks with that, too (ketchup!). The one thing that almost always tastes good is a chocolate milkshake, though sometimes it's a little much. We don't kid ourselves about how hard this will be, but we also don't kid ourselves about this: we will get through it. I couldn't do it without Elaine. Or without Tessa, who finishes the French fries I buy and never touch.

## Mikal Gilmore
## October 31, 2015

Friends, some Halloween suggestions, if you find yourself short: *The Innocents*. Not really a ghost story, but something worse. *Ichabod Crane* (Disney, 1949), which is still beautiful and scary after all these years. *The Whisperer in Darkness*: By far the best Lovecraft adaptation I've seen, as well as my favorite horror film of recent years. It's so spooky, my family bolted midway.

### The Albums—Part 1
### Mikal Gilmore

I have a large album collection that I began in 1967, when I was sixteen. At some point I started writing passages, bits and pieces, and turned it all into an outline of sorts, maybe for a long article, maybe for a book. Then I passed on the idea. Not sure why—I think I got some *Rolling Stone* assignments that were more immediately demanding, and truth is I forgot about it along the way. I also thought I couldn't really pull it off—that I'd fail it began:

It was a rainy late afternoon in downtown Portland, Oregon, the autumn of 1969. I had just been to a small classical music shop that also carried folk music, off 12th Street, where I bought the Library of Congress recordings of Woody Guthrie. Now I was headed to meet friends at a café near Portland State University, on the outer edge of the city's center.

The walk took me along a series of park blocks that led from downtown to the college area. This was always my favorite walk in Portland; the blocks formed a tree-lined pathway past the stately Paramount Theater and a pair of earnest art museums, through the series of brick and glass buildings that comprised the university. It was a romantic stretch, a long, narrow urban forest passage where friends and lovers met, sat on benches or the grass, talked, and where some adventurers wandered to groove on marijuana or psychedelics, and others sat on the grass to play guitars, flutes, autoharps or bongos.

Some sat on benches to talk about the war. What could we do to stop that monster—how far would we go? Would we risk freedom, even existence? Would we risk ruining the existence of others—both the guilty and the innocent? Gatherings like that went on in the park blocks every night and day, and even when they convened around dark purposes, they felt like new life.
This was a wet day, so as I walked I stuck close to the inner sidewalks, gaining a little dry from buildings and awnings.

Along one block of apartment buildings, you could occasionally see through the open-curtain windows of ground level residents—hardly a voyeur's vista, just people in their living rooms, watching TV or sitting down to meals.

This day, as I neared one window, open despite the rain, I heard the strains of chamber music, and as I looked inside I saw a middle-aged man seated in an armchair, reading in the light of a side-table lamp. Lining the wall next to him were shelves of LPs—vinyl albums—and on top of the shelves sat a Dual turntable—considered high-end at the time—playing the music I'd heard.

I caught a glance at a couple of album covers propped on the floor, against the shelves: a volume of Schubert String Quartets, plus the same Woody Guthrie collection I was now carrying. Maybe it was that latter coincidence. Or, maybe it was that this man looked content in his place, as if he was living inside the life he wanted to live in. Perhaps it was that I didn't at that time have a place in the world that I felt comfortable calling home. Or, it could have been just seeing the rows of albums, all that unknown music that might illuminate art and history and pleasure to me. But in that short-lived moment, the moment it took to look at this scene in passing, my ideal of my life was formed, and I knew it by the time I'd stepped beyond that window. This was what I wanted at some vantage in my life: a room of my own, where I could sit with music, comfortable in that self-containment.

It wasn't that this vision precluded anybody else—I was presently seeing a young woman I expected to marry—and besides, my friends and I already sat and listened to music together almost every evening, as so many other young people did in that time and in the times since. But I also realized, in that instant, that this reverie didn't rely on others. The ideal was to be in a place, a room, with music, to enjoy it and learn from it, and permission and dependency didn't have to fit in that room, not even love and companionship.

That might seem like a lot to realize in a moment, but these things happen to people all the time. You see somebody across a room, and unexpectedly you form a dream—a future of sex, love, maybe family, even company, creativity, action, until death. Of course, I was young then, eighteen, just beginning college. I wouldn't say I was innocent, but I didn't yet know what I would do in my life, that I would become a writer. I certainly didn't know the depths of the hopes and losses that would come, the pleasures, the fears, the deaths. Time and occurrence would give and take everything—knowledge and disillusionment. But that one particular instant, that glance into that room, I can truthfully say has always stayed with me, along with the hopes and sense of self that I formed directly.

So much of what has happened in my life followed from that—some of the best, and some of the most devastating. But my bearing, what I wanted for better or worse, I determined right then. Maybe it would have been different if I had understood the most essential direction of all—be careful what you wish for—but I doubt it. There are things you want no matter their cost.

In those days of 1969, I had enough albums to fill about two cardboard packing boxes—about one hundred LPs, that is. It was, I should admit, more than what most my friends had. I didn't have money. I lived on seventy-five dollars a month, which had to cover my food and rent, as well as entertainment and books, so the expense of an album—about five dollars then—was a real expense. But albums had come to seem essential, and so I often went without a meal or something else so I could have music.

For some music—say a new Beatles or Rolling Stones or Bob Dylan or Aretha Franklin album—I'd even pay rent or some other bill late. It was important to hear something of that magnitude pretty much the day it was released. It was like the news, and was a means of knowledge and experience that bound us together and made sense of the world we found ourselves in. And that, sometimes, aimed to transform that world, or at least to disrupt it. It was like the air. You breathed it if you wanted life.

Today, forty-eight years later, I have a large music collection—something like twenty-thousand vinyl records and over twenty-thousand CDs. (There's also at least another twenty-thousand albums or album-length collections stored in libraries across several hard drives. More and more I have come to count these digital audio files as a serious factor in my music collection. But a bad power surge or simple drive failure and half that could be gone any day. I've had it happen, and it's unrealistic to try to back up that many files.)

I know individuals who have larger music collections—like me, they are critics, journalists, historians or archivists—but few of the people who have been close to me have ever known those collectors. To my friends, even my wife, my collection has generally seemed immense and overwhelming. It's this thing that has filled the spaces I've lived, this thing that has always had to be accommodated, this thing that seems unreasonable, this behemoth.

Many friends have, of course, enjoyed the diversity and depth of the collection—they've appreciated finding music they thought they might never hear again, and more important, they've enjoyed discovering a singer or musical thinker, or an unfamiliar form, that they never knew before, just as I enjoyed hearing something surprising and exciting for the first time. Even so, few of these friends ever really get why I've kept and valued the collection. Aren't there a lot of albums, they wonder, that I could just weed out? (In truth I've eliminated far more LPs and CDs over the years than I've kept.)

Those walls of music are damn unsightly to most eyes, and even when the shelves of CDs and LPs are confined to rooms that are central to the living space, they still register as something that wastes other possibilities for those rooms. The truth is, some people I lived with plain hated my collection—it used money and territory, and it also used up attention, even love, they said.

That wasn't an unfair judgment. My record collection has been an absolutely crucial part of my life—central to my passions, and to my identity. My albums tell the stories of my life: what I believed in, who I loved, who I lost, where I was, what I learned—that is to say, what mattered and happened to me. And though I have much classical music and early jazz and blues and folk and country, many of my albums come from the times I've lived in. They document remarkable and combustible history—they are records, in any sense of the word, of change, hope, conflict, dissolution, renewal and wonder.

For me, living with my albums has, maybe foremost, been a way of living through and with history. Not just a personal history, but a larger, more reverberant one, born in the 1950s, heightened in the 1960s, transfigured in the 1970s and 1980s, and for all the ways it has been challenged and redefined in the decades after, a history not yet exhausted.

I have loved my albums, I have fought for them, I have kept a loyalty to them deeper than to some people in my life, and I have found a counsel and comfort in them, a companionability, that I have known nowhere else. For various reasons, I sometimes thought the albums had come to preclude any real family of my own. A few years ago, in 2001, through various circumstances I lost the collection. Then Elaine Schock, the woman I would marry, rescued them for me, at great cost to her.

We were not married yet, and wouldn't be for several years. It was a central cause for profound changes in my life. There were things that I'd no longer imagined were possible for me, but I now recognized new treasures, a romantic and erotic and intellectual union. And, with that, a family I'd never expected in Samantha, Preston, and Tessa. But a greater fear of loss—the nearness of death—was to come for both Elaine and me, for us all. Elaine and I still sometimes have cause to wonder if we're really out of the woods of that fear, but we also know we live with new blessings. Knowing you—or the person you love—might die has a way of focusing your mind and heart. It can cause you to reexamine how you use your time and temper, the effect of your kindness, the things you write about and how you write about them, the dreams you wrongly loved and the slights you wrongly nurtured, what you value. It has even caused me to hear music differently, more ruefully, more lovingly.

# NOVEMBER
## 2015

**Mikal Gilmore**
**November 4, 2015**
I am lying in bed, reading, and listening to the soft breathing of my wife beside me, and in this moment, I am utterly happy. Elaine Schock is my grace.

**Elaine Schock**
**November 7, 2015**
**"So it Begins Again"**
This is my weekly update on Mikal:

Yesterday was Mikal's second round of chemo. When we went to the oncologist after the diagnosis, the nurse offered us a tour of the chemo ward. We could only glance inside. It looked like an awful place. It was too scary to visit even for a few seconds. Of course I knew that we were going to spend a lot of time there, but not yet. Still we were in a rush to start treatment because that would lead us closer to Mikal's recovery.

Now the tumor on his neck had become disfiguring. That happened fast. And, there was no time to waste. Treatment had to be aggressive to save him. As frightening as that was, the good news is, it was a highly curable form of cancer. Even at stage 4, there is a high success rate.

I can't speak for everyone but when you get that kind of news, you panic. I read everything I could lay my hands on, googled everything that Michael Douglas said about his illness, because he had the same cancer as Mikal. I called the American Cancer Society pretty much on a daily basis for a week to get more info to find out what to expect. They sent me books and comfort. It was my job to be informed about cancer so I could help make the right decisions. It was Mikal's job to get well. But the truth is, everyone is different. Everyone has side effects, some more than others. You just don't know until you know. We learned how to combat most of those except the fatigue and weight loss, of course. That is just what it is. But after ending the first round, Mikal recovered nicely in a few weeks. Hydration every day and shots to raise his blood count worked really well. He got out a lot and drove himself to his treatments. it was almost like he was better, except we knew that wasn't true.

So now to round 2. The chemo ward is filled with comfy chairs and some private rooms. Mikal always gets a private room because his chemo treatment lasts for eight hours. After that he has a portable chemo bag that he wears for three days. It makes a whoosh sound every minute or so, and is kind of comforting.

We are only a few minutes from the hospital so I get Mikal there early, make sure he has a good breakfast, talk to the nurses, and leave for work. I will bring Mikal lunch and then pick him up at six. At this point he has regained his appetite and taste buds. That won't last, but while it does, we just go for it. I like and admire the nurses who are so diligent in their care. It is now a place that I no longer fear but revere.

And, so it goes. We will see how this week progresses. Fear is still a part of my life, but so is hope and a belief in people that I didn't necessarily possess before. Mikal has handled this with grace, dignity, and courage. I will post tales of this personal journey every week, or at least try to. It will be honest, sometimes brutal, and in the end victorious. I am eternally grateful to all of you who have cared so much about my husband.

> **Mikal Gilmore:** I second everything Elaine says here. This is the day after chemo, so the worst won't hit for another day or two, but I have good medications and daily hydration and near-daily Neupogen, a white blood cell booster. When I have an appetite, I take advantage and eat a lot; that carries over to water and beverages. I have to get better at eating small bites on the bad days, but I don't take risks with nausea.
>
> Elaine lifts and helps cure me every day, even on days she's had a nasty cold. And you, our Facebook readers, your continued kind wishes and strong examples help us both. We loved you anyway, now it's double.
>
> **Elaine Schock:** I don't really consider myself a caregiver. I give support and make sure that Mikal gets the best care. It is easy to say if someone is rich that he or she will get the finest care, but to be honest, that may be true on some level but on another it takes knowledge and the will to fight for what you know will help no matter what your income is. I learned that

lesson early on. Most people do not ask for what they need. This is for many reasons, including the fact they just don't know. They just suffer and endure until the end. It is my job to make sure that Mikal has the best possible outcome with the best possible quality of life during this really unusual time for us.

## Elaine Schock
### November 9, 2015

This is the great news about cancer. We have a vaccine that will protect against certain types of cancers including most cervical and tongue cancers. We will never actually get rid of all cancers, but we can hope to manage the disease better. I wish that this vaccine could have helped Mikal, but it will help the next generation. This kind of cancer can be caused by oral sex. Sex is a part of life, and it only takes one partner. So we need to get over this moral pretense and get to saving our children.

## Mikal Gilmore
### November 11, 2015

I want to say something about the courage I see every day in my wife. Elaine and I have formed a balance during my present experience with cancer—that is, each of us carries a weight. In my case, obviously, that weight is doing the best I need to do physically and mentally to cope with, and survive and recover, during the seasons ahead.

Elaine, though, has done much more, and with a courage that at times eludes me. She has devoted hours daily to learning about the history of this disease and its treatments. She has faced some difficult knowledge, and I have seen in her constantly lovely face the moments that her effort has pushed her into what must be scary territory.

I have been more apprehensive in these regards. My father died of colon cancer in 1962, when I was eleven. I knew he had a fatal diagnosis—my family knew—but he did not. He ran a publishing enterprise for the cities of Portland, Tacoma, and Seattle, and even during his last months he drove back and forth between our Portland home and a Seattle apartment. I was almost always with him; in fact, I was often the only one with him. I took care of his daily needs and hygiene, and tried to comfort his illness and confusion and pain. The things I saw and felt during those many long months have remained with me indelibly, etched in my memory every day since, and they have haunted me.

I became in some ways what my mother termed morbid after that. (She was no fan of Edgar Allan Poe, Bram Stoker, or Mary Shelley. She preferred Ibsen, and though I liked him too, he sometimes seemed to me as morbid as the Gothics.). Perhaps my tastes deepened my depression, though that had been inside me as far back as I remember anything. I didn't so much develop a fear of dying as I did of disease. After my father's sickness and death, cancer became my biggest fear, and though I took too many risks over the years, I nevertheless saw myself as somebody more prone to heart difficulties. That isn't how it worked out.

When I first received my diagnosis in mid-September, I was surprised at my reaction. I was not scared, except for its impact on my family. I didn't try to become calm, but nevertheless something close to calm and faith soon came to me. I know now that it was my wife and family. However, I also knew that I had limitations about this composure, that I could shatter it. I knew that if I looked too hard at what cancer is, at its images or its history, I might undo myself. It might cost me my equilibrium—and as we all know, mindset can be vital.

I didn't speak explicitly about this to Elaine until Monday night. As I say, she has been studying the disease and in the last few nights she watched a Ken Burns-produced documentary on the subject. I think she noticed that as she did this, I would slip on earphones or nap. Looking too closely at what cancer is and what it does is my fear, my cowardice.

Elaine has apprehension, but she does not have cowardice. She faces these dark truths better than I do, and I have no question that if she didn't, I won't survive this. She is saving my life. Still, I feel bad that she undergoes a certain terrible element of this that I'm too afraid to. Maybe I will get stronger in these ways and I can help her—and myself—by learning from her bravery. I hope to. I've maybe been a little better in that regard in the last day or two, but I have far to go.

I see in Elaine, every hour, the sort of remarkable person each of us would like to have on his or her side, fighting for us, giving us heart, even at a price. It is the greatest blessing of my life. At night, Elaine always falls asleep an hour or two before I do. I stay up reading or watching something, or working when I can, listening to music. In those moments, I realize I am the happiest I have been in my life. I sleep next to love, hearing its courageous breaths, and I know that though a second family came to me later in life than I ever anticipated, when it arrived it was as the grace that saves me, no matter what else comes.

**Mikal Gilmore**
**November 11, 2015**
I have a hat in case I lose my hair. Then, Elaine and I can't really see if that's happened.

**Mikal Gilmore**
**November 13, 2015**
There have been attacks in Paris. It isn't clear to me yet what exactly happened, or who committed these assaults or why, but our hearts go out to those who are in pain, fear or worse. (We later learned these incidents were coordinated terrorist attacks not only in Paris, but also the city's northern suburb, Saint-Denis. The first attack occurred outside the Stade de France in Saint-Denis, during a football match. It was followed by several mass shootings and suicide bombings at cafés and restaurants. In one horrific episode, gunmen executed another mass shooting and took hostages at an Eagles of Death Metal concert in the Bataclan theater. The assailants were shot or blew themselves up when police raided the theater.)

I can't claim to have a lot of guiding morals, but I do have one: don't hurt people. In fact, go out of your way to avoid doing so. It's not a golden rule—it's just a rule.

**Elaine Schock**
**November 14, 2015**
**"Every Cloud Has a Silver Lining"**
This is my weekly update on Mikal Gilmore:

Chemo hits hard. It has to. And some days are worse than others. Those days scare the shit out of us, especially me. Mikal is suffering from weight loss and ringing in the ears. Not the best side effect for a music journalist but we knew in advance this may happen. And, it was a choice we made. Most choices no matter how hard were the best possible ones to save his life. You don't play with advanced cancer, even if it is localized. These are tough times. Mikal cannot afford to lose any more weight so he is working harder at eating. He has gone beyond runway skinny.

We will be meeting with a nutritionist when I get back. I am currently in DC for work. I had to explain Mikal was not going to be the easiest of patients since even though he no longer could taste greens, he still hated them and would not eat them in any form. A feeding tube is the last resort. There are muscles you must work for quality of life after all this is over. Plus, he needs his lovely voice, which is as strong as ever, and a feeding tube could damage that.

These are chest tightening, pit in the stomach times. We just have to go through it. There is only one more round of intensive chemo before the radiation/chemo combo. Different treatment, but still harsh. This will continue until March. Seems like a long time but it also seems like forever since we started this.

I also know Mikal feels a stigma about having cancer. That surprised me. But it is something else we are working on. I don't know that all patients feel like that but your own family history can fuck you up on so many levels. And for further proof of that, you can read Mikal's astonishing book, *Shot in the Heart*.

Anyway, that was the cloud, here is the silver lining. The tumor is pretty much gone inside and out. It is all working beautifully. Mikal also feels well enough to get around himself. That hasn't changed at all. He even washed his car (OK, that is different) which makes mine look really dirty in comparison.

We have a lot to give thanks for this Thanksgiving. Mikal should have his taste buds back by then and we will have a big dinner with family. We believe remission is just a few months away, and we have so much hope for our future. Thanksgiving used to be a time Mikal hated before we were together. It has a different meaning now. Thank you all for caring about my husband.

It means more than you will ever know. For all of you who are going through the same thing, you are in our hearts.

**Elaine Schock**
**November 15, 2015**
I am leaving tomorrow to be a part of the festivities honoring Willie Nelson with the Gershwin Prize. No one is more deserving and I am so grateful to be there. Now, I have to pack and bring the right outfits. OMG! Even the size of the suitcase is confounding.

**Mikal Gilmore**
**November 16, 2015**
Elaine leaves today to travel to this event—which will be something special and memorable. Before leaving, she's already made all kinds of preparations with her family to make sure I'm okay while she's gone.

Travel in assurance that all is well at home, baby, and have a great trip. This is a once-in-a-lifetime occasion.

**Mikal Gilmore**
**November 16, 2015**
Sulamith Wülfing was an illustrator, born in 1901 to Theosophist parents. She claimed to have visions of fairies and angels—and dragons and religious suffering—and drew these subjects her whole life. Her work is clearly not for everybody's taste, but I always liked her hand, her detail, her palette. I also saw an occasional mix of innocent sublime and the dark sublime, in unexpected ways. I used to have a substantial collection of her art on German postcards. I think I still might.

**Mikal Gilmore**
**November 16, 2015**
It's chilly tonight.

**Mikal Gilmore**

**November 17, 2015**

Elaine Schock is at the Library of Congress luncheon. I don't want to get her in trouble, but I told her to steal that placard with her name on it. And to make them show her where my books are. (They're filed under "G.")

**Elaine Schock**

**November 17, 2015**

Willie tells the crowd he just recorded an album of Gershwin songs called *Summertime*. It went over well.

**Mikal Gilmore**

**November 18, 2015**

Elaine Schock gets to witness and partake in some good history.

**Mikal Gilmore**

**November 18, 2015**

For Elaine Schock, who is that someone for me. "Someone to Watch Over Me." Music by George Gershwin, lyrics by Ira Gershwin.

**Elaine Schock**

**November 19, 2015**

It was the highlight of an evening of magical moments. Good for Willie. Willie Nelson sings there's 'room for everyone' in America.

**Mikal Gilmore**

**November 19, 2015**

Elaine flies home today, and this song is perennial between us. The Shirelles' "Dedicated to the One I Love."

**Elaine Schock**

**November 21, 2015**

**"The Quality of Life"**

My weekly update on Mikal:

The chemo is wearing off, things are getting back to being a little more normal around here, but we are still off kilter. Mikal's white blood count wasn't high enough so he was prescribed two more Neupogen shots. Those also have side effects, especially headaches, but Mikal's nurse told him that she worked for The City of Hope for thirty-three years and she saw too many patients die from infections their chemo brought on. With this drug, she sees mostly survivors.

Though aggressive chemo remains heartless, at least the death rate has gone down considerably. Mikal feels the ringing in his ears is the worst side effect so we made the decision not to use Cisplatin—which is a heavy duty cancer drug and causes his tinnitus—for the third round of intensive chemo. That starts the day after Thanksgiving. Mikal will be given another drug with less toxicity. The progression of the effects of the treatment only get worse, and we need to consider his quality of life after cancer.

Mikal is still rail thin but he looks better. We normally do not fight but I was angry with him for not drinking the protein drinks we bought in bulk. I cannot fully comprehend that everything tastes dreadful, but that aside, eating is his job. It no longer has to be fulfilling or enjoyable. So now Mikal sends me photos of the high calorie nutritious drinks he has consumed and added various soups to his menu, which is smart on his part. His appetite is coming back. He is still fatigued, and his face and head are now baby smooth. We are saving money on razor blades, that is for sure. It is the chemo but the look works for him.

I was in DC for most of the week with Willie Nelson, my treasured client who has just received the Gershwin Prize. It never occurred to me not to go. I work as much as I ever have, if not more. There are a few good reasons for that. First and foremost is, I love my job, it keeps me grounded and focused. I have been working all my adult life and that will not change. Also, I have to pay bills. I have a successful career but when someone has cancer, you also have to face the fact that you are probably no longer a two income family. And treatment, even with insurance, can be costly. We are luckier than most in that regard. And, my family is nearby to help if and when I need them.

The next phase is chemo/radiation combo in mid-December. It is the thing that Mikal dreads the most. It is a five day a week seven-week ordeal.

You are fitted with a face mask for accuracy. He doesn't even want to discuss it. And, as awful as that sounds it is supposed to be easier than the aggressive chemo he is enduring now. To be honest, I don't know if that is true, but whatever it is, we will do the best we can.

I know Mikal will have to exercise his jaw and neck literally all the time to ease the scar tissue. And, not just during treatment but a long time after. I will have a yoga instructor come to the house to work with Mikal on these exercises. He will protest more than a little when he reads this, but it is not like he has to do the Downward Dog. And, he will eventually agree. I think. We will have a nutritionist in place so we can do our best to avoid a feeding tube. No matter what anyone says, that is a major goal of mine.

This is the journey so far. It isn't easy and it is often worrisome. I have to bite my tongue so I don't ask if Mikal is OK for the tenth time in an hour. I don't really know where this path will lead, but I have all the hope one can have. So thank you all for caring about my husband. It means so much to us. Please take good care of yourselves.

With love,

Elaine

**Mikal Gilmore:** Everything Elaine says here is fair, even the parts that freak me out. I'm more step-by-step, and Elaine is looking at the bigger and more long-term prospects. In general, I feel I'm doing better this round—I'm eating a lot more and I like the Ensure drinks. I consume several a day. The headaches are enervating but they don't worry me; I take Tylenol and sit in bed with Elaine, watching TV or reading. By far, the most difficult part for me is the hearing problem. I've lost all high frequencies, everything is muffled, and I have to ask Elaine and Tessa to repeat things all the time. I feel embarrassed about that. But my big question here is: what is the Downward Dog, and have I ever done it? It kind of sounds like something I should know.

**Elaine Schock**
**November 23, 2015**

Getting cancer is a frightening thing for everyone involved. There is so much to take in, and it can overwhelm your very being. You may want to run away, go someplace far from this disease, but there is no place to escape. You have to go through it. One step, one gut wrenching moment after the other until you hear the word, remission. And, sometimes you just snap. It happens and I am no saint. So you pick yourself up, dust yourself off and get through another day. It is better. There are so many questions and your doctor only has so much time, so I call the American Cancer Society who are always there, 24/7. I have to give an enormous amount of credit to them. I am telling you this because you may one day need the same comfort and information. I also called the City of Hope and certainly they have a different function, but they were dreadful. I had hoped for more from them. But, to be honest, I will call anyone for information. They don't have to be nice about it.

These are my experiences; others may have different ones. But, more important is that many of the answers and suggestions have come from Mikal's friends here who have experienced cancer or just expressed love and compassion. We are so grateful for you all. I hate this time so much, but in the end, we will prevail and get stronger. That is the least we can do. I was going to post this at the end of my Saturday update but I thought it should have its own post. Thank you for caring.

**Elaine Schock**
**November 24, 2015**

The Supreme Court is about to hear a Texas abortion case. It is crazy that men who know nothing about women or their health make these decisions. Of course, the new Texas law will be struck down by the court, but not without damage to the women it failed before the court can act. Compassion is something people pretend they have for the fetus but they don't really care about the mother—or the baby after it is born.

**Mikal Gilmore**

**November 24, 2015**

I've been far too slow to acknowledge the kind things people here have sent to me. There is a hat that Terri Huggins knitted for me. It has cats and it's remarkable. It took me a while to figure out how to wear it. Thank you, Terri. I love it. Sorry it took me a while to say that, but I'm kind of slow these days.

**Mikal Gilmore**

**November 25, 2015**

Chemo and radiation. Where I am right now.

> **Elaine Schock:** Mikal is home and doing well. I know what we have to do to get through this, and we will. It isn't easy and it certainly isn't fun but we are lucky because we can get to the other side of illness.

**Mikal Gilmore**

**November 25, 2015**

Today is the day Elaine Schock and I make a big decision. I couldn't do it without her. Maybe she will post more about it later. I will be doing medical stuff until evening. Not bad stuff, but there will be hours when I can't post. We love you all.

> **Elaine Schock:** This may be stage 4 but there is reason to believe that things will be fine sooner than later, whatever that means, but quality of life has to be a big priority even if there are risks. We are hoping for a long and uninterrupted life with few long term side effects, and I believe we can achieve that.
>
> Thank you, all of you. This isn't the easiest time for us but you sure make it so much better. I read every word carefully, if not once, then twice. I take it all in and wonder, how did we get so lucky? I will never forget the kindness here and other posts. It is a crazy world—except here.

**Elaine Schock**
**November 25, 2015**
This is a comment from Mikal on my Facebook page, regarding an article he wrote on the band Queen: "This is the most recent article I've had published in *Rolling Stone*. There are others in the works, but they will necessarily be months away. When this appeared in print, I realized: If for any reason this ends up being my last contribution, I'll stand proudly with it. It is the best thing I've written for *Rolling Stone*, and writing the last few paragraphs changed me in lasting ways I didn't fully understand until more recently. I wouldn't have known it was posted anew on the magazine's site if Elaine hadn't let me know."

**Mikal Gilmore**
**November 26, 2015**
My daily prayer of thanksgiving: may yours be the last face I see.

**Elaine Schock**
**November 26, 2015**
It's Thanksgiving and I have much to be grateful for this year. I have had opportunities to see places few get to see and work with the best people in the world. I have great children and they have happy lives, and my old dog Indie is still alive. Yes, so are the cats. I also have a most extraordinarily beautiful marriage to Mikal Gilmore that is truly for better and for worse. And, a family that has our backs when we need them. I have discovered so many people are caring and good and in this crazy world, that is everything. Even though it has been a little challenging lately with Mikal's health, we have many wonderful friends who give us positive thoughts and love on a daily basis. I will never be able to repay their kindness. I am also grateful for Obamacare. You don't know how valuable that is unless you need it and we needed it this year. Life and death are not just words to us. They are our reality. Mikal has an incredible and caring medical team and it gives us hope for the future. I wish you all a wonderful Thanksgiving with much love and gratitude.

**Mikal Gilmore**
**November 26, 2015**
Thanksgiving wasn't always a day I've looked forward to. In my family, in the 1950s and 1960s, it was often the most turbulent of days—turkeys being thrown off the table—and I gathered a conviction that Thanksgiving was a day when people gathered who should never gather.

That's all changed now. My wife, Elaine Schock, has given me a new family, and this year I found myself looking forward to the holiday more than ever, because it will give me invaluable hours with them. I have much to be thankful for—more than any year prior. I have learned a tremendous amount about family, protection, health, hope, kindness and grace. Without Elaine, I might have been more fatalistic in recent months—but the moment I told her about my diagnosis, and saw the look that crossed her face, that changed. I wanted to live to heal that look and to justify her love. I still like the dark stuff—I always will—but the blessings Elaine and the little Shockmores have given me in recent years have helped make the whole spectrum of love and fate more comprehensible and sympathetic to me.

I also have a life which has given me opportunities to do work that has been continually meaningful for me. This is work that lets me pay testament and historical perspective to music that excited and enriched me and millions of others; music that is aesthetically and culturally remarkable, and that shaped me in moral and political ways as well.

Finally, both Elaine and I are grateful on an hourly basis for our friends here—most of whom we didn't know before joining Facebook. This is truly a living place, and as it breathes, laughs, quarrels and shares support, it has become indispensable to us. We love you more by the day.

Happy Thanksgiving to all, and to your children who will outlast us. They will work in an ongoing history to make a better, kinder, more tolerant world—especially for those who feel ill or lonely or hurt or confused or endangered on days like this, and days like tomorrow.

**Mikal Gilmore**
**November 27, 2015**
It's dark in the bedroom. I'm getting dressed. I mistakenly thought Fubar was

my wadded up jeans on the bed and tried to put him on. He did not like this. I'm surprised he didn't waken Elaine.

**Mikal Gilmore**
**November 27, 2015**
I'm at Kaiser Woodland Hills Oncology. I'm a little early. Story of my life.

**Mikal Gilmore**
**November 27, 2015**
My mother used to tell me how horrified she was when people were rounded up and sent to camps. She was a Mormon with a Catholic husband who truly believed he was born Jewish. He wasn't, but you can see how that combination proved to be a concern when they lived for a brief time in the American South, in either the 1940s or 1950s. Quite a lot of people from those religions had been murdered in the South over decades, simply for the identity of their faiths. Eventually my parents hurriedly left the South, during an unnerving night, when my father became fearful for them. My father was one of the people who used to recite the "first they came for the Jews" allegory.

From *The New York Times*: For Japanese-Americans, Resistance to Syrian Refugees Recalls Long-Ago Fears; The dark memories of seven decades ago have bubbled to the surface in recent weeks for many people who were sent to Japanese internment camps.

**Mikal Gilmore**
**November 27, 2015**
Fuck. More terrorism and wanton murder. Fuck. This time in Colorado at a Planned Parenthood clinic.

**Elaine Schock**
**November 27, 2015**
I don't worry about radical Islam, but I do worry about our homegrown terrorists. We never call them what they are but they are exactly that. Terrorists with guns. They don't want you to have freedom over your bodies or freedom

of religion or anything else. They are truly evil. They prefer to kill you. So what do we do about them? Do we have weeks and weeks of TV coverage. No we pretend they don't exist but that doesn't make them nonexistent.

**Mikal Gilmore**
**November 28, 2015**

I've received some art gifts recently. This first one is by John E. Williams, who gave an original of Elaine Schock and me to Elaine when she was in Washington, DC, for Willie Nelson's honors at the Library of Congress. Thank you, John—especially for rendering that hottie who's behind me. I can't compare.

**Mikal Gilmore**
**November 28, 2015**

Another incredible piece of art we received recently was from Michael Cano (married to Patsy Faragher). Thank you so much, Michael. I'm flattered.

**Elaine Schock**
**November 28, 2015**
**"It's a Great Day to Be Alive"**

This is my weekly update on Mikal Gilmore:

Mikal just underwent his third round of intensive chemo yesterday. It didn't take as long as it normally does (eight hours), because we decided not to use Cisplatin any longer. It has been effective, but the side effect of hearing loss could not be tolerated any longer. It would have gotten much worse. So hopefully, this will do what it is supposed to without the drug and we push on.

The doctors seem very optimistic. I feel good about the treatment and its success. So fingers crossed and maybe some toes too. Mikal still has to wear his chemo bag for the next three days. We all have gotten use to it by now, including the cats who use to freak out when the bag made a whoosh sound every few minutes.

There is hope and fear. What if? And, of course that shakes me to my core. But then, I bring myself to a better place. It's not that I don't allow myself to have these thoughts. I have given myself that right, but I don't give into the worry for very long.

It has been a pretty up week. Mikal got his appetite back and gained at least fifteen pounds and he has become addicted to Ensure Plus. We had fourteen people over for Thanksgiving, and it was wonderful. I wanted it to be perfect, especially for Mikal. And, it was. Everyone made their best effort not to discuss Donald Trump for too long, even though we had at least one Republican in the house and a conspiracy theorist. (And yes, even though I wasn't on the moon to see it first hand when it happened, there was indeed a landing.) Yet we all got along and my eyes did not stick when I rolled them. Mikal wore a suit, with a white shirt and white tie. The classic two button collar fit his neck perfectly (it was the shirt he wore when we got married). No tumor is visible at all. That was not the case just a few months ago. It was just a pleasure to look at him. Wonderful food, good company, laughs and enormous love. It was a great day to be alive.

Next week is busy for Mikal. There is the mask fitting with tattoos for radiation accuracy, which will be rough because he dreads that so much. Also a dental visit complete with getting the jaw exercise equipment. And, his regular hydration and Neupogen shots to fight infection. These therapies have made a world of difference in being able to tolerate chemo. And, a visit to the audiologist is scheduled to see about repairing the hearing loss. I have been busy at night studying radiation/chemo. The chemo helps the radiation work. The doctor assures us that the aggressive chemo Mikal is receiving now is the hardest part of treatment. Wouldn't it be nice if that were true?

We are watching CNN's documentary about the sixties. Mikal was interviewed for that series but had become so sick on the set, he had to stop. The interview continued after Mikal composed himself. We realize now that was the first manifestation of his illness. It took another year, though, to actually get the right diagnosis. A year is a long time to be misdiagnosed. Christopher Hitchens said, "I'm not fighting or battling cancer, it is fighting me." He had a point but in our case, we can fight back. And, you know we intend to win.

**Mikal Gilmore:** Elaine is unflinching in her reports. She has a courage I don't possess when it comes to facing this experience, and I'm indebted for it. I have always thought she is the more natural writer between us—and the funnier—but when I watch her as she composes, she's every bit as meticulous as I try to be when I'm working on an article. Writing is a good thing to worry over, but when you have a voice—as Elaine does—then trust it and work with it.

I know this much, and I've known it since September: If anybody beats this for me, it will be Elaine. I would've been lost weeks ago. Her no-nonsense, tough advocacy has guided me every day, even when I tried to run counter to it because I'm afraid. When this goes into remission, it will be due to her as much as the good medical team we have (thank you, President Obama, for the ACA). I'm trying to take the lead on the auditory problem, because it's more graspable, and looking at it is more familiar and less scary for me. But hearing doesn't work without living, and Elaine is the one who commands that bigger picture and battle. I am more grateful to her every hour than I adequately express.

**Elaine Schock**
**November 29, 2015**

I post updates on Mikal's illness every week. When I first posted, I did it to give Mikal's friends an idea of what was happening. I was writing to a lot of people and I was a little nervous about my ability to convey what it was like to deal with cancer from my end and what Mikal was going through. I am not a writer, and knowing a great one doesn't give you talent, but I have been trying to do my best. If I sounded dopey, OK, it wouldn't be the first time. But what we got back was so much more than I ever could imagine. Literally hundreds of people would be in our corner. That stunned and humbled me. My oldest and dearest friend asked me today if I had a therapist to deal with the fears and uncertainty of tomorrow. The truth is, you are all my therapist. People have reached out with love and great advice. And, I have my work. I've said this before and I will continue to say it. Thank you for caring about my husband.

**Mikal Gilmore:** I will come through this because of Elaine. I don't even know if I'd have made it this far. There were two or three quite scary nights in the early phase. She saved me then. I have been transformed by the kindness and support of our Facebook friends. Elaine's incentive has made all the difference. I'm not sure I would ever have posted about this problem had it not been for Elaine. I'm more grateful than I can adequately express for your offerings throughout this, especially the encouragement and grace you have offered to my wife. It means the world to me. Thank you.

**Elaine Schock**
**November 30, 2015**
On January 22, 1973, the U.S. Supreme Court handed down its landmark decision in the case of Roe v. Wade, which recognized that the constitutional right to privacy extends to a woman's right to make her own personal medical decisions—including the decision to have an abortion without interference from politicians. Over forty years later, Americans are still standing by this decision—with seven in ten Americans believing Roe v. Wade should remain the law of the land. And, no amount of terrorism or deliberate ignorance or theology will change that. We will fight you back. You will not win with your intimidation and lies.

## The Albums - Part 2
## Mikal Gilmore

This narrative is to some extent coexistent with that period in my life covered in *Shot in the Heart*, but it isn't a retelling of those events. It also goes beyond that timespan by decades, and hopefully amounts to its own story about the obsessions and people one loves as a way of making it through life—and what happens when you lose those touchstones.

When you feel you've lost everything more than once and have to ask yourself, what do I do now? How do I dare get older living without a companion's hand, and without the guideposts that got me through the rough past? How do I find the will to redeem whatever I have left of my heart, my mind, my time? It took me a while to appreciate that many people responded to *Shot in the Heart* not so much because it explored where devastation comes from, but rather because it also raised an immediate question. How do you live with the knowledge and effect of devastation? I never imagined I'd be able to fulfill that question for myself until Elaine let me into her life and body and home and heart. Maybe some parts of this new account will resonate for others as well.

The Albums, as an idea, alludes to something more than a physical mass. My lifetime collection of recorded music is a large, amorphous thing that took on both metaphorical and metaphysical dimensions for me as time went along, and events went north and south, then south and north and south again. My albums were, for a long time, a way of representing the meaning of my life— and then, at a certain point, this bulwark of hope and history and ideals and pleasure was gone.

Then, because Elaine now loved me and accepted this was a loss for me, the albums came back, in hundreds of boxes. They stayed in those boxes a long time, until Elaine built me earthquake-proof shelves in the garage. As I looked at those boxes, then unpacked them one by one over a few weeks and saw them as a massive library that filled the walls, bottom to top, the collection reminded me of the rifle that drives the narrative in Anthony Mann's great and defining western, *Winchester .73*, or like the piano that finally sinks at the end of *The Piano*. That's to say, it's an object of great price that can obsess and define those who own or covet it so much that it can undo their well-being.

But this is also a story about living with rock 'n' roll and its relations. Popular music, all said and done, has been among the best friends—and one of the confidants—I've known in my life. Whereas you could talk to and confide and hope and trust in a lover, that lover might still leave or betray you. A great song, by contrast, would talk to you—and its truths would never betray you. At three A.M. in the morning, outside of the greatest intimacies of love, there was nothing that could mean as much as a pop song that told you secrets about your own fucked-up and yearning heart.

Mainly, this is an account of a life, how this writer's was lived and determined largely by the particulars of musical moments that proved to be so much more than moments, but instead proved a lifespan cavalcade. My albums also became, quite early in that span, a living library. They represented the formation and uses of knowledge, were a means by which to shape a worldview, and to mark and weigh experience. Music of course wasn't the sole inspiration in these regards—historical events, books, art, film and TV moments figure into that accrual—but for generational and other reasons, music wielded a special influence for me.

After all, rock in the 1960s and onward took on the functions, the purposes, of literature. It became the arena, for some time, where many of the most interesting and reflective writers went. Some albums took on the effect and role of novels or collections, and some sequences of albums worked like a trilogy or quartet. Which is to say, the albums I collected functioned as an accumulation of cultural works (in particular pop culture works), in tandem with lived moments in history, sifting through it all for understanding and value. The albums themselves are like a character that takes on a presence in our cultural story that helps determine various events.

If this expands, it might also be somewhat a social, cultural, and political history, a classic chronicle of how and why music's meanings changed in the last few decades, how it developed and mattered. Some of this will be meditations on particular albums or songs, and on the artists responsible for those works. Maybe other parts will unfold personal memories of some of the artists I've encountered. (This is the sort of material that never makes it on to the printed pages of profiles and interviews, but that sometimes is even more telling.)

Maybe I'll look at a some of the history of musical albums, how 19th century compositions, slave and folk traditions, and early 20th century blues and vaudeville performances got documented on gramophone 78s. And, how they then yielded to long-playing phonographs, which in turn gave way to the rise of CDs. That's one way of tracing how sessions and recordings eventually transformed into albums, and how labels like Blue Note, and artists like Miles Davis, John Coltrane, Frank Sinatra and the Beatles further transfigured albums and their stories and meanings for audiences, the times and history.

I guess I could say what many people of my age—or people who are younger or even older—might be able to say: I grew up with popular music encompassing my life. It played as a soundtrack for my youth. It enhanced (sometimes created) my memories. It articulated losses, angers and horrible (as in unattainable) hopes, and it emboldened me in many, many dark hours. It also, as much as anything else in my life, defined my convictions and my experience of what it meant (and still means) to be an American, and it gave me a moral (and of course immoral) guidance that nothing else in my life ever matched, short of dreams of sheer generous love or of sheer ruthless rapacity or destruction.

I can remember my mother playing piano, singing to me her much-loved songs of Patsy Cline and Hank Williams, or singing an old-timey Carter Family dirge, accompanying herself on harmonica. As I remember it, she wasn't half-bad, though of course I'm forming that judgment through a haze of long-ago memories and idealized longings.

It was my older brothers, though, who brought music into my house—and into my life—in the ways that would begin to matter most. I was the youngest of four boys; my oldest brother, Frank, was eleven years older than I, Gary was ten years older, and Gaylen, six years older. As a result, by the time I was four or five in the mid-1950s, my brothers were already (more or less) teenagers—which means that they were caught in the early thrall and explosion of rock 'n' roll. They had been born at the perfect time. In the 1950s, rock 'n' roll meant disruption. It was the clamor of young people, kicking hard against the Eisenhower era's public ethos of vapid repression.

As far back as I remember hearing anything, I heard (either on one of the house's many radios, or on my brothers' portable phonographs) early songs by Bill Haley & His Comets (also known as Bill Haley and The Comets), Carl Perkins, Johnny Cash, Fats Domino, the Platters, Buddy Knox, Chuck Berry, the Everly Brothers, Sam Cooke, and Ricky Nelson, among others.

But the biggest voice that hit my brothers' lives—the biggest voice that hit the nation—was, of course, Elvis Presley's. In the mid-1950s, every time Presley performed on nationwide TV (on the Milton Berle, Steve Allen, or Ed Sullivan shows), it was an occasion for a family gathering—and was among the few times my family ever collected for any purpose other than to fight. Those times we sat watching Presley on our old Zenith were, in fact, among our few occasions of real shared joy.

The appearance I recall best was Elvis's 1956 performance on the Dorsey Brothers' Stage Show (which was also the singer's national debut, and was followed by six consecutive appearances). I remember sitting tucked next to my father in his big oversize brown leather chair. My father was not a man who was fond of youthful impudence or revolt (in fact, he was downright brutal in his efforts to shut down my brothers' rebellions). At the same time, my father was a man who had spent the better part of his youth working in show business, in films and onstage and in vaudeville and the circus, and something about rock 'n' roll's early outlandishness appealed to his show-biz biases (though his own musical tastes leaned to opera and Broadway musicals).

After watching Presley on that first Dorsey show, my father said, "That young man's got real talent. He's going to be around for a long time. He's the real thing." I know how cliché those remarks sound. Just to be sure my memory wasn't making it all up for me, I asked my oldest brother, Frank (who has the best memory of anybody I've ever known), if he remembered what was said after we'd watched Presley on that occasion. He repeated my father's declaration, pretty much word for word. I guess my father had a little more in common with Colonel Tom Parker than I'd like to admit, but then, like Parker, my father had also once been a hustler and bunco man.

So rock 'n' roll as popular entertainment was welcomed into our home. Rock 'n' roll as a model for revolt was another matter. When my brothers began to wear ducktails and leather motorcycle jackets, when they began to turn up their collars and talk flip and insolently, likely as not they got the shit beat out of them. I guess my father recognized that rock 'n' roll, when brought into one's heart and real home, could breed a dislike or refusal of authority—and like so many adults and parents before and since, he could not stand that possibility without feeling shaken to the rage-filled and frightened core of his being.

I never got to have my own period of rock 'n' roll conflict with my father. He died in mid-1962, when I was eleven, when "The Twist" and "Duke of Earl" were the picks to click. Hardly songs or trends worth whipping a child until he bled. The song I would most identify with my father was one I heard playing on the radio, as I rode with my brothers after the funeral to the graveyard. It was "Point of No Return," by Gene McDaniels (Georgie Fame recorded a pop-jazz-R&B version as well, and in my memory that's the version I cling to). "I'm at the point of no return," the song said, "and for me there'll be no turning back." I was growing up feeling like an outsider because of how my family saw itself in position to any surrounding community. But from this time on I began to see myself as an outsider within my own family; I felt that this wasn't really where I belonged.

It turned out that being born a few years after my brothers gave me a fairly different entry on history. A little over a year after my father's death, President John Kennedy was shot to death in Dallas, Texas. It was a startling event, and it froze the nation in shock, grief and a lingering depression. Winter nights were long that season—long, and maybe darker than usual. I was just twelve, but I remember that sense of loss that was not merely my own—a loss that seemed to fill the room of the present and the space of the future.

If I look back at any one time that politicized me, clearly that was the one. Politics quickly seemed like the great ground for the future and for jeopardy. There wasn't anything that unusual about a twelve-year-old kid feeling that exigency. After the great void caused by Kennedy's murder, every stir in the nation felt political. The stakes were exceptional—these were arguments about destiny and betrayal, and about something crucial that had been cut off from us, about the ruin left behind that we couldn't puzzle out. This injury dominated us. It didn't so much permeate our popular culture as it haunted it. Our movies, our novels, our TV dramas, even our comedy couldn't let it go. We had to come to terms with this, but it was nothing that could be solved. History had shifted too irrevocably in that season. Something big, something that might be ultimate, was going to happen in these fast-coming times. It's only fitting that when it did, it came in ways nobody might have anticipated.

In this period, my brothers were hardly ever home. Gary and Gaylen were either out at nights on criminal, drunken, carnal activity, or in jail. My mother had the habit of going to bed early, so I stayed up late watching old horror movies, talk shows, anything I could find. I remember—in January 1964—watching Jack Paar's late night show, when he began talking about a new sensation that was sweeping England, a strange pop group called the Beatles. He showed a clip of the group that night—the first time they had been seen in America. It's a ghostly memory to me now. I don't remember what I saw in the clip's moments, but I remember I was transfixed.

Weeks later, the Beatles made their first official live U.S. television appearance, on February 9, 1964, on *The Ed Sullivan Show*. The date happened also to be my thirteenth birthday, and I don't think I could ever have received a better, more meaningful, more transforming gift. As romantic as it may sound, I knew I was seeing something very big on that night, and I felt something in my life change. In fact, I was witnessing an opening up of endless possibilities.

In 2006, those three 1964 appearances by the Beatles on *Ed Sullivan* were finally issued (for the first time in any form) on DVD. To this day, they remain remarkable. You watch those moments and you see history opening up, from the simple (but not so simple) act of men playing their instruments and singing, and sharing a discovery with their audience of a new youthful eminence. The long dark Kennedy-death nights were over. There would be darker nights to come, for sure, and rock 'n' roll would be a part of that as well. But on that night, a nightmare was momentarily broken, and a new world born. Its implications have never ended, even if they no longer mean exactly what they meant in that first season.

The Beatles' appearances on *The Ed Sullivan Show* proved momentous; they broke modern culture and history wide open. The broadcast that night drew over seventy-million viewers—the largest TV audience ever, at that time—an event that cut across divisions of style and region, and drew new divisions of era and age; an event that, like Presley, made rock 'n' roll seem an irrefutable opportunity.

In those minutes—especially in the first appearance, on February 9th—you see two formidable forces meeting for the first time: the Beatles and American youth. There's an overpowering mutual delight in the encounter, and there's also a clear sense of power being born in the moment—a power that would be shared (not always easily) by the band and its fans over the next several years. It was a cultural and entertainment event, but it was also an important moment of political upheaval.

When the Beatles stepped before that Manhattan audience in the winter of 1964, many things about our history and promises changed—and one of the most immediate and startling changes was that we were witnessing the social and cultural power that a pop group and its audience could now feed one another and share. That dynamic alone helped create whole new possibilities for what would happen as the decade developed, and artists and audiences and leaders and followers formed new (and sometimes precarious) alliances. The moment was about more than charisma or star-worship. It was about discovering—and asserting—a new mode of youth mandate.

Coming together in theaters, stadiums and outdoor amphitheaters in those days felt like we were forming our own little cities of youth, brimming with expectation and desire. It's amazing to realize how much power actually coalesced in American arenas on days and nights like those, whether we understood it or not.

This was back in a brief time when young people could still gather and scream in the dark and not meet with fear, distrust, resentment and retribution, before everything around us—the politics, the nation, the culture and the music—turned into wellsprings of division and dread. You could scream those days in a shared awareness: that life might be good after all, and if nothing else, you were lucky enough to be living it in a time when a band like the Beatles' every gesture seemed to illuminate your world.

DECEMBER
2015

**Mikal Gilmore**

**December 3, 2015**

This is where Elaine will be this weekend: The John Lennon Tribute Show to Feature Steven Tyler, Willie Nelson, Eric Church, Brandon Flowers, Tom Morello, Sheryl Crow and others. I will miss her, of course, but I'm always glad for the events and history she sees. I'm also looking forward to her photos and reports.

**Mikal Gilmore**

**December 4, 2015**

I'm honored to have some notes included in Bruce Springsteen's *The Ties That Bind: The River Collection*, released today. I haven't yet heard or seen everything included in the set (though what I've seen of the historic November 1980 Tempe, Arizona concert DVD certainly conveys the sound and impact of his expanding performances during this period), but by tonight I will.

In the mid-1980s, while working as a music critic at the *Los Angeles Herald-Examiner*, I probably wrote more about Springsteen than any other artist. Long reviews and commentary—some pieces over three thousand words, I believe—covering his epic shows, music's role in politics, questions of patriotism and community, labor unions, and the rising destructive wave of Republican conservatism in the wake of Ronald Reagan's 1980 election. I haven't looked at those articles in years (I could maybe find them at the library), but my bet is that they hold up better than most of my writing then.

The notes here focus on the period prior: the complex making of *The River*, and the complex life and meaning it took on after the album's release, as Springsteen took the music on stages across America, into the nation's realities and meanings. He found new depths, a new point-of-view voice, and showed a concentrated and smart courage that changed his music—from earlier to onward—forever. I have never seen a better live performer. I'm especially excited to watch the Tempe concert with my family. With the band's sound, with his body and nerve and personality, Springsteen made something heroic and monumental night after night. It gave many of the rest of us priceless heart during the dark Reagan years, and for all the years after.

Elaine Schock

December 5, 2015

"It Don't Come Easy"

We are halfway through treatment. I'm told the hardest part is over and for now it is. After the third round of aggressive chemo, Mikal is doing good. His appetite is returning and he eats pretty well, mostly pastas and soups. It is wonderful to see his weight returning to normal. His head and face are smooth but he still has his eyebrows. It's a good look. We have come a long way and learned a lot since the first round.

Mikal gets some sort of treatment daily. Kaiser has become his second home. They provide comfort, healing and live music. But it is work to get better. You have to have the right attitude because that is also part of the job and it don't come easy. You are in a ward of cancer patients and you can't help but see and feel their pain and anger with the hand they have been dealt. They are now Mikal's peers.

It can be hard to keep your spirits up, but Mikal has overcome that with a few self doubts here and there. Though I know there is still a long way to go, this time, this week feels hopeful. More than even last week. I'm in New York with Willie covering The John Lennon Tribute concert and TV special. As I was driving to the airport, I found myself missing the times when Mikal was feeling well enough to drive me to the airport and be at least an hour early to pick me up when I returned home. Yes, I miss that a lot. Thank you again for caring about my husband and for your kind words about me.

**Mikal Gilmore**

**December 5, 2015**

I miss those airport drives too. I look forward to doing them again.

Yes, I have been feeling better during this last chemo round. There were a couple of rough days—back pain, other stuff—but that has resolved for the present. Daily hydration helps, along with Neupogen injections. But what helps me most is seeing Elaine's face and hearing her voice. When things are good, she radiates. When they're less than good, she still manifests hopefulness. It is true that seeing people suffer at the hospital inspires some hard meditations and feelings. Many are going through worse than I am. They are hurting and brave, and I always summon my equivalent to a silent prayer when I see them, which is daily.

Elaine is busy right now gathering photos of holiday lights and trees in Manhattan. Lights and trees used to be my favorite part of the holidays. Now, my family. They look beautiful in the glow of the lights I place around the house.

## Mikal Gilmore
### December 8, 2015

My fear isn't that Donald Trump will become president. Rather, my concern is that when—not if, but when—his ongoing and worsening rhetoric results in bloodshed, it won't concern him; he won't regret it. He'll quickly find a way to boast about it. This man has a Vlad (the Impaler) Tepes lust for absolute power.

## Elaine Schock
### December 9, 2015

We have the most beautiful Christmas tree. We bought the lights and decorations. The house looks lovely and most festive. It is not a religious holiday to us even though it is for many. For us it is a celebration of life, love and family. We got thrown a curveball this year but it is not going to stop us. We are planning for this to be our best Christmas ever. Well, until next year.

## Mikal Gilmore
### December 10, 2015

Dear friends: Do some of you have experience or knowledge of hearing aids? As you might know, my chemotherapy has caused tinnitus and has cut off my high frequencies, and that won't change. Things sound like a tin can din, and I frequently have to ask people to repeat what they've said. I'm now investigating hearing aids—hopefully something that will allow me to wear over-the-ear headphones when I listen to music, and that will improve the experience of listening to music.

Some of you might have similar problems or know those who do, and perhaps there are musician friends here who have had to deal with the same problem. All advice is welcome. In addition, specific brands and names or models of particular hearing sets would be helpful as well. If possible, please post your comments rather than through private messages. As too many people know, I am miserable at private messages.

**Elaine Schock**

**December 10, 2015**

Mikal did the lights and I put up the star. Believe me, I got a lot of direction on that. Tomorrow we do ornaments. It's a big tree.

**Elaine Schock**

**December 11, 2015**

I put on my wedding ring for the first time pretty much since the ceremony. Truth is, you can't wrap your hands with a ring, and I am a boxer who trains several times a week. So I'd take it off and think I lost it. Then I just took it off for good. It didn't make me less married. But I am wearing it again and hope it works out. Not the marriage, that is fine, but the ring wearing.

**Elaine Schock**

**December 12, 2015**

**"Ray of Light"**

Our home looks lovely. The Christmas decorations are done—well, mostly. It even smells like Christmas. Mikal put the lights on the tree. That was a major feat because we didn't think he would be strong enough, but he was and did a beautiful job. And, for the first time since the diagnosis, we both believe that we will spend another Christmas together. Yes, it was a good week.

The thing that Mikal dreaded was the fitting for the radiation mask. But it went fine and was remarkable to watch. It is a thin clear plastic square that magically turns into a net like mask in a few minutes. It is warm when the technicians put it over your face and neck and they fan it with real fancy hand fans to cool it down. I don't know if that is how it is always done, to be honest, but it works. Mikal will have to wear the mask during his radiation treatments.

I was concerned how he would handle the fitting. He was terribly anxious to begin with but everyone at Kaiser was so kind and cheerful, it made things seem OK. He will be ready to start radiation/chemo on Dec. 21 for seven weeks, and maybe after all this is over, Mikal will be in full remission. He has worked hard at getting well. We see the doctor on Monday and will have an idea of where we stand but I think the news will be fine.

Mikal looks wonderful. Being bald works for him and he has gained the weight back. He looks healthy; even the nurses at the oncology center complimented him. There is still a long way to go, but we can finally see a ray of light at the end of the tunnel. There were days where there was no end to the darkness. Mikal should be feeling better for a few weeks so we will take this holiday and enjoy the hell out of it. And, I guess that is really all you can do, no matter what your circumstances are. Enjoy the time you have because you never really know when that time will end.

**Mikal Gilmore**
**December 12, 2015**
Two of my favorite Frank Sinatra recordings from the 1960s were "Summer Wind" and "That's Life." Years ago I'd sometimes see a local saloon singer who did a medley of the two. Sinatra identified and prided himself as a saloon singer. Though his greatest acting role is no doubt *The Manchurian Candidate*, his performance that always affected me most was in *Young at Heart*, in which he plays a depressed and self-destructive saloon singer. There's a gripping and frightening scene near the film's end that's as good as any acting I've ever seen. Sinatra doesn't say a word. The entire meaning comes through his face, and a movement of the wrist.

**Elaine Schock**
**December 14, 2015**
As Mikal Gilmore wrote in his liner notes for Bruce Springsteen's *The Ties That Bind*, "In effect, this was the tale of the real ties that bind: a faith in love's meaning, despite inevitable mortality. Wrap your arms around life and love, Springsteen was saying. Realize its span and its blessing." I knew Mikal's writing was poignant when I read it months ago but I had no idea at that time how much those words would mean to me and how it is exactly what I feel. Thank you for all your good thoughts about my husband.

**Mikal Gilmore**
**December 15, 2015**

*Ikiru* (Akira Kurosawa,1952) appears to be the story of a man who knows he is dying, though the title translates as *To Live*, or *To Live Again*. The central character, Kanji Watanabe (played by Takashi Shimura), is a man whose wife died twenty years before; he has since led a stultifying bureaucratic life, to raise a son who seems indifferent to him. One day Watanabe realizes he is dying of stomach cancer—he has a year at best. He is frozen with horror and regret. He's a nowhere man, with no experiences or amusement, but suffering and fear now drain him. The story takes Leo Tolstoy's *The Death of Ivan Ilyich*, then reforms and unfolds it by Kurosawa's own narrative.

One night, after seeing a windup hopping bunny toy, Watanabe realizes what he can do to make his last months something more than fearful paralysis. He hits upon a useful purpose that might redeem him by extending a good work to others. For me, this is Kurosawa's best film. It has an unusual structure that is hard to turn away from at any moment, because there is a mystery that needs to be answered, through memories and argument, right up to the final moments—not unlike *Citizen Kane*'s Rosebud. Watanabe's song, sung in freezing snow at film's end, is life's instruction. *Ikiru* is devastating and heartening like no other film of the 20th century, as well as a fitting rumination for our holiday season, though there's nothing religious in its meaning or divulgences.

**Mikal Gilmore**
**December 15, 2015**

Masaki Kobayashi's *The Human Condition* is one of the greatest achievements in cinema, in terms of craft, story, meaning and effect. It is, to be brief, the story of a man's sojourn through love, nationalism, war and the worst human darkness, in the World War II period. The human condition is not something humans easily survive or transcend, and that truth accumulates throughout this nine-and-a-half-hour film (divided into either three or six parts). It also stars one of Japan's most intense and handsome actors, Tatsuya Nakadai. And here's the best bit. It is available for streaming on Hulu, where you can also find a number of other matchless Japanese classics.

**Mikal Gilmore**

**December 15, 2015**

Apparently, America is quite fearful right now. Seems whupped up by shameless politicians and craven media. Even though there have been numerous mass shootings in public places, I am not afraid of malls nor public events. There are no guarantees of safety in this land.

**Mikal Gilmore**

**December 15, 2015**

Best day at the hospital ever. Some amazing therapy dogs, Tibetan Mastiffs, came to visit me.

**Mikal Gilmore**

**December 16, 2015**

In addition to being one of the defining samurai-legend filmmakers, Akira Kurosawa was perhaps Japan's best film noir director—and no place else in his career do crime and consequence cut more meaningfully than in the 1963 tale of a kidnapping, *High and Low*. The film unfolds in movements. The first--presented like the opening act of a play—depicts the news of the horrendous theft of a child for ransom, and the terrible choices that the main character, a wealthy businessman (Toshiro Mifune, in maybe his best role), must face. In this section, each decision redefines the man's morality and suffering.

The next movement is largely a police procedural (the original story is taken from *King's Ransom*, by Ed McBain), a thrilling movie-within-a-movie (with Tatsuya Nadakai) about the investigation and pursuit of the kidnapper. (There's an unusual chase scene that will rivet your nerves.)

Ultimately, the film comes to its revelation: the confession of the kidnapper. In a dialogue between Mifune and the criminal, it all comes out, in agony—why one man wrecked the lives of others. You can watch this film for its suspense all the way through, until you get to that ending—and its complex weave of class, hatred, fate and choices of redemption and inexorable damnation that are not that far apart—and then you will wonder what the hell just happened to you as the viewer? How did this crime tale come to hurt and confuse us so much?

In the end, Kurosawa has turned it into another Shakespearean tragedy. (*High and Low* was later remade in America as *Ransom*, with Mel Gibson and Gary Sinise—a miserable and cheapening rendition that fucks up all the devastating morality.)

**Mikal Gilmore**
**December 17, 2015**

Another Shakespearean noir by Akira Kurosawa—this time derived from *Hamlet*. In a way, that might be as much plot description as necessary (though I think *The Bad Sleep Well* has a better pace and structure than *Hamlet*). That's to say, deadly ends are in store for some characters, though not for others. After all, the bad sleep well. This is a complex and merciless tale—the opening scene of a wedding cake in the shape of a building, with a rose protruding from its seventh story, portends secrets that can't be survived if known. No lives or virtues are sacred here. It's a long film with a relentless pace, and Toshiro Mifune embodies layers of virtuous deception and irrefutable fate that convey his resourceful intelligence as an actor. You can't look away until an ending that, no matter what you expect, will shock you every time you see it. The bad sleep well.

**Mikal Gilmore**
**December 18, 2015**

Yasujirō Ozu was one of the greatest filmmakers of the twentieth-century. He had a feel for family, misbegotten love, heartbreak, human glimpses of eternal truths, plus a sympathetic view of the power of youth, that's never been topped by anybody. *Good Morning*, though, is maybe the best place to start with his work. It is a beautiful and hilarious film about two boys who take a vow of silence after their parents refuse to buy them a television set.

You might think that this is a thin precept for a gripping movie, but one of the ways that Ozu made it so involving was the camera perspective he employed. *Good Morning* was filmed from the viewing height of the boys. The other gift is that it ended up being much more than a story about whether the boys prevail in their strategy, because from their angle they don't miss much that is going on around them.

This is an ideal film for holiday viewing. Ozu was a humanist, and humanism deepens and enriches how we come to live with indelible traditional celebrations; secular values—even commercialization—can be beneficent compared to religion or the state's demands of observance. By example, we can laugh our asses off, as this lovely film causes us to do. Available for viewing on Hulu.

**Mikal Gilmore**
**December 18, 2015**

Though I met Elaine in 1977—and loved her immediately—we didn't come together as a couple until 2001. We never dated or romanced before that, though I thought my interest had to be apparent at times. Instead, we became indelible friends. We shared a lot of unspoken affection, devotion and humor simply by seeing each other over the years, despite our exclusive joys or pains. That only deepened for twenty-five years.

When we came together in late 2001, it was at a time when I believed that any ideal romantic love was fool's gold—it was as much my failing (if not more) as anything else. The possibilities of friendship and caring sex would have to be meaning enough. When I realized that Elaine was perhaps truly interested in a relationship, everything changed and never stopped changing. She has given me all of these verities and pleasures and lessons, and so much more. She is a teacher—a tough teacher—and I am rather certain I wouldn't have made it this far alive without her. More than anything, I want her face to be the last thing I see in this life, whenever that might be.

**Mikal Gilmore**
**December 18, 2015**

Ever since I first saw Elaine Schock, in 1977, I've wanted to make her face smile. It is something to see.

**Elaine Schock**
**December 19, 2015**
**"On the Road to Find Out"**

Mikal's PET scan (a type of imaging test using a radioactive substance to look for disease in the body) has come up clear. That means there are no signs of a tumor or tumors. Now, that doesn't mean he is cancer free yet, but the aggressive chemo has worked. So we go on to the next phase which is radiation/chemo combo starting Monday. Mikal gets a tattoo, which is sadly not cool like Johnny Depp's, just a dot to make sure his mask fits correctly. He will take a shuttle every morning to the hospital. The ride is longer than the treatment.

It seems like a long time ago since this battle started but it has only been about three months. A very long three months. There were days when things were dire, especially when Mikal's weight plummeted to 129 pounds and he was so fatigued that fatigue is an understatement. The hearing loss and tinnitus are still an issue. And things got worse before they got better, but they did get better. Mikal was able to get medicines and hydration to help with the side effects. The disfiguring growth on his neck disappeared. He liked Ensure Plus when smoothies no longer were tolerable, and he started to look like himself again. His appetite has returned and though that will probably only last a few weeks, it is long enough for a Christmas dinner celebration. Hallelujah for now—with a little trepidation.

We are on the road to find out what happens next on this journey. Fingers and toes crossed, it won't be a very difficult one. Mikal had been misdiagnosed for a year. He had been sick well before that. His first doctor was careless and perfunctory. Tragically that happens way too often. But we have an enormous amount of respect and gratitude for the doctor who did finally diagnose him——almost as soon as he walked into her office—and got Kaiser in gear immediately to save Mikal's life.

Next week Mikal will drop off a single white rose and a letter to let her know we will forever be in her debt. Thank you all for caring.

**Mikal Gilmore**
**December 20, 2015**
There is no other song that intimates Elaine Schock to me more than The Beatles "In My Life."

Love remembered, treasured and foreseen. Thank you all for your daily kindness to us both.

**Elaine Schock**
**December 20, 2015**

The HPV vaccine has been available for years now and they are extending who can be inoculated. That being said, there are certainly a lot of cancers we still don't know the cause of or why some people get cancer and others do not. And, that last part of the equation gives permission to smoke cigarettes and other risky behaviors. It is a fool's gamble. But knowledge is power. We won't stop the disease completely but maybe we can manage it better.

**Mikal Gilmore**
**December 20, 2015**

I've always wanted to have a real Santa suit and hat. Sometimes I feel like somebody tries to hide the Santa hat I got long ago, my $3.99 grocery store special. I'm sure all will be happy to know that I found it tonight, at the bottom back of a dresser drawer.

**Elaine Schock**
**December 23, 2015**

I'm Jewish and Mikal Gilmore is a Mormon (neither of us practices our religion) but we celebrate Christmas and maybe this year more than any other. Thank you all for being here with us.

> *And so this is Christmas, I hope you have fun*
> *The near and the dear ones, the old and the young*
> *A very merry Christmas, and a happy New Year*
> *Let's hope it's a good one, without any fears*
> —John Lennon

**Mikal Gilmore**
**December 21, 2015**

M Travis was one of my mother's three favorite country artists (Johnny Cash and Hank Williams were the others, though she was fond of Jimmy Dean and George Gobel, too). I've heard "The Christmas Song" (Merry Christmas to You), written by Mel Tormé and Bob Wells, and popularized by Nat King Cole, since I was a kid. I can't imagine not having lived with it.

**Mikal Gilmore**

**December 23, 2015**

Waiting for Elaine, with a smile.


**Mikal Gilmore**

**December 23, 2015**

The first time I recall hearing a resonant contrasting statement about Christmas's meanings was some time in the early 1960s. My mother was playing Johnny Cash's Christmas album, which featured "I Heard the Bells on Christmas Day," a song based on Longfellow's poem "I Heard the Bells." It's a notable poem, steeped in loss and necessary ambivalence.

In the 1860s Longfellow had lost his wife after her dress caught on fire. (Longfellow had tried to put the fire out and suffered burns severe enough to keep him from attending his wife's funeral.) In November 1863, Longfellow's son had been seriously injured during a Civil War battle. On Christmas Day that year Longfellow wrote his poem about a world of injustice and war that mocked Christmas's perceived promise:

> I heard the bells on Christmas Day
> Their old, familiar carols play,
> and wild and sweet
> The words repeat
> Of peace on earth, good-will to men!
> And thought how, as the day had come,
> The belfries of all Christendom
> Had rolled along
> The unbroken song
> Of peace on earth, good-will to men!
> Till ringing, singing on its way,
> The world revolved from night to day,
> A voice, a chime,
> A chant sublime
> Of peace on earth, good-will to men!
> Then from each black, accursed mouth
> The cannon thundered in the South,

*And with the sound*
*The carols drowned*
*Of peace on earth, good-will to men!*
*It was as if an earthquake rent*
*The hearth-stones of a continent,*
*And made forlorn*
*The households born*
*Of peace on earth, good-will to men!*
*And in despair I bowed my head;*
*"There is no peace on earth," I said;*
*"For hate is strong,*
*And mocks the song*
*Of peace on earth, good-will to men!"*
*Then pealed the bells more loud and deep:*
*"God is not dead, nor doth He sleep;*
*The Wrong shall fail,*
*The Right prevail,*
*With peace on earth, good-will to men.*

By the time the poem made it to song (English organist John Baptiste Calkin adapted the poem with a melody that became the standard), the lines had been condensed effectively:

*In despair I bowed my head:*
*"There is no peace on earth," I said,*
*"For hate is strong and mocks the song*
*Of peace on earth, good will to men.*
*Then pealed the bells more loud and deep:*
*"God is not dead, nor doth he sleep;*
*The wrong shall fail, the right prevail,*
*With peace on earth, good will to men."*

That first verse, sung by Cash in his sepulchral voice, seemed revealing and authoritative to me; Cash's conviction carried more effect than the reassuring rejoinder. The blessing, the promise, seemed strained by comparison.

Even as a kid I knew the proof was in the doubt. In the 1950s and early 1960s, we were constantly aware of the possible immediacy of war and destruction—we drilled for it regularly, we worried over bomb shelters. Christmas's assurances couldn't survive the bomb.

So Christmas was a dilemma. There is no peace on earth, yet we have this season or day when we insist or proclaim there is. But Christmas's promises never seemed equal. The peace means different things to different people. To some, true peace; to today's Evangelicals, true hellfire; to others, nothing. But if you've grown up with this dilemma—or just with healthy skepticism or lack of faith—you feel it in this season. Christmas is as much about darkness (reality) as about peace or love (hope, mythic claim). You simply have to look at the stories in the Gospels.

Jesus was born and immediately King Herod had hundreds or more baby boys slain as a guarantee to eliminate the threat of a rival. In short, Jesus escaped; other babies were put to the sword as the price of his birth. Either that's not a good way to begin a holiday's history, or it's the truer way, the more realistic one. Christmas is not about equal blessings; perhaps it's about hoping you and yours are blessed and remain blessed despite the wailing and death of the world around you.

The claim that there is no peace also resonated with me due to my own experience. Like anybody else, I looked forward to the holiday for its gifts, lights, shopping atmosphere, the magical holiday radio show Cinnamon Bear (broadcast from Portland), the lights and music, decorations, the snow (on the rare occasions when it happened), movies, TV specials—the basic human things—and of course the possibility of family harmony. But in my family's case, that was fool's gold.

Our mornings might start well enough, but by dinner time my father would goad my brothers or my brothers would voice their resentments, and my mother would jump in, ostensibly to restore the peace, but with barbed comments that only served to ramp up the conflicts. These quarrels erupted in shouting, frequently in violence, and my father would haul me out of the house, off to a motel for the night, my presents stuffed in a bag or two. I remember sitting on the grimy floor of a motel room, playing repeatedly with a metal ski jump toy I'd hoped for (my Rosebud), missing my family and thankful I wasn't with them. Those Christmas nights promised murder. There is no peace on earth.

I still enjoyed Christmas for the good feelings with friends, for the lights (especially the lights), for the inexplicable excitement and fulfillment of a tree (especially pink ones). Then the anticipation of a good Christmas came true, in my fifties. I didn't really experience the holiday as a family communion again until I moved in with Elaine and her children, Samantha Schock, Tessa Schock, and Preston (and his wife Claudia) Schock. I've tried to add to the pleasure and love and goofiness of the day for them by working hard on decorations and gift organizing, though I know I exhibited some of my original family's tensions and unkindness. But I've tried to get better with time, and to be an essential part of the warmth, and now that warmth has become essential to my happiness and well-being.

That has extended to the rest of Elaine's family, including her sister Linda and everyone else. I've learned family can be that elusive peace—or its meaningful equivalent—that the song doubted; that community sustains me. I can put my arms around my wife and her family, and in those moments—always too brief, never long enough—I find peace, and grace, on earth. As Elaine has already noted, this will be our best holiday to date.

**Mikal Gilmore**
**December 24, 2015**
When babies are born at Kaiser in Woodland Hills on December 24 and 25, a special tone plays throughout the hospital. I heard two such tones while there today.

**Mikal Gilmore**
**December 24, 2015**
I was thinking this morning about a quirk Elaine has: she can't stand tags inside shirts. They drive her crazy. She tears them out. I always poke fun. This morning I'm wearing an Arm the Animals T-shirt with a tag that is driving me nuts. I wonder if Elaine pasted it in there.

**Mikal Gilmore**
**December 25, 2015**
I have a new hat, from Elaine, and it doesn't mess around.

**Mikal Gilmore**
**December 25, 2015**
Ken Shane has nominated me to undertake the seven songs in seven days challenge. The idea is to post one song a day for seven days that has meaning. I think the best I can do is to pick daily whatever seems to suggest itself. This will overlook any true hierarchy of taste, but hopefully will result in some worthy choices.

Tim Buckley was one of my favorite singers and songwriters (and bandleaders), and "Song of the Siren" (co-written by Larry Beckett, from 1970's *Starsailor*) is his most haunting song. (In 2007, Beckett said, "It's a perfect match of melody and lyrics. There was some kind of uncanny connection between us.") The LP version is eerie and uncanny, but getting a chance to see Buckley sing it was invaluable.

The song's actual pedigree is pretty interesting. Buckley introduced it on the Monkees' final TV broadcast on March 25, 1968 (available, I believe, on *Morning Glory: The Tim Buckley Anthology*). But, the first cover version—preceding Buckley's own recording on his *Starsailor* album—was by Pat Boone, from 1969; Boone (a more interesting recording artist than often recognized, and one of the people I'd most like to write about) sang it as almost a sea shanty.

In 1983, I'd flown to a concert in San Francisco—the Clash?—and flew back to Los Angeles around three in the morning. A thick fog had settled over the parking lot, and that fog persisted all the way up along La Cienega through its weird oil fields. A bit after three I heard This Mortal Coil's version for the first time. With fog the only thing I could see, I felt like I was driving on the moon, and would soon be heading through to Mars' murky canyons. I was fine with the notion that the song and the drive would last for eternity—as far as necessary to answer its lyrical invitations. As a side note, David Lynch used This Mortal Coil's track in 1997's *Lost Highway*, and said that the band's recording inspired the first two wondrous Julee Cruise albums.

Lynch also once told me—well after his film was finished—that he'd never heard of Hank Williams' recording of Leon Payne's "Lost Highway." (That version was Williams' best recording.) There have been many other interesting covers. It's one of those songs that lives up to its title's invocation.

Elaine Schock
December 25, 2015
"Days Like This"

We are a week into this phase of radiation/chemo treatment. Mikal has never looked better. At least to me. It is perhaps a little ironic that he is done with all of this on his birthday, Feb. 9th. Mikal is feeling pretty good but we got a call saying his red blood count is too low and we need to watch it carefully. That was a bit of a setback. So you make a choice, either you curl up in a fetal position anticipating the worse or just enjoy every day.

We opted for the latter. That was actually a conscious decision. I know it sounds crazy but it is not an automatic thing. And the holiday has been so lovely. We had a delicious Christmas Eve dinner, great fun opening presents and then a visit to my brother's house to celebrate with our extended family. It is always wonderful to see them and eat just a little too much. So the evening ends and we are grateful for our incredible family and friends. It is a gift and we have learned to appreciate days like this more than ever before.

Mikal is doing everything he can to get better. He goes on the shuttle bus to radiation treatment every morning at seven A.M., and after that will spend another few hours getting other treatments to help minimize the side effects. It is a full-time job to get well. The bus seats twenty, but since Mikal is the newbie, he is relegated to the back of the bus. There is a hierarchy and no one shares seats.

All ten passengers got a small gift bag for the holiday, which included hand sanitizer, a coffee flavored lollipop and a lottery ticket. The leader of the pack makes sure that all patients are aboard and OK. He is a teacher by profession, and told Mikal that he has been given two years. He is OK with that and right now feels fine. Just getting his affairs in order so his family is taken care of. He said it almost matter of fact, but it threw Mikal. This is not your ordinary bus; it is one where you face mortality each ride. So we count down another day. Just thirty-one radiation treatments to go. Thank you for your thoughts and prayers. You mean so much to us.

## Mikal Gilmore
### December 26, 2015

My second in the seven songs challenge is "Peace Piece," by pianist Bill Evans (a sometime soloist who led superb small bands and played with Miles Davis on *Kind of Blue*). I first heard this recording in the dark, around four A.M., terrified out of my mind, in about 1970 or 1971. I was in the back of a van, lost on country roads, in a terrible mental state, and the friend driving the van (we were coming back from a rock festival) was debating whether or not to take me to a hospital.

As he drove, this track began to play on a jazz station. It's a solo improvisation by Evans, who used modal scales more effectively than perhaps anybody. The piece begins in a lonely and meditative state, but soon inches out beyond the sane cosmos, into unknown places, deep in fragmented madness. I felt the music pull me further apart inside, and then strangely, as it touched ever more discordant space, it pulled me back together. At the end of its few minutes, my mind felt integrated again. The road to peace traveled through uncertainty and fear.

A few days later I went into a local record store and described the music to the person working there. That manager, Michael Sugg, knew immediately the recording I was talking about and directed me to *Everybody Digs Bill Evans*, from 1958. So the music was twice wondrous. It saved my mind from disintegration, and brought me to one of my best lifetime friendships. Michael Sugg has taught me more about music than any other friend, listener or critic I've ever known.

Evans improvised "Peace Piece" based on the song "Some Other Time" from the musical *On the Town*, music by Leonard Bernstein, lyrics by Betty Comden and Adolph Green. Evans subsequently recorded a lovely version of "Some Other Time" with singer Tony Bennett. (*Where has the time all gone to / Haven't done half the things we want to / Oh well, we'll catch up some other time / This day was just a token/Too many words are still unspoken / Oh well, we'll catch up some other time.*)

Chuck Israel, who later played bass with Evans, said of the song: "'Peace Piece' is an example of the depth of Evans' compositional technique. It is an ostinato piece, composed and recorded long before the more recent superficial synthesis of Indian and American music; in fact, it owes more to Satie and Debussy than to Ravi Shankar. The improvisation starts simply over a gentle ostinato, which quickly fades into the background. Evans allows the fantasy that evolves from the opening motive (an inversion of the descending fifth in the ostinato) more freedom than he would in an improvisation tied to a changing accompaniment.

"He takes advantage of the ostinato as a unifying element against which ideas flower, growing more lush and colorful as the piece unfolds. Polytonalities and cross rhythms increase in density as the ostinato undulates gently, providing a central rhythmic and tonal reference. The improvisation becomes increasingly complex against the unrelenting simplicity of the accompaniment, until, near the end, Evans gradually reconciles the two elements."

"Peace Piece" is my favorite piece of music. Though others (Herbie Mann, the Kronos Quartet, Richie Beirach, Liz Story) have tried to record it, they shouldn't. It was a moment, and its epiphany belonged only to Bill Evans and those who heard it.

## Mikal Gilmore
### December 27, 2015

I was just listening to a combination humanist-deist-scientist on KCRW, as he related that he'd been at the death bed of famous people who'd never given a thought to dying until it was too late. I am not sure what his point was—we don't fear the end, or God's insecurities, enough?—so I could only react from my own reference. I'd thought about death every day of my life since I was sixteen—feared it, obsessed over it. That changed in September, the day I got my diagnosis. I stopped fearing or thinking about death. It wasn't a noble or conscious choice. Instead, I'd seen the look on Elaine's face, and what took over my awareness was that I wanted her to be okay, and not to fear. I wanted her to be assured about our future. I wanted to live for her and our family.

There's a certain irony here, as most of you know. Elaine has taken care of me every hour of every day since; she has done it by worrying and loving and, most of all, assiduously thinking her way through each day's worries. She does it for both of us, and for her children. Still, I'm grateful for that moment when I understood that what mattered overwhelmingly in my concerns wasn't so much what happens to me but rather the welfare of the people I love, and what their future brings them. Dylan has this wonderful song, "Lord, Protect My Child:" *While the earth is asleep/You can look at it and weep/Few things you find/Are worthwhile/And though I don't ask for much/No material things to touch/Lord, protect my child.* I play that song in my head every day now, and "child" equates to "family."

**Mikal Gilmore**
**December 27, 2015**

Here is my third in the seven songs choices in seven days challenge. After his time with Buffalo Springfield, Neil Young made three varied and brilliant albums from 1968 to 1969—*Neil Young, Everybody Knows This is Nowhere*, and *After the Goldrush*—then in 1972 he made *Harvest*, an album that damn near ruined him by turning his quirks and power into mainstream sound.

Maybe he scared himself, because the four albums that followed—*Time Fades Away*, *Tonight's the Night*, *On the Beach* and *Zuma* (1973 to 1975)—strike me as a perfect quartet, the best sequence of four albums by any rock 'n' roll artist. They were honest portraits of social, idealistic and personal dissolution. In the years that have followed, Young's brilliance has been consistently hit and miss. Maybe the Doom Quartet was even scarier than the mainstream gambit, because he never again came close to those mid-1970s lethal straits. (As far as I know, *Time Fades Away* is available only as part of an expensive vinyl box.

The sole CD versions I've found are bootlegs. It's incomprehensible to me that *Time Fades Away* doesn't seem to be available in Young's catalog, but then Neil can be a bit of an odd duck. I'm picking "Drive Back" from *Zuma*. It's a vicious sounding track, with the best guitar sound that Young ever achieved, and its lyrics always sounded like memory to me.

There isn't a day I don't think of *Zuma* and this song.

**Mikal Gilmore**
**December 28, 2015**
My fourth song in the challenge (actually, I'm cheating by selecting two songs today, but then, I can) is from thinking about people I've lost. "Canon" by Charles Mingus—one of the twentieth-century's great musicians and composers—plays in my mind. When I hear Hendrix's "Bold as Love," I catch music's will to life as it soars.

**Mikal Gilmore**
**December 28, 2015**
I'm not at all clear about who will "capture" the GOP nomination, though I know one candidate I hope won't: Trump. The media likes to talk about how he's reinvented all the rules this year, but that's Emperor's New Clothes horse-shit; he's "reinvented" nothing. He has no real political sense, and he has no ground organization—and the first few real states (i.e., not Iowa, which only matters on the night of Iowa) will make that plain. Polls don't equal votes—they equal pipedreams-for-business. Plus, while I'm at it, I'm not at all convinced that Bush won't end up as the nominee. He can afford losses and humiliation. Trump cannot.

**Mikal Gilmore**
**December 28, 2015**
In Oncology I just heard a nurse say, "We're still awaiting Mr. Smith's testicles." My ears perked right up—but in the wrong direction. Turns out she said, "We're still awaiting Mr. Smith's test results." Man, that Cisplatin has really fucked up my hearing.

**Mikal Gilmore**
**December 28, 2015**
Another hearing typo. Here in Oncology they've all been awaiting the arrival of their playlists. Naturally, I was interested. Playlists for us, or for the nurses? Well, they just arrived. In plastic bags. "The platelets are here." Damn.

**Elaine Schock**

**December 29, 2015**

This is the thing about boxing, about fighting. It isn't easy and you get knocked down and have to endure pain. Body shots are the worst. It takes courage just to get in the ring. Losing is not an option, but one person *will* lose. You need confidence, courage, mental and physical strength, and you get hit hard. Those punches will always be felt. This one is for you Mikal Gilmore. The Ali vs Foreman fight is considered one of the greatest, but I think maybe the greatest fight is closer to home.

**Mikal Gilmore**

**December 29, 2015**

Something I learned in my 20s: If you go through loss, death, depression or suffering and don't gain better compassion—I don't mean mere sympathy, I mean understanding—for others, then you've missed a meaningful opportunity. If you come away from your experience with anger above all, then you deserve compassion for that too, and hopefully that will help.

**Mikal Gilmore**

**December 29, 2015**

My fifth (I think) in the seven-songs-choices-in-seven-days challenge that I inherited from Ken Shane. Years ago, shortly after the release of his *Street Hassle* (1979), I spent many hours throughout that year or longer interviewing Lou Reed, in San Francisco, Los Angeles, and on the phone. I later adapted some of that in a collection of my writing, and added this to the end of that entry: "If I had to pick my favorite lines [Lou Reed] has ever written, they would be these: *It was good what we did yesterday / And I'd do it once again / The fact that you are married / Only proves you're my best friend / But it's truly, truly a sin* (from 1969's "Pale Blue Eyes"). Also, these: *With a daytime of sin and a nighttime of hell / Everybody's going to look for a bell to ring* (from 1979's "All Through the Night").

It seems to me that in his best music—even in his darkest, most broken-hearted reveries—Lou Reed has always rung a bell, loud and clear, pealing a clarion call of hope that the glory of love, despite (or because of) our daytimes of sin and nighttimes of hell, might see us all through yet. During dinner and drinks one night, Reed asked me what I thought his best song was. I told him "Pale Blue Eyes," for its sad truths and beauty, for its personal resonance in my life, and for my favorite guitar break on any record of his or the Velvets'.

That night he surprised me by singing the song on stage. He was often looking for something inside that song—something that explained what was taken and lost. I think of "All Through the Night" as revealing what became of the sin and hurt and need of "Pale Blue Eyes." *You feel so lonely, when it's in the afternoon / And you gotta face it, all through the night / Don't it make you believe that something's gonna have to happen soon? / Oh, baby, all through the night, All through the night / With a daytime of sin and a night time of hell? / Everybody's gonna look for a bell to ring / All through the night/And they do it, all through the night, baby, All through the night / Said: 'oh, babe got to celebrate,' all through the night / Made me feel so sad, I cried all through the night / I said: 'oh, Jesus,' all through the night / If the sinner's in and the good man's gone / Then a woman can't come and help him home / It ain't so much when a man's gotta cry / To get a little loving, and some peace of mind / Said: "hey, baby give it to me," all through the night / Some people wait for things that never come / And some people dream of things, they've never been done / They do it, oh, baby, all through the night / Why can't anybody shed just one tear? / For things that don't happen all through the night.*

## Mikal Gilmore
### December 30, 2015

My sixth (?) in the seven-songs-choices-in-seven-days challenge, though there's more than one song and singer here. These are in fact three diverse vocalists whom I hear in my head every day. What they have in common is singular tone and vision. Judee Sill saw dependency, pain and God (and it was God who fucked her over tragically); Helen Merrill saw the expanse of blue loneliness; Jeri Southern saw sex, wit and her own variant of blues, and she never kidded herself about how seductive and perilous that combination was.

Her selection here, "The Cabin," was written by Paul Bowles and Tennessee Williams (from their Blue Mountain Ballads song cycle), and like Judee Sill's "The Kiss" and Helen Merrill's "When Flamingos Fly," it will haunt you for what was hoped for and then replaced by unforgettable loss. From Sill's "The Kiss." *Once a crystal choir/Appeared while I was sleeping / And called my name /And when they came down nearer Saying, "Dying is done"/ Then a new song was sung / Until somewhere we breathed as one / And still I hear their whisper . . . Lately sparkling hosts/Come fill my dream / descending On fiery beams / I've seen 'em come clear down/Where our poor bodies lay / Soothe us gently and say / Gonna wipe all your tears away / And still I hear their whisper . . . Love, rising from the mists / Promise me this and only this / Holy breath touching me, like a wind song / Sweet communion of a kiss.*

**Mikal Gilmore**
**December 30, 2015**

I have no business forgiving the extremist couple that killed fourteen co-workers in San Bernardino on December 2, 2015—that would be up to those directly affected, and why should they? However, sitting here watching CNN, I realize I can't forgive the media either. They have exploited and unnecessarily increased fears and potential for panic. Most likely we are not all going to die at midnight tomorrow. Nor should we be told to worry over such a possibility, or to examine every stranger in public as a threat or suspect. What happened to fearing fear above all else? Here's what happened to it: ratings competition. Be afraid, be very afraid, because to disempower our better sense is to empower an ideology that needs to sell us fear—which is to empower another form of terrorism. We have met the enemy, and it wants us to submit to its hysteria twenty-four hours a day. This is the worst year for American media that I've experienced firsthand, but don't expect American media to report that truth to you.

**Mikal Gilmore**
**December 30, 2015**

This is a terrible admission, but I'm no saint. I'm sitting in the lobby and I hear a nurse say to somebody, "Are you sick? Here, sit next to this gentleman." (Me!) Before I can do anything, this poor guy sits down next to me and picks up my hat, and moves to put it on.

I say, "That's okay, I'll take that."

He says, "I might die. Right here, right now," and moves again to put on my hat.

"That's terrible. Can I have that hat?"

Yes, I talk about compassion, but . . . my hat! I've retrieved it, but I haven't put it on. This poor man gets up, walks all around, coughing. Suddenly I notice, there are coughers and bloody noses all over the lobby. I'm going upstairs. If all they find of me is a puddle, the iPad Pro is Elaine's. What I've learned in the last few days is that death does *not* take a fucking holiday, at least not without company. I'm going to hell. With my hat.

## Mikal Gilmore
### December 31, 2015

My seventh and final song, though (again) there's more than one song here. (I'll be posting something a little later today about passing the torch.) My choices have comprised whatever came to mind day to day—songs that have had some place in my taste or memory—though on this last occasion I've allowed taste and historical consequence to correspond.

It's reasonable to make a case for Mamie Smith's "Crazy Blues" (by Perry Bradford, from 1920) and Billie Holiday's "Strange Fruit" as two of the most important recordings of the twentieth-century. "Crazy Blues" was the first blues hit, and though some will argue that it wasn't a true blues song, that's terribly shortsighted. The lyrics are about loss, anger, sex, abuse, violence, depression and murder, and about music that battles (or succumbs to or celebrates) it all. Perry Bradford's composition codified blues more immediately than the "father of the blues," W.C. Handy did—and just as authentically—and Mamie set the way for two other great Smith blues singers, Clara and Bessie.

Beyond all this, "Crazy Blues" is a wonderful recording, and it still holds a tale of mystery and madness. The song changed America perhaps more than any other song of its time, and its lyrics still convey that weigh: *I can't sleep at night / I can't eat a bite / 'Cause the man I love / don't treat me right / He makes me)feel so blue / I don't know what to do / Sometime I sit and sigh / And then begin to cry / 'Cause my best friend / Said his last goodbye / There's a change in the ocean / Change in the deep blue sea, / my baby I'll tell you folks, / there ain't no change in me / My love for that man will always be / Now I can read his letters / I sure can't read his mind / I thought he's lovin' me / He's leavin' all the time / Now I see my poor love was blind / I went to the railroad / Hang my head on the track / Thought about my daddy / I gladly snatched it back / Now my babe's gone / And gave me the sack / Now I've got the crazy blues / Since my baby went away / I ain't had no time to lose / I must find him today."*

Lyrics that have been questioned: *"I'm gonna do like a Chinaman, / go and get some hop / Get myself a gun, / and shoot myself a cop / I ain't had nothin' but bad news / Now I've got the crazy blues / Those blues.*

Billie Holiday's "Strange Fruit"—from a poem by Abel Meeropol, set to music by his wife, Maura Duncan—is among the bravest and scariest songs ever written. Holiday feared that singing it might cost her life. Holiday's producer, John Hammond, refused to record "Strange Fruit"; Holiday turned to her friend, Commodore Records' Milton Gabler.

From Wikipedia: "In her autobiography, *Lady Sings the Blues*, Holiday suggested that she, together with Meeropol, her accompanist Sonny White, and arranger Danny Mendelsohn, set the poem to music. The writers David Margolick and Hilton Als dismissed that claim in their work *Strange Fruit: The Biography of a Song*, writing that hers was 'an account that may set a record for most misinformation per column inch.' When challenged, Holiday—whose autobiography had been ghostwritten by William Dufty—claimed, 'I ain't never read that book.'"

Horribly, the lyrics still resonate: *Southern trees bear strange fruit / Blood on the leaves and blood at the root / Black bodies swinging in the southern breeze / Strange fruit hanging from the poplar trees / Pastoral scene of the gallant south / The bulging eyes and the twisted mouth / Scent of magnolias, sweet and fresh / Then the sudden smell of burning flesh / Here is fruit for the crows to pluck / For the rain to gather, for the wind to suck / For the sun to rot, for the trees to drop / Here is a strange and bitter crop.*

## Mikal Gilmore
### December 31, 2015

Last night Elaine and I finally had a couple of hours to watch Bruce Springsteen's 1980 Tempe concert, from *The Ties That Bind* box. It is a transfixing, rapturous and heartbreaking show—a document of the moment that Spring-steen turned from focusing on personal heroic and angry statements to epiphanies of communities in shared need, cut off from the kindnesses of society and government.

Tempe also works as an example of the period in which Springsteen was moving afield from being an operatic singer to a folk voice. He could always sing coloratura when necessary (and still can), but he never again wrote in the grand-sweep style that tied "Born to Run" and "Thunder Road" to hot-rod rockabilly, Roy Orbison bel canto, Mozartian embellishments, Little Richard hyperbole, and existential crisis, with Copland on the horizon of "The Promised Land."

I didn't see the entirety of this DVD before working on the liner notes, and I'm grateful because the beauty and mastery of this would've been overwhelming. This is a special moment from the best band that rock 'n' roll has ever produced, and it's not a bad New Year's Eve companion. As Elaine noted when we were done with the first half, "Not a moment of this is dull. Not a moment. It's all charisma."

**Mikal Gilmore**
**December 31, 2015**
I have used up a lot of my wishes this year but I think I get one more. I wish you all a Happy, Safe and Fearless New Year. With love.

## The Albums - Part 3
### Mikal Gilmore

The 1960s was an exciting and eventful time to live through, though it would soon become (just as obviously) a complex and scary time. It was a time when almost every new song was shared, discussed and sorted through for everything it might hold or deliver—every secret thrill or code, every new joyous twist of sonic texture. "Respect." "The House of the Rising Sun." "Stop! In the Name of Love." "Help Me, Rhonda." "Mr. Tambourine Man." "(I Can't Get No) Satisfaction." "Positively 4th Street." "Help!" "California Dreaming." "Good Lovin'." "When a Man Loves a Woman." "Summer in the City." "Sunshine Superman." "I Want You." "96 Tears." "Paint it Black." "Over Under Sideways Down." "Ode to Billy Joe." "Good Vibrations." "The Letter."

It was also a time of many leaders or would-be leaders—some liberating, some deadly. Mario Savio. Lyndon Johnson. Robert Kennedy. Julian Bond. Richard Nixon. George Lincoln Rockwell. George Wallace. Martin Luther King, Jr. Malcolm X. Hubert Humphrey. Eldridge Cleaver. Shirley Chisolm. Jerry Rubin. Tom Hayden. Gloria Steinem. Abbie Hoffman.

There were also the other leaders—some who led without desire or design, but who led as surely (and sometimes as liberatingly or as foolishly) as the political figures. The Beatles. Bob Dylan. Mick Jagger, Brian Jones and Keith Richards. Timothy Leary. Jimi Hendrix. Jane Fonda. Jefferson Airplane. Aretha Franklin. James Brown. Marvin Gaye. Sly Stone. Jim Morrison. Charles Manson.

As you can tell from those lists, the 1960s' ideals, events and moods grew darker—and they did so earlier than many people would like to acknowledge. In the early 1960s, America was a nation wrestling with how to define and accommodate its liberal conscience. The rising struggle for the civil rights of American blacks was meeting with some vicious resistance, erupting in numerous murders of peaceful black and white activists working and demonstrating in the nation's South.

The administrations of John F. Kennedy and Lyndon B. Johnson gradually moved to protect and facilitate this movement, but it took years of bloodshed to make a real difference. In addition, Kennedy, and then Johnson, became increasingly entangled in campaigns of militant-anti-communism, resulting early on in Kennedy's embarrassing attempt to help Cuban insurgents rise up against Fidel Castro, in the Bay of Pigs fiasco, and later in Johnson's devotion to tragic actions in Southeast Asia. In reaction to all this, a new activism found momentum among students in American universities, to galvanize young people toward trying to reclaim American liberalism.

All of these developments transformed me—transformed everybody I knew near my age—if not precisely in the moment, then soon enough. My parents had been, more or less, liberal. For a time in the early 1960s, I flirted with the beliefs of conservatism (it may seem I was too young at the time for all this, but it never felt that way—politics was in the air as much as was music), but the emergence of the new rock 'n' roll sensibility that came along with the Beatles and Bob Dylan closed off that possibility forever for me.

To be meaningfully young then, to be part of that fast-changing rock 'n' roll generation, was to be liberal, and in ways that went well beyond clear-cut politics. How you wore your hair, the colorful clothes you adopted, marked you as a part of a different tribe with different values and hopes. The music you listened to, that you took into your mind and heart much like others took religion into their soul, formed a fraternal sense of shared convictions deeper than the bonds of any political party.

The drugs we would take, and our eagerness to take them, would constitute genuinely revolutionary acts that deeply changed America. And perhaps most of all, knowing that you were of draft age, that much of your entire generation was being called to deadly and futile service in Southeast Asia, deepened your sense of standing apart. It hardly seemed coincidental that so many of us who were turning rebellious could also be easily killed or ruined. We would be running all sorts of risks; the changes we caused met all kinds of resistance.

There still was joy; profound fun and discovery was, for a long time—or what felt like a long time—our daily portion. Since this is a story about an album collection, I should point out that until the summer of 1967, I didn't have one. I didn't even have a single album. For that matter, I didn't own a record player (the ones that had belonged to my brothers had long since disappeared). But I also didn't yet need any such things. I've said, probably more than once, that in these years music and its credo of change was in the air.

That's hardly an idealized description. Radio was, whether it meant to be or not, the widespread network for a fast uprising. Everywhere, you heard the Beatles, the Rolling Stones and Motown, to mention some of the most obvious movers, and by 1965 some of these artists were saying different sorts of things than popular music had said before: notions of unease and audacity. I remember that in the summer of 1965 I was working in a strawberry field, picking berries with scores of other kids my age. It was tiring and dirty work, and we had to get up far too early to do it, but it was a way of earning money for clothes and dances.

Despite the mud and back pain, radio often made the chore incomparable fun. We would all bring our transistors, hang them on the handles of the baskets we dragged through the rows of berries, and tune into the local top pop station in Portland, KISN-AM. The summer of 1965 was perhaps the best season of popular radio music I can remember. Remarkable charges of innovative and vibrant sounds bounced across the fields by way of our transistors, and we regularly registered our assessments of each new song.

When a song like "(I Can't Get No) Satisfaction," by the Rolling Stones, came along that summer, the reaction was an immediate shock wave. This was more than about a restless libido. This was about a discontent that was bubbling under but rising up. We all felt it.

There were even better ways to share our collective thrill. That same summer, the Beatles made their second major tour of the U.S., and I was lucky enough to win tickets to one of those shows. Being a fourteen-year-old kid in mid-1960s America and having a pair of Beatles tickets show up in your mailbox unexpectedly? It was prize enough for a lifetime.

I'd been to other pop concerts—Herman's Hermits, the Dave Clark 5, the Beach Boys, and I'd soon see the Rolling Stones—but nothing before or since held the excitement I felt among that crowd on that afternoon. We were like our own country, brimming with expectation and desire.

The concert took place at Portland's Memorial Coliseum—a twenty-thousand-seat sports and convention center, just outside city center. There were two, three, maybe four other acts on the bill. I'm trying to remember, was Gerry and the Pacemakers one of them? Or Roy Head, of "Treat Her Right" fame? I can't be sure—so much of that afternoon felt like a fever dream of some sort. This much I recall with clarity: At a certain point, a small legion of Portland policemen assembled in front of the stage. (I counted roughly two hundred. By contrast, there were maybe fifteen cops several months later, when the Rolling Stones played the same venue.) We all knew what it meant when the officers formed those lines. The moment was imminent.

The house lights went down, but so many flashbulbs were suddenly going off that you could see the Beatles moving through the darkness, taking their stage positions. The band vaulted into its first number as the spotlights came up—but to this day I couldn't tell you what song it was. The truth is, you couldn't really hear the Beatles—you couldn't catch George Harrison's witty riffs or Ringo Starr's adept snare and tom rolls, and you couldn't distinguish Paul McCartney's ecstatic croon from John Lennon's creative howl.

All that you could hear—instantly, and with enough fierce intensity to shock you—was the amassed shriek of the audience. It was a full-throated, uncontained celebratory and needy cry, and it never relented for a single second during the next half hour. If anything, the colossal yowl grew louder the longer the band was in front of us. At first, I was annoyed. I wanted to hear the Beatles. After all, if you look at some of the concert footage from that tour or play the long inexplicably out-of-print *The Beatles at the Hollywood Bowl* album, you realize just how damn good (tight, clever and dynamic) the band was live; in the center of those public storms, they were four very cool cats.

At an actual concert, though, you understood that the whole fucking gestalt of being in that room with the Beatles and their ululating audience was all that mattered. This wasn't just about hearing great music—it was about being in the presence of an experience that genuinely felt like living revelation. You couldn't separate any of the parts of that experience—the band's looks and sound combined with the crowd's concentrated fervor, and your own submission to the headiness of that fusion—and still have the fullness of the mystery. At one point I realized my own voice was screaming along with all the other voices around me—and I was startled. I felt embarrassed for a moment, yet I couldn't help it, I couldn't stop it. I had to scream, I felt so full of life and pleasure.

These were overwhelming moments, watching the Beatles through the flickering luminescence of flashbulbs, moving and playing and singing in the fractional lights of history. The poet Allen Ginsberg attended that same performance I did at the Memorial Coliseum and rendered the experience in his poem "Portland Coliseum."

Ginsberg understood what he was witnessing. Mass fervor that great—especially from the young—has always felt threatening. That's because it can seem unruly, powerful enough to upset traditions and values or to incite dangerous action. There had been small riots at rock 'n' roll concerts in the 1950s—chairs thrown, fisticuffs—but the threat implicit in 1960s music was something else. It was about setting things loose, about changing or upending the world. The barricade of policemen I saw that day at the Beatles' show—the same line Ginsberg had seen—certainly acted as if they were seeing something more than mania. The scream the Beatles brought forth in America was just too unforeseen and too big. It could help shake the order of things, and in time it would.

JANUARY
2016

**Mikal Gilmore**

**January 1, 2016**

This is a column I wrote for the *Los Angeles Herald-Examiner* in the 1980s. It corresponds to a YouTube link I posted earlier tonight, to the film *Hank Williams: The Show He Never Gave*:

IN THE EARLY 1980s, a young Canadian director, David Acomba, made a film called *Hank Williams: The Show He Never Gave*. It's among the best—certainly among the most unforgettable—music films I have ever seen. It uses pop music as a means of contemplating (even entering) imminent death, and in the process resolving, explaining, and perhaps redeeming the drama of one man's public life and sorrowful end. Shot in Canada, *The Show He Never Gave* opens its story on New Year's Eve, 1952, Hank Williams' final few hours on earth. A night-blue Cadillac is traveling on a lonely, snowy road. In the back seat, the lean, grim figure of Williams (played by Woody Guthrie-influenced Canadian folk singer, Sneezy Waters) stirs fitfully. On the radio one of Williams' pedal-steel-laden hits is playing. Leaning forward, he abruptly snaps it off.

Williams begins to rue the loneliness of the night. "I wish I didn't have to be playing that big concert arena . . . tomorrow night," he mutters to himself. "Tonight's the night I should be playing . . . one of those little roadside bars we're goin' by right now." He gazes out at the blue darkness as if he were looking at a long-desired woman.

Moments later, Williams' ruminations become reality: We see him pulling up to a jam-packed honky-tonk, his five-piece band finishing the strains of "My Bucket's Got a Hole in It," a crowd of old rubes and young rowdies in semi-religious awe of this country legend. With self-conscious meekness, Williams takes the small stage and begins to play his exhilarating and broken-hearted minstrel songs—"Half as Much," "Hey Good Lookin'," "Cold, Cold Heart," "I Can't Help It If I'm Still in Love with You," "Kaw-Liga," "Lovesick Blues," "Your Cheatin' Heart," among others. He also talks to the audience self-deprecatingly about his alcoholism, muses over his separation from his first wife, worries that the audience at this little wayside stop may reject him. Indeed, the one injunction that every important voice in the film—devil or keeper—tells him is, "Give 'em a good show." Williams looks paralyzed at the mere suggestion.

Not much else happens. There are brief bouts of flirtation, camaraderie, and self-destructiveness backstage, some more icy self-reflections in the back seat of the Cadillac. And yet it becomes apparent that we are witnessing a man struggling to account for himself—his hurts, his hopes, his soul, his terror, his deviltry—in the measure of this handful of unpolished songs.

And that's what happens. When in mid-show Williams begins to reminisce about his first wife, Audrey, and then moves into an unaccompanied reading of his haunting folk ballad, "Alone and Forsaken," the movie provides an emotional wallop that we never quite forget. From that point on, the crowd in the barroom watches Williams more heedfully, more perplexedly, as they gradually become aware they are privy to the confessions of a man with a heart so broken that he may never get out of this world with his soul intact.

By the end, we have come as close to a reckoning with dissolution, death, and judgment as film—or pop music—has ever brought us. "It might seem funny that a man who's lived the kind of life I have is talking about heaven when he should be talking about hell," Williams tells his audience before moving into a desperately passionate version of his gospel classic, "I Saw the Light." Moments later, in the lonely, fading reality of the Cadillac's back seat, Williams admits to himself: "Only there ain't no light. I tried, Lord knows how hard I tried, to believe. And some mornings I wake up and it's almost there." The moment is more frightening and desolate than might be imagined. Williams indeed sees the light, walks toward it, and we know there is no return from God's fatal graces.

As good as *Hank Williams: The Show He Never Gave* is, I'm afraid you might have to look damn hard to find it. Acuff-Rose, the Nashville publishing firm that owns the rights to Williams' extensive songbook, withheld permission for the filmmakers to use Williams' songs, thus in effect barring the film's U.S. release. Acuff-Rose's response was a little hard to fathom. After all, Williams' excesses were not merely pop legend—they were a matter of record. Roy Acuff himself was a member of the country gentleman Nashville establishment that expelled Williams from the Grand Ole Opry because of his drinking, drug use, intoxicated performances, and occasional gunplay.

Maybe Acuff came to regret Nashville's staidness so deeply that he preferred to see its history go unpublicized, or maybe he never quite forgave Williams for refusing to keep his demons private and thus marring the smooth façade of Nashville's decorum. In 1983, Wesley Rose of Acuff-Rose told me: "What I didn't appreciate about the film—because Hank was a personal friend—is the part where they show someone give him the needle. I never saw Hank take a needle. It isn't what you call expert criticism; it's what I call personal criticism. [The filmmakers] stressed the weakness of the man, rather than the greatness that rose from his work."

To my mind, *Hank Williams: The Show He Never Gave* did just the opposite: It got as close to the artist's greatness as any biographical or fictional work might. The only thing that gets closer is the frightened yet lucid soul of Williams's own songs. "The lights all grow dim and dark shadows creep." *The Show He Never Gave* takes us right into those shadows—and maybe that's not an easy thing to forgive.

### Elaine Schock
### January 2, 2016
I'd not heard of the movie before Mikal wrote about it. Then I had to see it. You should, too. Hank Williams made unforgettable music and Mikal Gilmore can write better than just about anyone else. I love Hank and I love Mikal.

### Elaine Schock
### January 2, 2016
For the record, one of Mikal's bus drivers is a big asshole. She doesn't get flowers or even a smile from me. I don't care what her motives are, but I doubt they have anything to do with separating herself from the heartbreak of cancer. She leaves those patients waiting for her for quite some time while she does something that has nothing to do with her job. The patients just had treatment and some are terminal. She could care less about the fact they are weak, exhausted, and cold because the bus is locked and they are outside in 40-degree weather. She knows their schedule, so she knows perfectly well they are waiting for her once again.

There is no place for the patients to sit while they wait. I guess they could collapse and take the pressure off their legs, and one or two have done so already. She never turns on the heat for them but if she feels a bit warm she will blast the AC. The people are already cold and the ones up front now get to freeze. None of the patients want to give her anything but the middle finger. I am happy to do that in solidarity, of course with an extra dose of kindness. She is lucky I don't clench it and punch her, but that is not my style. Most of the time. Now, I get that most people on this thread cannot fathom that kind of callous behavior because they are kind and good, but it exists right here in River City and Woodland Hills.

## Mikal Gilmore
### January 2, 2016

I inadvertently made one evening this last week more difficult for Elaine and Tessa. I came up with the idea of Indian Chicken Curry. Two bites in and my esophagus froze completely, and I couldn't talk at all, only make weird noises. I knew I'd be fine, but I couldn't assure them. Elaine got me some water and I stood up to go into another room. As soon as I did, that somehow solved the problem—I could swallow, breathe, and talk again. But the hard part is that both Elaine Schock and Tessa seemed scared—Elaine especially. It had her shaking the rest of the night. A lesson partly learned. Use common sense. Some things won't be edible for years again, if ever. Now Tessa researches the content of everything I eat before I do, and either allows me or forbids me.

## Mikal Gilmore
### January 2, 2016

This is Saturday, which means it's the day for Elaine Schock's weekly update about my medical progress—and in this case, our state of family as well. I think it's her best commentary to date.

## Elaine Schock
### January 2, 2016
### "Move On Up"

Mikal's doctors have told him that he is doing better than expected. They say his attitude makes all the difference. He is still warned of the possibility of terrible side effects, so that is underlying. But they note how good he looks. Mikal even jokingly asked me if he was getting fat. (At least I think it was a joke?)

We brought in 2016 the same way we have done every year since 2002, together with family. My children are all at the house this week and sleeping under one roof. They are safe and happy. And, this year we have new family members, the loving partners of the older children.

Mikal has started writing again and has a genius idea for a book. I couldn't ask for more, so it was baffling to me that at the stroke of midnight, I got emotional. I don't know what came over me. I thought I would be able to hide my tears, but my sister, who notices everything, pointed it out loud to the room. She has always been a snitch. I tried to escape unnoticed, but at least three members of my family followed me out of concern, which made it worse of course. But I pulled myself together and went back to celebrate the New Year.

Mikal's routine to remission is steadfast. Radiation every day and chemo once a week. Five more weeks to go. They increased his chemo dosage because he is doing so well, and his red blood count went up considerably. One less worry today. Mikal travels on the bus with the other cancer patients from Woodland Hills to get treatment at Kaiser on Sunset. He is still relegated to the back of the bus. No move on up for him yet. As I have mentioned, the patients have a careless and somewhat cruel bus driver. I think they don't say anything to her for fear she will leave them behind, and most are very weak from their illness. So, the riders carefully pick their battles. Me too. I have offered to have a nice chat with her but Mikal worries about that. He is no fool; he knows me. Still, if she doesn't become a bit more of a considerate driver, we will meet soon. Things will change.

Thank you for all your prayers, thoughts and concerns. It helps us a great deal and makes me believe the world is a better place.

**Mikal Gilmore**
**January 4, 2016**
Hard things come to those who wait—and wait. I'm amazed at what so many health care professionals have to witness, and what so many of their patients

endure for so long. When mortality hovers in a room or roams the halls, or even sits on the bus, it is no small presence. It tends to draw company.

## Mikal Gilmore
### January 5, 2016

As a Mormon, I've been wanting to say something about the Mormon aspect of the current standoff debacle at the Malheur National Wildlife Refuge in Harney County, Oregon. Militants have seized the refuge to make their case that the United States Forest Service and Bureau of Land Management are constitutionally required to turn over most of the federal public land they manage to the individual states. It's an extremely complicated issue, with criss-crossing roots all the way back to anti-Mormon persecution during the Joseph Smith era (the Mormons that I shared an outsider identity with).

Things got more compromising in the early 20th century, as the church became less liberal and more die-hard conservative. One result of that compromise is that Mormons gradually became law-fearing, upright citizens—the Mormons I found myself in conflict with since I was sixteen—who learned to declare fidelity to the laws and leaders of the land, and who see themselves as patriots. (The church itself will disenfranchise same-sex couples, though the church nonetheless says that state and local governments must abide by the Supreme Court's ruling, and should not refuse same-sex marriage rights.) This is to say that the Oregon hooligans are a fringe minority, and the Mormon Church would never countenance their foolish disrespect of federal and local laws—if for no other reason than they are deeply embarrassing to church leadership.

However, this is what has caught my interest in all this: Apparently there are members of this confederacy of dunces who identify themselves as members of a Captain Moroni movement. Some even call themselves Captain Moroni. The big-name, famous Moroni was one of the significant characters—a prophet, and the son of Mormon—in Joseph Smith's grand-vision American novel, *The Book of Mormon*. Moroni essentially compiled the writings that became *The Book of Mormon*, according to the book's own legend, and centuries later Moroni appeared as a ghost-angel and transferred those records to Joseph Smith. (Moroni is the angel you see on top of Mormon temples.)

That Moroni, though, was not Captain Moroni, a figure earlier in *The Book of Mormon*'s chronology. Captain Moroni was a fierce military commander and ideologue who did more for war than for peace, though Smith touted him in his novel as a man who stood up for liberty (Captain Moroni summarily slaughtered dissenters.) This earlier Moroni has in recent times become a symbol for fringe-Mormon anti-government and survivalist groups––the fundamentalist equivalent to the Al Qaeda and ISIS movements that have attempted to represent Islam. So far these would-be Moronis are unintentionally self-parodying, but they are indeed itching for a confrontation in bullets. If they come out of this embarrassed, they will likely also come out of it more deadly, or would hope to seem that way. There's no solution for this kind of idiocy; it likely perpetuates through generations.

My advice is, if you see them coming down the street, cross the street. They are itching for trouble.

**Elaine Schock**
**January 6, 2016**
I just watched a *CBS This Morning* roundtable discussion on cancer with some important specialists. They thought it was so smart but it was not. They mentioned prevention a bit (smoking and sun), but never mentioned that eleven to twenty-six year olds (I believe they will expand the age) can get a vaccine for HPV that can eliminate HPV cancers. There is an epidemic. Mikal is suffering from HPV related tongue cancer. His oncologist is seeing ten new patients a week who have the same disease—mostly young men—and it is the primary cause of cervical cancer. If these are the doctors running the show for a cure, it is no wonder why we haven't gotten farther.

**Elaine Schock**
**January 6, 2016**
I will continue to bang the drum. Other research shows that the most common reason for adolescents not to receive the HPV vaccine isn't parental refusal; it's a lack of physician recommendation.

**Mikal Gilmore**

**January 6, 2016**

Elaine Schock travels for us both. She goes to interesting places and sees fascinating, sometimes historic, events. I miss her like mad, and it's exhausting for her, but she constantly sends me photos and accounts that make it real for me. I used to travel a lot—work, family, friends—but in the mid 1990s, during a book tour, something snapped. I was visiting places I'd wanted to see, but I wasn't seeing them. Plane, car, hotel, event, the same the next day. For weeks. I don't know why I came to feel so depressed by it, but I did. Maybe I would've enjoyed it by car, but planes became exhausting.

In 2001, I more or less stopped traveling. In part because that's when I (finally) got together with Elaine, and didn't want to take long trips away from home anymore. I've been on planes a few times since. I'm not afraid to travel, and if it was a visit overseas, I'd enjoy that. As it is, I rarely drive miles from home (I've told Elaine I have my borders: Reseda, Victory, Topanga, and nothing south of Wells). The worst moment in learning about my treatment was being told I'd have to visit Hollywood five days a week for seven weeks. That's a lot of time and miles on a shuttle. Almost stomped my foot right then, but one doesn't stomp a foot when Elaine is doing her best for you.

**Mikal Gilmore**

**January 7, 2016**

From the *New York Times*, How Donald Trump Loses article: "There is no credible scenario in which a consistent 30 percent of the vote will deliver the delegates required to be the Republican nominee. So for Trump to lose, he doesn't actually have to collapse; he just has to fail to expand his support. And in the states where candidates are actually campaigning, voters are paying the most attention, and the polling screens for likely voters are tightening, he hasn't expanded his support meaningfully since he first climbed into the lead."

**Elaine Schock**

**January 7, 2016**

I read as much as I can about HPV-related cancers. If you think you won't be affected by this disease, think again because I didn't think that either.

**Mikal Gilmore**

**January 8, 2016**

During radiation they stream music I request. (They're tapped into Pandora, Spotify, and YouTube.) So far I've had Al Green, gospel, hip-hop, jazz, and nu soul, among others, and today I had Muddy Waters at Newport. Maybe I'll ask for Goldfrapp on Monday.

**Mikal Gilmore**

**January 8, 2016**

For me, Jefferson Airplane was always the best of the San Francisco bands—especially live. This is from my favorite song of theirs, "Crown of Creation." (For what it's worth, *Bless Its Pointed Little Head* is my favorite Airplane album, though *Crown of Creation*—the album this song appears on—isn't far behind.) *In loyalty to their kind / They cannot tolerate our minds / In loyalty to our kind / We cannot tolerate their obstruction!*

**Mikal Gilmore**

**January 9, 2016**

Elaine and I were talking yesterday about Jefferson Airplane, and our favorites among their albums. They were such a great and startlingly inventive band. The one person I think could have truly saved the Airplane was co-founder Paul Kantner, but instead made the saner choice. I spoke to him for a couple of hours once on the phone years ago, for a project I never finished, though I believe I still have the interview on tape. I should transcribe that, along with some other unpublished or unexpurgated interviews from over the years, before it's too late. (Note to Elaine: Please remind me to look for these materials. I believe they're here somewhere.) Kantner, Barry Melton, Robert Hunter, Peter Albin—these are some of my favorite interviews, all unpublished.

**Elaine Schock**

**January 9, 2016**

**"Wouldn't it Be Nice"**

Mikal is going into his third week of radiation/chemo. He leaves the house every morning at seven to ride the shuttle to Kaiser on Sunset. We have had a lot of rain and it is chaotic trying to get back to Woodland Hills in time to see the doctor and receive the other treatments. One more month to go. So far so good. Mikal looks great and the doctors are impressed with his recovery. We have been warned the next few weeks might be difficult. But wouldn't it be nice if the side effects didn't much worsen? So we just count down another good day and keep hoping for the best.

Mikal has been promoted to the middle of the bus. Passengers come and go. Some have completed their treatment, and some are new. It is a close community with rules and a cast of characters. Each one with a story to tell and advice to give. Some have been here before.

The bus driver was once again late on Monday and the patients were waiting in the cold and rain. However, they were not alone; her supervisor was waiting as well. He took her aside and had a talk. She is late no more. At least for now.

It has been nearly five months since our lives were turned upside down. And, although there is always a shadow hanging over us, it hasn't stopped us from having a good time. We try to live as normal a life as possible. I work every day and the family always has dinner together. For numerous cancer patients the disease not only impacts their health but financially it can be devastating. Mikal hasn't been able to work for a while but that is slowly changing. We are converting part of the bedroom to his work space today. We have been fortunate that he has excellent health insurance and I have a successful career.

Many don't really know all that much about HPV related cancers. People and much of the media—and even some doctors—don't like to talk about a sexually transmitted virus that can cause cancer. I have made it my goal to inform. It is not always easy dealing with the proud science-deniers. I am working on being more tolerant. Anyway, thank you again for all your thoughts and prayers. It always touches our hearts.

**Elaine Schock**
**January 11, 2016**
When Tessa Schock came to me with this headline: David Bowie Dead at Age 69 After Battle with Cancer, I felt sure it was a hoax. I didn't even tell Mikal. I wish I had been right.

**Mikal Gilmore**

**January 11, 2016**

On the bus today, en route to radiation, there was only one subject of discussion: the death of David Bowie. The news hit this mortal capsule like a sledgehammer.

**Elaine Schock**

**January 11, 2016**

*No man is an Island, entire of itself;*
*every man is a piece of the Continent, a part of the main;*
*if a clod be washed away by the sea,*
*Europe is the less,*
*as well as if a promontory were,*
*as well as if a manor of thy friends or of thine own were;*
*any man's death diminishes me,*
*because I am involved in Mankind;*
*And therefore never send to know for whom the bell tolls;*
*It tolls for thee.*
—John Donne

**Mikal Gilmore**

**January 13, 2016**

*My death waits there in a double bed / Sails of oblivion and my head / So pull up your sheets against the passing time / But whatever lies behind the door / There is nothing much to do Angel or devil, I don't care / For in front of that door there is you.*
—Jacques Brel, "My Death," a song covered by David Bowie.

**Mikal Gilmore**

**January 13, 2016**

I just got to pet a Chocolate Lab therapy dog. Plus, volunteer sketch artists came by and offered to do my portrait or draw anything else I'd like. I strongly considered Scrooge McDuck, but then I always do at these moments.

**Mikal Gilmore**

**January 13, 2016**

It's a prayer to a love, or to a needed God? Sometimes they're the same. *Lord, I kneel and offer you my word on a wing / And I'm trying hard to fit among your scheme of things / It's safer than a strange land / But I still care for myself / And I don't stand in my own light / Lord, lord, my prayer flies like a word on a wing / My prayer flies like a word on a wing / Does my prayer fit in with your scheme of things?*

—"Word on a Wing," by David Bowie

**Elaine Schock**

**January 13, 2016**

When I heard Rock and Roll Hall of Famer Bernie Worrell had cancer, I contacted his wife Judie to ask how I could help. I was in a unique position to do so, as I have worked with Bernie over the last few years and know what it is like to love someone with cancer. To say it is emotionally and financially difficult is an understatement.

**Mikal Gilmore**

**January 14, 2016**

Elaine and I have noticed that as my hair is growing back, it's also growing darker. But not in all places, and not evenly. I will be a patchwork.

**Mikal Gilmore**

**January 14, 2016**

I recently dug out some old T-shirts. I don't plan to wear them to radiation treatment (though, ahem, the techs there have said more than once, "This guy always wears the coolest shirts"). Instead, I'll wear one, maybe both, for tonight's Republican debate.

**Mikal Gilmore**

**January 14, 2016**

If you live in or near Santa Fe, George R.R. Martin's Jean Cocteau Cinema has this upcoming event: "Jean Cocteau Cinema is very lucky to have received one of the only DCP editions of *The Man Who Fell to Earth*, David Bowie's starring role. We share the world's sadness at Bowie's passing, and we wanted to pay tribute to this one-of-a-kind artist. This Sunday we will host a David Bowie Tribute and American Cancer Society fundraiser. Sunday's tickets sales for *The Man Who Fell to Earth* will go straight to the charity. The free event after the film screening will include live music, a sing along, and some karaoke. Join in the fun and help us raise some money for the fight against cancer! We will be taking donations for the American Cancer Society all evening. Cancer has taken too many of our friends and loved ones, and every donation—no matter how small—is a big help."

**Mikal Gilmore**
**January 15, 2016**
I'm at Denny's. A guy in the booth next to me is reading the Tarot to a woman wearing a dubious expression. It's part business and part courting.

**Mikal Gilmore**
**January 15, 2016**
For Elaine, who is this wife to me. Me only. It's nice to say that. David Bowie, "Be My Wife."

**Elaine Schock**
**January 16, 2016**
**"Work Song"**
Mikal has started to work again. We cleared part of the bedroom to add a work-space and he has two immediate assignments. It is nice to see him write again. January 17th marks the anniversary of his brother's death. It is never an easy day. On that date, this Sunday, Mikal will preview a written work in progress called "Unfinished Heart (a prologue)" on FB. I think it is a beautiful piece and people who were touched by *Shot in the Heart* will love it. And, like that book, this passage is quite dark. If you are not familiar with *Shot in the Heart*, you need to read it. It is a true story about family, love, and murder. It is Mikal's family history. I had hoped for years Mikal would write about the next chapter of his life.

We are also just into week four of chemo/radiation. The doctors are quite pleased and say Mikal is doing well. He even drives places he needs to go. He is the only one of the bus riders to do so. One more day down, one less day to worry about the side effects we have been warned about. Mikal's sense of taste is off, as well as his stomach sometimes, and radiation hurts his throat, but he is eating. He is at a good weight. His hair has started to grow back. It is darker than it was. It is time to buy him an electric razor (doctors say to be careful of razor blades right now). Chemo can change the color and texture of hair. Strange but true.

Mikal gets treatment of one sort or another everyday for hours. Ed, the leader on the bus to Kaiser Sunset, has finished his treatment. There is no one to take his place so newbies take a seat where they want. They don't know the protocol. Mikal may never graduate to the front. But, the bus driver is on time.

The death of David Bowie threw us. For me, this unexpected death from cancer was like a kick to the gut. For Mikal, it held an even deeper meaning. You will get to read about that shortly. February 9th is the last day for radiation. It is also Mikal's birthday. If we do nothing, it will still be an enormous celebration. He is working hard to get better. As always, your thoughts, prayers and comments mean so much to us.

**Mikal Gilmore**
**January 17, 2016**
Today is the thirty-ninth anniversary of the date that my brother, Gary Gilmore, was executed for murder, outside Provo, Utah, in 1977. Though I've written about that event in a book and in a few articles, I've only occasionally mentioned it here on Facebook. It seems I addressed it in final terms for myself in those earlier writings, and I don't want the subject leaking into unrelated conversations here. The other day, though, I noted that January 2017 will be the fortieth year since that pivotal event in my life, and maybe I should think about whether I had anything I might want to say to people here on that date. Then I thought again. I don't know where I'll be in 2017, so if I'm going to say something, now's the moment.

I didn't know, though, what I wanted to say. So, I tried an approach I only tried once before, in *Shot in the Heart*. I sat down and started to write, to see where it might take me (all my other writing is thoroughly outlined in advance). What resulted surprised me. As soon as I began, I realized I was making my way from one mortal story to another, though I felt better about the new one that was emerging, even if it turns out more mortal. I debated about whether to post it, but I trust Elaine's judgment. There will be more, though I can't yet say when.

**Unfinished Heart: Prologue**

I didn't feel afraid. I didn't feel stunned or devastated. If anything, I felt a kind of relief, in the way that certainty—knowing an identity or cause or end, rather than puzzling over a malady indefinitely—can bring relief. Say, somebody has gone, disappeared. Is that person dead or alive? They find the body. There is grief, maybe rage, when that knowledge comes, but perhaps there is also a relief—unless the doubt gave you hope.

In May 2015, a lump developed quickly on the right side of my neck, just under the jaw. My wife and I were driving to visit her mother, and I felt a strangeness in my throat, then I felt the lump. It hadn't been there minutes before. By the evening, it had grown large. I'd had cyst problems in the same area several years before, and they had been removed without trouble. I assumed this was the same. When I saw my doctor, he thought ice packs would bring the swelling down. They didn't. Months later I saw a neck and throat specialist. She took one look at the mass, then looked inside my mouth. She said she wanted to take a biopsy of the tumor.

"Tumor? Could this be cancer?"

"It's one-hundred percent cancer," she said.

She was angry at my previous doctor's misdiagnosis, and promptly referred me to radiology and oncology. Within a couple of weeks, I was diagnosed with HPV-related throat cancer, stage four.

As mentioned before, after my father died, cancer became my biggest fear. I took many risks over the years, but saw myself as more prone to heart disease than to cancer. That isn't how it worked out. As life went along, concerns other than death worried me more. Recently, they seemed constant and deepening. Was I a good husband? Did I deserve my wife, Elaine Schock, and her children? Did I contribute to or hurt their lives? These were my greatest fears, rather than death. Also, did my work still matter? I hadn't seen much evidence of interest from my editors of late—ideas went nowhere. I'd gone through dry periods before, sometimes for a year or more with no writing. But I was younger then, and I could recover or resume from those dry stretches. I was now sixty-four. At this age, things didn't necessarily resume with ease, if at all.

This all piled up, at moments into panic, a kind of madness and depression that screamed inside or me for hours a day, though I tried to keep it from being apparent to my family, this internal screaming. Sometimes I lay in a dark room and willed myself into a dazed sleep, wondering at what had gone wrong, wondering at an end. I dreamed at times of a sidewalk ditch near our house. I would crawl into that ditch, in the rain, in the deep of night, with a pillow and a covering, and I would accept whatever came. This was deep down, face down.

Now, if anything, I guess I knew what was coming. That was the relief. In that knowledge. I felt a great burden or cloud lift—I literally felt it as I left the hospital. All lives end, and I realized I didn't fear my own, nor did I any longer desire it. I was in the moment, and that was the only place I would ever be. It was the first time in years I felt depression dissolve. No more thought of ditches. If this recent bout of depression had been some unconscious sign of the disease, the knowledge of the disease might have reduced that depression to ashes. I worried a bit about that, assuming depression was gone. I'm sure it had still to be there, watching from the corner of a window, biding its best moment.

As I crossed the long parking lot, I thought of my brother, Gary, who had been put to death in 1977, for two murders he'd committed in Utah the previous summer. In his last months, he still had rage. He still plotted, deceived, and caused hurt, and I still hated and loved him. He had no fear of his impending death, after receiving his sentence. It was a better purpose than he'd had in his life, he would say. In fact, he insisted upon that end, and upon the mechanism of a Utah firing squad to accomplish it. In the moments he talked about that nearing fate, he was a different man than I'd known him to be. He was calm—not proud or hopeful or false, just calm. "It's a great gift," he said, "knowing when and how you will die."

I didn't believe him. I couldn't understand it, any more than I could understand how he had let himself shoot to death two men he did not know. Life, I argued with him in our last conversations, is all we have—it's the only way we can redeem ourselves. I was twenty-six, when I said this to him. He was thirty-six. He looked at me with a strange smile, and shook his head with the knowledge of one who knows better. I don't know if he hated life—he had hours, even days, he seemed to relish near the end—but he no longer wanted to live with life's pain and anger and guilt and failure. He especially no longer wanted to live with its imprisonment. Five days after we had that conversation he was dead. I never understood how he went to his deserved death so calmly. It wasn't that I thought he should fear he was headed to punishment—all of that got fulfilled in his death. No gods or hells await us, though I learned that he did believe in some after state. "Death will not be unfamiliar," he said.

As I left the hospital that day, and crossed the parking lot, I knew I'd already come to a better and shared understanding with him. Perhaps he had won the argument; he certainly had decisive methods. His last words to me, face to face, were, "See you in the darkness beyond," not that I particularly wanted to.

Though I didn't know the hour of my death—perhaps that would have terrified me—it seemed it was now on a horizon. I couldn't imagine I'd possibly survive this disfiguration. It didn't seem possible. For whatever reason, I didn't feel fear. I didn't feel depression; I felt a calm. However, I also instinctively knew that if I looked too hard at what cancer is, at its images or its history, I might undo myself. It might cost me my equilibrium.

I headed home. I still had work to do. More important, I had to tell Elaine. The abiding task or purpose ahead of me was to make this knowledge as easy for her and our family as I could. That was the best possible thing I could hope to accomplish, to give them love and leave them with peace, as our mortal embraces fell away.

My wife, instead, taught me that the horizon I'd seen as I left the medical hospital wasn't acceptable. She taught me, instead, what I had tried years before to tell my brother. Life is a gift worth fighting for. It is not merely that we live, but it is the obligation and kindness we owe to the best part of our world, to those who love us or who might still benefit from us.

I now had a family. In some ways that had been the last thing I'd expected. It sneaked up on me, and stole my night.

**Mikal Gilmore**
**January 17, 2016**

Dear friends: Thank you for all your kind attention and words today. I intend to reply to many of your comments, but I have to finish an article by midnight, and that will necessarily occupy my time. Please know that Elaine and I are grateful for your presence and support. We love you.

**Mikal Gilmore**
**January 18, 2016**

The final performance of the final Ziggy Stardust and the Spiders from Mars show. This is the moment that forever secured David Bowie's meaning for the audience that he'd uncovered and assembled. Its significance rippled out and never stopped. For me, it's one of the most inspiring moments in all rock 'n' roll. "You are not alone."

**Mikal Gilmore**
**January 20, 2016**

The alarm went off at 6:15. I thought, "Rrrrrrr." I'm not a morning person. "Fifteen more days of this."

But that passed quickly. Getting ready to head off to the radiation bus and vault, I realized what I realize every day. Since I learned of this condition, I've had a decent mindset. I'm not sure why, and though there have been lapses, they've been brief.

I live with a great family, in a home that my incredibly caring wife, Elaine, provides us; I've been doing work I care a lot about; and I have the remarkable, helpful support of friends here. And then there's Fubar, Mr. Unconditional.

Yes, there are some pains and tiredness, moments of mental "what the?" Plus unexpected worries, both in and out of the illness. But if you ask me, it's a wonderful life today.

**Mikal Gilmore**

**January 21, 2016**

*Every man has a black star / A black star over his shoulder / And when a man sees his black star / He knows his time, his time has come / Black star don't shine on me black star / Black star keep behind me, black star / There's a lot of livin' I gotta do / Give me time to make a few dreams come true / Black star.*

"Black Star," by David Bowie

**Mikal Gilmore**

**January 21, 2016**

My friend Michael Sugg has some matters before him for a while, so I am bequeathing the seven-songs-in-seven-days challenge to my beautiful wife, Elaine Schock. This will be great.

**Elaine Schock**

**January 21, 2016**

From divorce to work woes to Mikal's cancer, I have listened to this song with a new understanding each time. Jimmy Cliff's vocals are incredible with just the right amount of heartbreak. Life can be a struggle and sometimes it really is only your will that keeps you alive. "Many Rivers to Cross" is from the soundtrack, *The Harder They Come* released in 1973. Every song on the album is a gem, but this is my favorite. Mikal Gilmore gave me this seven songs in seven days challenge and it is hard to turn him down. So here you go, Mikal.

**Mikal Gilmore**

**January 22, 2016**

So far I've lost all my stocking caps, on the bus, in clinics, the chaos of my closet. I'm down to my last one. Time for a trip to Hot Topic, yes Elaine?

**Elaine Schock**

**January 22, 2016**

Years ago I was the director of publicity at Chrysalis Records in New York and was fired because I decided to have a second child. They didn't sugarcoat it or pretend there was another reason. It was also perfectly legal. I was let go six weeks after my son was born. I had two babies and no income. How would we survive this? What I didn't realize after I got home and crawled into a fetal position was that I was appreciated for the work I had done for the artists on the label. Within a week, I got a call asking me to listen to a demo of this amazing singer Sinead O'Connor, and would I be interested in representing her? The song on the tape was "Troy." That day I started Shock Ink. Within a few months, at least three more artists on Chrysalis asked me to work with them. I was now earning more money as an indie publicist working with the same artists, and I had a lot more power. The head of the company was eventually fired and he sincerely apologized to me. So maybe being fired wasn't the best thing that ever happened to me, but it was close. "Troy" is the second song in my seven songs in seven days challenge from Mikal Gilmore

**Elaine Schock**
**January 23, 2016**
**"Alright for Now"**
We now have less than three weeks to go. Twelve more days of radiation (five days a week) and a real hope for remission. I never know what the next day or even the next hour may bring, but we are all right for now. Mikal is still handling radiation and chemo well. Thank goodness for all the medicines that have made having cancer easier to bear and beat, and for Ensure Plus.

Three patients finished treatment this week. It is bittersweet. They are a close knit community but will most likely never see each other again. That part of their lives is over. Protocol calls for a small gift of fruit or cake to be given to each rider from the person leaving, and it must be individually wrapped. We are already planning on what we will give.

The big news is that after five months, Mikal is working again. His cover story in the next issue of *Rolling Stone* about David Bowie is just lovely. I worried when Mikal accepted the assignment. It was going to be a lot of work in a very short period of time. What if this set Mikal back in his recovery? But he admired Bowie's music and was the perfect person to do the feature. His previous cover story on Bowie as Ziggy Stardust was well received. Probably more than anyone else, Mikal understood what Bowie might have gone through toward the end of his life. Every night for a week, I would go to sleep and Mikal would still be working. It was an uneasy feeling. Mikal is downright heroic.

We also appreciate anyone who read the Unfinished Heart post, as well as shared it. The response was beyond wonderful. It also brought attention to the book, *Shot in the Heart*, one of my favorites. We know we are not the only ones who have suffered because of cancer. For all of those people, our hearts are with you. Thank you for caring about my family.

## Elaine Schock
### January 23, 2016

I love the Supremes. I was such a huge fan that when I was younger I wanted to be one of the Supremes. I had no idea then that I didn't have any musical talent—and it didn't exactly work without that. I knew every song by heart and every dance move. We lived in Chicago and my grandparents used to fly to Las Vegas to gamble. One year my grandparents took me with them. The Supremes were playing at our hotel. I was too young to go to the show but that didn't matter, I was so happy just to be in the same vicinity. As luck would have it, we saw Mary Wilson when we were having lunch. She was so beautiful (even more than on TV) and dressed to kill. Just looking at her was intimidating. And as much as I wanted to, I did not have the nerve to go up to her and tell her how much she meant to me. My grandmother did, though, and told her about her biggest fan. Mary Wilson took the time to come over to our table and talk to me. It has been a long time now, but I will never forget that moment or how lovely she was. "Come See About Me" is my third song of the seven songs in seven days challenge that Mikal Gilmore gave me. It is my favorite Supremes song.

## Elaine Schock
### January 24, 2016

When I returned home from London after working at Island Records in the late 70's, I got a job at Casablanca Records. Neither company was your average record label. One sold few records but was totally cool, and the other was controversial and had a policy of making sure every record shipped platinum. Even though large numbers of records shipped out, it might not have had much to do with sales, and there still might be basements filled with Ace Frehley's solo outing, among other releases. However, Donna Summer was the real deal. No one was bigger in disco music. And, like it or not, disco changed our culture. So *Rolling Stone* decided to send their new reporter Mikal Gilmore to do the cover story on Donna.

I had never met him before but I had heard about him. I guess most people had. It was my job to help him get the research materials in our files. He looked pretty cute to me, so I flirted a bit. We became good friends from that moment on and never lost touch, not even when I left Los Angeles to move to New York City. Through good times and bad, Mikal was often my first call. Years later I moved back to LA. Really long story short, our friendship turned deeply romantic and we finally got married in 2009. But I think it was this song that started it all for us. They say every picture tells a story, but in my life so does every song. This is the fourth song in my seven songs in seven days challenge that Mikal gave me. "Last Dance"

## Mikal Gilmore
### January 24, 2016

If you haven't yet had the chance to read Elaine's song-choice for today (Donna Summer's "Last Dance"), I think you'll enjoy it. This is further testament that we saved the last dance for each other.

## Elaine Schock
### January 25, 2016

After I graduated high school, I went to London. I wanted the adventure and romance of being someplace far away from where I lived in the San Fernando Valley. I had one hundred dollars in my pocket and knew one person. London was magical. Music, art, fashion, and pubs. I was staying.

Now, I needed a job, but I was still a teenager. Who on earth would hire me? I wasn't even legal to work. But as luck would have it, I met someone who had a connection at Island Records and they needed help in the publicity department to file press clippings. I got the job. Island was like no place I have ever worked. It wasn't even an office building. It was a mansion in Hammersmith. Artists and label were family. We hung out together. It was how the label functioned. When Bob Marley came to town to perform, he was an un-deniable force. You could feel the excitement in the air. Everyone wanted to be at his shows at the Lyceum. And, for good reason. You knew it was going to be a musically historic performance. It was also a defining moment for me. Working in the music industry was what I wanted to do. No pretense of college or another calling. The album, *Live!* (recorded at one of the Lyceum shows) remains on my top ten list and "Get Up, Stand Up" is the song I love the most. This is my fifth song from the seven songs in seven days challenge.

### Mikal Gilmore
**January 25, 2016**

I just went through the best moment of the last five months. In our last regular meeting for some time with my oncologist, the relatively—and of course cautious—positive news he gave us produced the most beautiful look I've ever seen on Elaine's face. That alone almost made me cry. It's really something to see. I hope my future results do the same for her.

### Elaine Schock
**January 26, 2016**

It was the mid-90's. My marriage was over and I just had my third child. I wasn't scared or anxious. To be honest, I was glad it was over. It had been on life support for years. Sometimes people are not meant to stay together, but do because of the kids or finances or obligation. That wasn't me. I had my own career and money, which gave me independence. Plus, I owned the house. Don't get me wrong. It is hard being a single mom, especially with an infant, but I was determined to make it work.

Funny story. Months earlier Mikal Gilmore was in Manhattan promoting *Shot in the Heart.* He was always crisscrossing my life and this time I picked him up to drive to a friend's house. Out of nowhere, he says,"We should get married. It will be great." I was sure he was kidding and said, "No, I'm still married." He didn't know, but I was pregnant with number three. I remembered that moment and thought about it a number of times over the years.

Still, fate has a funny way of stepping in. I moved back to Los Angeles after a senior vice president stint at RCA and started my publicity firm Shock

Ink up again. My family is here and I wanted them to be a part of my children's lives. I hung out with Mikal a lot, as his book was being made into an HBO feature film. I never regretted the move or any of the decisions I made at that time. My father died a few years after I came back and I was glad we got to spend time together. And, as you may know, I got married again. The song "Not Gon Cry" resonates with me. I must have played it a thousand times. It's about betrayal, divorce, and survival soulfully sung by Mary J. Blige. It is my sixth song in the seven songs in seven days challenge. Tomorrow is the last song.

## Elaine Schock
### January 27, 2016

I was a single mother with a successful PR firm when RCA Records offered me a job I couldn't refuse. The money and prestige of being a senior VP of a major record label was something I wanted. And, I could buy my dream house. I had just gotten a divorce and it was time for change. In the mid-90's things were not exactly progressive and I was only the second woman in RCA Records' history to achieve that title, and the first in the creative division. I also got to take my Shock Ink staff with me. It was a good time to ask for everything. RCA was a moribund label and had fired everyone including most of the artists. It was so bad, the higher ups in corporate wanted to change the label's name. I told them that would be idiotic, in a nice way, of course.

Still, we had a clean slate and nothing left to lose. If this didn't work, the label was gone for good. Thankfully, RCA succeeded beyond the industry's wildest dreams. We broke N'Sync, Christina Aguilera, and The Dave Matthews Band (though they were on their way) and brought bands like the Foo Fighters to a new level of popularity.

Success also breeds contempt and we had plenty of that at our marketing meetings. It was brutal. I used to gear myself up for these meetings by listening to DMX and Mobb Deep's "Quiet Storm" before I went to work. Just like a fighter who mentally pumps himself up to win. I was about as badass as it gets. But in truth, I was unhappy. I didn't want to be that hard. After five years, it was time to go. I had another year on my contract but all I wanted was to get out, be in LA and start Shock Ink back up.

I finally got my wish. Hip hop music helped me survive all of it. It still does. "Juicy" is another song I must have listened to a thousand times. I related to the message that success is the best revenge. Rest in peace Biggie, and thank you. This is my last post for the seven songs in seven days challenge. Thank you for reading them. Every song is a little chapter of my life. I haven't picked a successor yet, but I will.

**Elaine Schock**
**January 27, 2016**
Life is beautiful. It is just the stuff in-between that can suck. "That's Life" is as true a song as I know. We can only hope to come out on top. Here is the real end to my seven songs in seven days challenge. Now, I do realize it is my eighth song, but I couldn't leave it out.

**Elaine Schock**
**January 27, 2016**
You all need to read this cover story in *Rolling Stone* by Mikal Gilmore. If anyone could relate to David Bowie's struggle toward the end of his life, it is Mikal. You can feel it in the story. I worried about Mikal doing the story. How would his equilibrium handle Bowie's death from cancer? Would writing this impact his health? He had not written in five months because of the side effects of chemo and radiation. It wasn't easy. The feature is not only a testament to David Bowie, but Mikal as well.

**Elaine Schock**
**January 28, 2016**
I just like seeing Mikal Gilmore's byline on the story. I really hope you will read it.

**Elaine Schock**
**January 28, 2016**
Energizing the Trump movement are voters who call themselves the "silent majority." These individuals feel strongly that white people, too, face discrimination in this country, and that they are often wrongly accused of being racist.

*Above: Mikal in side yard of Johnson Creek Boulevard home in Portland, Oregon, 1955, one year before Elvis Presley transformed America.*

*Left: Earth Wind and Fire inside cover for the album, Faces.*

*Right: Eiaine in high school, pretending to be a model.*

*Below: At the backstage entrance of Madison Square Garden for the Go-Go's show.*

**Below: Elaine and a canine friend in Banff, Alberta, Canada.**

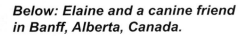

*Above: Fluffy, studying Mikal's research.*

*Left: Our beautiful Foofie.*

*Samantha, Tessa and Preston Schock.*

*MIkal's self-portrait the night of his diagnosis.*

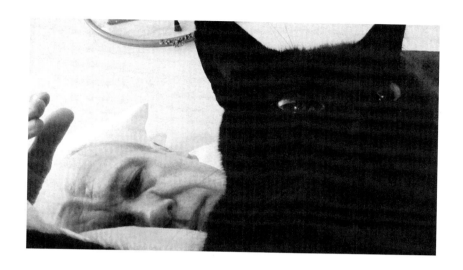

*Above: Fubar with Mikal during treatment.*

*Left: Mikal awaits Tessa Schock's hat approval.*

*Above: An early boxing photo of Elaine.*

*Right: Mikal, during treatment.*

*Right: Mikal, after recovery.*

*Below: Mikal at Pioneer Square, in Portland, Oregon*

*Above: An artist pass for Willie Nelson's Farm Aid concert. Elaine is WIlie's publicist.*

*Above right: Elaine in the snow.*

*Mikal Gilmore, Neville Johnson (Cool Titles co-publisher), and Elaine Schock sign the* Stay With Me *publishing contract.*

This is stirring anger at the Black Lives Matter movement. They aren't wrongly accused of being racist. They *are* racist and Trump speaks to them and for them. He cannot do anything wrong as long as he runs his campaign on racism. It doesn't matter if he goes to a debate or not. They don't care if he fakes being religious. They know he is not. It is like a rich George Wallace came down from the heavens to embrace them after all these years, giving them freedom to be hateful in the open. This is what they believe will make America great. And news flash: they aren't silent or the majority.

## Mikal Gilmore
### January 29, 2016

Today is the birthday of my wife, Elaine Schock. I love her because I've always loved her, from the moment I met her a long time ago. I love her because of how hard she works to care for her children and for me (I wouldn't be as okay as I am right now without her advocacy). I love her because she's the funniest person I know. And I love her because I get to see her face every day. May hers be the last face I ever see.

## Elaine Schock
### January 29, 2016
#### "7 and 7 is"

We are finally in the home stretch. Mikal's last chemo is on Monday and there are just seven more radiation treatments. He will then get his port removed, which is how he receives chemo and other treatments. These are such meaningful days. His doctors say Mikal looks really good. Better this week than even last. Usually at this point in radiation, things get worse. It is a roller coaster ride for us with steep drops. Mikal does everything right. He spends most days in the hospital getting radiation and hydration. Eating is part of the job too, and it doesn't matter that he has no real taste buds and his throat is raw, or that he is literally a red neck.

Mikal's treatment is longer and more extensive than anyone else who is on the shuttle to Kaiser Sunset, which makes sense given the stage of his cancer. But he is stronger, and drives to Kaiser Woodland Hills to catch the bus. Today, there are only five passengers left. That will change next week. Someone else will be diagnosed with cancer. But for now, Mikal can sit anywhere he likes. As protocol requires, we will give the others a parting gift when he leaves. Mikal's heart will always be with his fellow passengers, especially the most fragile. I see the pain in his eyes when he speaks of them. And we won't forget the incredibly kind and caring nurses who have been with Mikal every day during this process.

We will also keep his radiation mask, and I want to have it painted. It will become a beautiful piece of art. I like the idea of this transformation. The mask fitting was filled with trepidation for months. Now it is relief.

My birthday was yesterday and I have made my wish. We will hold off celebrating until we can both do it together. It wouldn't feel right otherwise. I don't really know what the future holds for us, but I feel hopeful enough to believe there is one. This has been a painful and scary time but all of you helped make it easier. We are so grateful for your support.

**Elaine Schock**
**January 30, 2016**
I have to say how much I love that people appreciate Mikal Gilmore's cover story on David Bowie. I have heard that it is selling out.

**Elaine Schock**
**January 30, 2016**
Mikal is the brave one. I don't think I could endure what he does every single day, and then write the Bowie piece while going through all of that. It is all the very definition of courage. This has been a very long process and it isn't over yet, but we are getting close. And every day, I am not sure that my heart can stand it, but somehow it does. Watching Mikal do the Bowie story certainly put it to the test.

## The Albums - Part 4
## Mikal Gilmore

In the fall of 1965, a month after seeing the Beatles at Portland's Memorial Coliseum, I started high school, in Milwaukie, Oregon. I began on uneasy ground. I had thrived in junior high (after years in which my father dragged me from town to town, an average of three different schools per grade), but I didn't feel on steady ground in this new domain. My brother Gary was in prison, and I was entering a setting where another brother had been a notorious student, and both of these more or less marked me from the beginning.

My brothers' exploits, along with my father's death three years earlier, left the family fairly poor, though my mother certainly did her best to keep me outfitted for school in all regards. Also, I was a Mormon at the time. Mormons in those days seemed like strange birds outside of their natural habitats. I found friends slowly and carefully in school, and it would not be until my sophomore year, when an English teacher took interest in my development, that I began to find a security that would allow me to thrive. This English teacher, George Bouthilet, insisted on teaching sophomores as if they were seniors, and he saw in me that I was a reader—I was already familiar with much of the syllabus he required. He would teach me in different classes in my remaining years there, and he had a profound effect on me, to say the least. He opened up whole vistas of literature, history and philosophy for me, and for others.

I think I owe George Bouthilet, along with a few other teachers—especially Grace McGinnis, who taught writing—my life. I had begun to feel like an outsider in the same ways my brothers did—as an outcast, looked down upon by a community—but these teachers affirmed for me the idea that the life of the mind could make for a success and redemption all its own. To be honest, that's maybe the only redemption I've ever known, from which other wonders and triumphs (and mistakes as well) flowed. The albums became for me another library of knowledge, but before I had them, and before I learned how to read their contents for meanings and mysteries, I made use of more conventional libraries.

There was, of course, plenty else going on, for us all. In 1965, after waging the most successful "peace" campaign in America's electoral history (with college youth support), President Lyndon B. Johnson began actively committing American troops to a highly controversial and deadly military action in Vietnam, and it quickly became apparent that it was the young who would pay the bloodiest costs for this lamentable war effort. This changed everything in America, and everything in this story.

In April of that year, Students for a Democratic Society (SDS) organized the first national anti-Vietnam War march in Washington, drawing over fifteen thousand people, most of them students. In the next three months, the national membership of SDS grew to several thousand. But while the war began to motivate young people, the maddening, bloody and recalcitrant nature of that war also helped change how youth would enact its new politics.

Sixties rock 'n' roll had already given young people a sense that they possessed not just a new identity but also a new empowerment, numbers that might have more than just marketing clout. Now, Vietnam began to teach that same audience that it was in danger, that its government and parents would willingly sacrifice young lives for old fears and distant threats—and would even use war as a means of diffusing youth's new sovereignty. The contrast between those two realizations, between power and peril, between joy and fear, became the central tension that would define 1960s youth culture. And, as rock reflected that tension more, it also started forming oppositions to the jeopardy of the war.

Whereas groups like SDS articulated doctrines, policies, goals and theories, rock 'n' roll began to represent harder and harder social and political truths, and that representation became its own form of action. It wasn't so much that rock and radicalism merged in any formal way (in fact, that never happened), but that rock 'n' roll began to subsume more extremes and signify real and extraordinary power.

This mingling between activism and popular culture wasn't always comfortable. Many politicos still had real contempt for what they saw as the mass cultural and ephemeral nature of pop music, while many smart and self-determined rock figures, like Bob Dylan, refused to be co-opted by any organized or militant political movement's agenda. Still, a vital interplay was underway, and the ways in which rock 'n' roll would incorporate and drive that change would prove one of the most innovative and consequential turns in the decade.

The degree to which all this happened perhaps seems unthinkable today, and even in that time it caught almost everybody off guard. It wasn't painless to feel at odds with your country and its stated principles, nor was it always easy to withstand the withering disdain you would draw for proclaiming protest or dressing differently. I put those two actions alongside each other for a purpose. In the years that have followed, a myth has grown that some great gulf separated young political radicals from other young people who seemed more intent on the pleasures of rock music and youth fashions, many of whom would soon be known as "hippies." Maybe that division existed, but as often as not it all felt like one continuous groundswell. I saw many of the same faces at demonstrations that I saw at dances, and as I've already said, most of us understood that the new sounds we liked, along with our lengthening hair and curiosity about marijuana, were if not intentional political choices, then were certainly making for a new social alignment.

If you were of high school age in those years you might feel all this with a special intensity. In part that's because being young at a time of great social novelty that revolved so much around youth couldn't help but prove exhilarating. But also, high schools were battle grounds in their own way. They were a place where authority was supposed to have all the sway, yet they were also places where the most daring rock 'n' roll and fashions had the power of active codes. These were the things that set you apart, from both the social rules that the school structure was supposed to inculcate among its young learners, and from that great number of students who had no interest in taking part in all the cultural and political upheaval.

I got beat up by young people my own age more than once for simply having long hair. I also got thrown off speech teams because authorities didn't want a student with long hair representing our school. To this day, I can't say which dismayed or hurt me more.

None of that, of course, was enough to stop me. Change happened fast in those days and was never less than exciting. Music got more far out and sex grew closer. For me, it all came together in the summer of 1967. We began to hear some especially adventurous music coming from San Francisco, where bands like the Jefferson Airplane and Grateful Dead were part of an already legendary scene in the Haight-Ashbury district. Like that neighborhood, the music coming from it was steeped in the psyche of hallucinogenic drugs—psychedelics like LSD and mescaline.

Nothing else, not the mounting youth opposition to the war, not even increasingly widespread sexual activity among teenagers, would frighten so much of America or seem so radical as the use of psychedelics. They represented real (though vastly overstated) risks of mental confusion, even imbalance, but just as threateningly, both the act and the effect of taking these drugs signified breaking the bounds of possibilities and permissions. These sorts of hazards could reach beyond a confined neighborhood or past demonstration barricades, into homes and schools, where they might wreak social disruption at the most local and personal levels.

I wasn't there yet. I hadn't taken LSD. I hadn't yet smoked dope or even had a taste of liquor. Some of this, I'm sure, was a residue of my Mormon rearing, though it was also simply a reasonable wariness. We heard so much about what could go wrong on psychedelic adventures, or the life straits that marijuana could lead to. But as it developed, that summer of 1967 opened all sorts of possibilities for me. Likely I would have tried drugs in time anyway—curiosity about them was like a virus—but what made it a more or less certainty, and what shook my world and that of so many others, was the Beatles' *Sgt. Pepper's Lonely Hearts Club Band*.

The Beatles had been growing and changing along with the times and their audience—speaking out more clearly on social and political matters, for example, and the effects of psychedelics on their music had already been manifest in the previous year's *Revolver*. It was full of remarkable sounds—including non-Western harmonies and instrumentation, tape-loops that helped shape intense electronic trances, disorienting guitar reveries that curled backwards—unlike anything heard before by a massively successful pop group. Now, in 1967, first with "Strawberry Fields Forever," then with *Sgt. Pepper*, LSD informed both the ambiance and the meaning of the work, permeating everything about the record, from its illusory perspective and imagery to its sonic formations. It was about being both enlightened and ensnared within the psychedelic state of experience; about the possibilities and limits of the drug.

*Sgt. Pepper's Lonely Hearts Club Band*, of course, was about many other things as well, including the effect on its audience in that particular historical moment. The day I bought the album, the day of its release in America, June 1, 1967, I didn't yet own a record player. Having the album was the essential thing; it was like a talisman. Days later I scraped together enough money to buy a cheap portable player, in a slim plastic case with a handle, and with a small, built-in monophonic speaker. I became transfixed by the album, and I heard it everywhere I went that summer. *Sgt. Pepper* hit a nerve in 1960s popular culture as nothing before had; it was era-defining and form-busting, and intentionally or not, it tapped perfectly the collective generational mood of the times.

"For a brief while," critic Langdon Winner famously wrote, "the irreparably fragmented consciousness of the West was unified, at least in the minds of the young." Real or not, this was seen as an occurrence of, or a call to, community. In some ways, the Beatles had represented this ideal, fused with the value of generational change, all along. They made plain that we had entered a different age, that young people were now free to invent themselves in completely new terms. With the Beatles we witnessed the social and cultural power that a pop group and its audience could create and share, and because *Sgt. Pepper* was all about new heights, potentials of all sorts felt boundless.

Now that I had a record player, I began to buy albums—all the prior ones by the Beatles, Bob Dylan, the Rolling Stones, as well as any new ones. From then on, I also bought whatever tapped the pulse of the moment, the pulse of change or discovery or argument. In that year, it was music by the Jefferson Airplane, the Doors, the Grateful Dead, Jimi Hendrix, Pink Floyd, the Yardbirds, Tim Buckley, John Coltrane, Otis Redding, Aretha Franklin, Donovan, the Byrds, Moby Grape, Buffalo Springfield, Big Brother and the Holding Company, Cream, the Mothers of Invention, Wes Montgomery, Muddy Waters, Tim Hardin, Phil Ochs, Joan Baez, the Who, Miles Davis and the Velvet Underground, among others.

There was also plenty of other vital music that I continued to absorb mainly through radio, including songs by the Mamas and the Papas, the Temptations, the Supremes, the Turtles, Lovin' Spoonful, Wilson Pickett, Procol Harum, and the Monkees, and fine pop by the Fifth Dimension, Tommy James and the Shondells, the Association, the Seekers, Herb Alpert and the Tijuana Brass, Sergio Mendes and, yes, Frank Sinatra.

With few exceptions, though (the Beatles, for example), I was not somebody who collected 45 rpm singles, until the punk era, and only then for a few years. This, of course, set me apart from many collectors who regarded singles as the holy grail of any serious archive. The beginnings of my own collection reflect an important truth about that era in that we had now crossed over into the age of the album—that is, long-form statements that set out to explore themes or extended musical explorations. The traits that characterized this blossoming medium would change over the years (by the end of the following year, in fact, the Beatles were celebrating the negation of theme with their sprawling and masterly "White Album"), but as the prevailing medium, albums would hold sway into the 1990s.

The rule that would evolve for me was to buy each new work by an artist I felt was contributing something important to the moment we were in and to how we might progress, which obviously entailed artists like Bob Dylan, the Beatles, the Rolling Stones, the Velvet Underground and Miles Davis. But that rule also made for an ever-expanding list which quickly became exponential. In those years, that made music the top priority in my budget. If I had to forego a day's meal for an album, it seemed an obviously necessary sacrifice. Music was, and would always be, a sustenance.

FEBRUARY
2016

**Mikal Gilmore**

**February 1, 2016**

Here's the plan: finish chemo treatments today, work in the afternoon, then have dinner with Elaine while we start watching the Iowa primary results. I wonder if there will be any surprises. I guess I'm resigned to Trump taking the largest percentage, but in Iowa (and New Hampshire) second and third place can present big upsets. This could be a night when third place counts for more than first.

**Mikal Gilmore**

**February 2, 2016**

We will read and hear a lot in the next week about last night's Iowa results. Some of it will be astute or intriguing, and some will be defensive and wrongheaded. Here's why I believe Trump lost (and was never going to win). He wears thin. He has loud appeal but no constituency that can truly be organized, because he has no real political system (and he has no viable ground organization; he can't win without that). He can be fun or maddening to watch, but he's never had the solid numbers and momentum that pollsters and pundits declared—right up to the moment the caucuses started.

Talking heads had decided that the huge turnout guaranteed Trump's momentum, all the way to the nomination. In fact, the large turnout guaranteed his defeat. Those voters turned out not simply to vote for Cruz or Rubio, they turned out to stop Trump. The polls, though, won't stop. They will lurch on—often untrustworthily—even though state polls are more like augury than anything dependable. I don't think Trump will win this nomination. Americans in great numbers do not want a self-obsessed blowhard for president. They want somebody who can effectively work for their beliefs and security.

Trump is an entertaining sham. That and the embarrassing poll claims created his appearance of immensity that was a surge; it was never really there and it never will be. He is a dead slump walking. I don't know whether we saw the eventual nominee in that top three last night. I think the media hasn't been paying enough attention to the strategies and organizations and gathered endorsements of those who knew that Iowa was fruitless, and instead chose to concentrate on New Hampshire.

## Elaine Schock
### February 2, 2016

These last five months have been the hardest times of our lives. The uncertainty, the sheer physical pain and will to survive on a daily basis is just about coming to an end. The last day of chemo was yesterday. Mikal Gilmore has five more treatments of radiation to go. The combined effects are hard. But it looks like we are going to make it. The fact that Mikal was able to do his cover piece on David Bowie is an astounding testament to his courage. There will have to be some recovery time but it won't be long before we have real dinners and a normal life and put this all behind us. Mikal will look healthier than before this all started. I cannot wait. And, even with all that, we are the fortunate ones, Mikal has good medical care. The fact that some people still think that is too great a luxury for their other citizens is beyond me and borders on monstrous. There is something missing in their souls. Cancer can happen to anyone. It doesn't discriminate.

## Elaine Schock
### February 2, 2016

I will be in Denver tomorrow at a summit, and am looking forward to meeting new friends and hanging out with my old ones. The summit is about something I care a great deal about, the cannabis industry and legalization, and I'm not going to defend that opinion. As an adult, I believe I can make my own decisions. Certainly there are many medical possibilities that need to be explored, but sometimes recreational is also medicinal. And, sometimes a growing industry needs a woman's touch.

## Mikal Gilmore
### February 4, 2016

Tonight, Elaine isn't here. She's in Denver, with snow. I'm sitting up in bed, working. I have my bedside desk piled with music and books and note-marking pens (I like colors). My desk is piled with medicines, too. Except for the medicines, this moment reminds me of many years-long moments when I was younger, during times when I lived and worked like this. I got by, I had what I called a good life (also what I sometimes saw as an abject life). But every night I'd wonder why

I didn't have beside me the partner I'd idealized since I was quite young—friend, lover, somebody to share the funny and sad and bewildered and hopeful hours with—someday who would always mystify me with a smile. I'd done something wrong along the way. It took a while to reach out and touch that person, but now I touch her just about every night. This is a good life, no matter what develops.

**Mikal Gilmore**
**February 4, 2016**
Elaine Schock: "I was asked to pose for Earth, Wind & Fire's *Faces* (1980). On the inner sleeve, I am the one with a smile and umbrella. Rest in peace, Maurice White."

Elaine was still living in Los Angeles at this time (I did an Earth, Wind & Fire feature for *Rolling Stone* at some point in those years, but I don't remember exactly when). Elaine and I hung out a lot, and I could never get enough of that face and smile. Still can't. That smile means everything to me.

**Mikal Gilmore**
**February 6, 2016**
This is Elaine Schock's regular Saturday update about my ongoing medical treatment and our shared spirit at home. I especially like this one.

**Elaine Schock**
**February 6, 2016**
**"Love and Happiness"**
We are almost there. After five months of aggressive cancer treatment, there are only three more days of radiation. We are done with all of this on Mikal's birthday, February 9th. I guess you can call it a re-birthday. The fears coming into this were worse than the reality, and luck was on our side. That's not to say this was easy. Far from it. Mikal's hearing loss is difficult for him, and treatment causes emotional and physical pain. Mikal managed to avoid a feeding tube by his own sheer will. And, his voice is clear and strong. He has been able to drive to the hospital each day and the doctors are very impressed with how well he is doing. Though he is runway slim, he is a decent weight. Best of all Mikal is writing, better than ever. Not only can we see the light but we

are almost out of the tunnel. Now there is nothing left to do but get going with the healing.

Mikal has been on the shuttle to Kaiser Sunset longer than anyone else. None of the original Ruff Riders are on the bus anymore. We need to figure out a healthy gift to give the passengers on Tuesday, when he graduates.

Next week will be my last regular update. We have to wait until April 11th to know if Mikal's cancer is in remission, but I have every reason to hope there will be only health, love and happiness. For all of our friends suffering with this horrible disease, our thoughts are with you. The kindness given to us here has been humbling and wonderfully surprising. We are better people for knowing you. It is good to remember how decent and empathetic human beings are. I have read every comment at least twice, always with my heart in my throat. Thank you for caring about my husband, his family and his work. Thank you for making this dark time in our lives bearable. We look forward to better days.

**Elaine Schock:** I started writing these updates to keep Mikal's friends informed. I didn't see how we could deny that Mikal had cancer, nor did I want to. He was going to have to have aggressive chemo and radiation to keep him alive for over five months. He had a disfiguring tumor that was growing. It all meant he couldn't work for most of that time. We had no idea how his treatment would affect him. There is also a stigma attached to the disease even though it affects so many. Mikal has HPV related cancer and this is becoming an epidemic. No one likes talking about that. Even to the point of not giving HPV vaccines to young people because it is an uncomfortable conversation. Michael Douglas went public a few years back and he was ridiculed, and his own family made him step back on why he got the disease. But pretending it doesn't exist will only ensure more people will get this form of cancer.

It is my goal to change that.

The other thing I want to say is this is what cancer looks like through my eyes. Maybe you or someone you love is experiencing what we are. The diagnosis comes as a shock. What do you do, where do you turn? I want you to know, you are not alone. In these updates, I tried to include some medical information as well. Each week was a different experience. There are always good and bad times, but there was a progression. I never in a million years thought I would be writing so personally about our lives, but you never really know where life will take you.

**Mikal Gilmore**
**February 6, 2016**
Elaine has been able to face and speak about much of what I still find frightening and difficult about having cancer, given my family experience when I was eleven, and the lifetime fear that developed of the word cancer.

**Elaine Schock**
**February 6, 2016**
Because prevention is possible. Mikal Gilmore has HPV related cancer and it is not easy to detect. He was misdiagnosed for a year, until he was stage 4. I will try to give whatever information I can on this dreadful disease. It is really only now that HPV related cancers are getting media attention.

**Elaine Schock**
**February 8, 2016**
I was awakened by a thumping noise coming from downstairs, then I heard it again and again. It was three A.M. Mikal wasn't in bed, so I went to look for him and met him on the stairs going back to the bedroom. He had been downstairs for reasons I couldn't guess. When I found him, he was unsteady on his feet and barely recognized me.  I tried to get him to bed but he insisted on letting go of my hand and said he was fine. He said I should just leave him alone. He fell again, hit his head, and lay there for a minute, and then started to get up again only to fall. Mikal refused any help. He kept getting up and bumping his head on the cold bathroom tile. Not hard, but it looked painful.

I love Mikal and he was very ill. I told him in my most serious voice that if he didn't listen to me, I would punch him in the throat, and he knows I can throw a punch. Of course, I would never do that but I was angry and desperately frightened. That did the trick. I got him to go to bed but I was unsure of what to do next. Did I call an ambulance, which would have caused complete havoc in our household? I didn't think he was injured badly enough. I decided to let him sleep off whatever the hell it was. I also tried to call the doctor but couldn't reach him.

I stayed up the rest of the night checking on Mikal. I was worried he might have done damage to himself that I couldn't see, or that he would try to get up again. But, he slept peacefully the rest of the night. I called the oncologist in the morning. Maybe this was a chemo event, or an adverse side effect to some medication? We didn't know, and it never happened again. Mikal doesn't remember the incident, but it was one of the worst nights of my life. He was a little bruised but that was the extent of it. Just another night of gotcha in cancer treatment.

I didn't write this when it happened in October, after Mikal's second round of chemo, because I just didn't understand what actually occurred or why. But it has never left my mind.

## Mikal Gilmore
### February 8, 2016

Elaine remembers that night better than I, but she has never given a full account until just now. One of two things happened. I do remember my stomach had been in terrible pain for hours, and I'd been up and down the stairs. I have no recollection of how I ended up on the bathroom floor, though I assumed at the time that I took too many sleeping pills. Counting the pills later, though, I no longer believe that was the case. I think the pain simply caused me to pass out.

Other than that, I was dazed and bewildered. I'd never fainted before. I'd never before been out of my mind. I'd never lost full consciousness in my life. It was a strange and frightening way to wake up. When I came to I was bewildered and surprised. Was I dying? Was this it—this indignity on the floor? Elaine's voice was getting through—loud—but I couldn't figure out what she was saying until I realized I was hitting my head on the marble floor and she wanted me to stay there until she could get me up. Even in my worst nights of drinking years ago, I never passed out, I never forgot anything, and I never injured myself. I think Elaine handled it the way she did out of fear and love and anger, but it was not a good night.

I didn't recall, and still don't, that she threatened to punch me in the throat. I've wished she hadn't told me about that because the image has stayed with and haunted me ever since. Sometimes I awaken from a bad dream of the event, and I wonder, did I faint again? This was during the first week or two of heavy dosages of chemotherapy, and that was probably our toughest period. I was pretty undernourished and was more or less passively refusing to eat, but Elaine seized the bull by the horns the next day.

We haven't had anything that bad, or remotely that bad, since. The next day Elaine whisked me off to see my oncologist. He didn't seem very concerned about the matter, but at Elaine's insistence he ordered daily infusion treatments and regular Neupogen injections. I credit those treatments with helping to save my life. Which is to say, Elaine did the right thing and corrected the course of my treatment.

## Mikal Gilmore
### February 8, 2016

I've been fascinated about voting since my parents made me watch everything related to the 1960 campaigns. Regardless of my own politics (which developed to be leftist by the time I was sixteen), I enjoy following each cycle, and I've developed my own perspective. I usually do okay, though not always. The first thing I disregard is polling—especially on state levels. (It shouldn't be conducted nationally until the conventions.) Polls are unreliable indicators.

I've paid attention to the Republican ones this time because there are several candidates, plus the polling is its own confederacy of dunces. (I don't pay attention to any polls about the Democratic race. That nomination is a done deal, no matter what any of us think of it.) Two or three different Republican candidates could have a big effect by winning New Hampshire, but Trump is not among them. He has lost his vomit-shine, and he has no path to a delegate count for the nomination short of deporting other candidates. If Rubio does well tomorrow, it will be interesting. It makes him a considerable lightweight—I guess. If Kasich does well, that would have impact that might also aid Bush. I doubt that the media is adequately prepared for Tuesday's outcome. So far its coverage has been unwise on every level.

**Mikal Gilmore**
**February 8, 2016**
Does anybody here have recommendations for lightweight electric guitars? In my current condition my Fenders are a bit weighty, hard to spend much time with, though I especially enjoy my Telecaster. When I was young a friend had a Gibson SG, and it was always fun to play; I also remember it being easy to carry around. There may even be lighter solid body guitars now that are just as good. Since I play only for my own fun, it would just need to be a guitar that feels good in my hands and that sounds decent through an amplifier.

**Mikal Gilmore**
**February 8, 2016**
Dear friends:
Since this page will likely be busy in the next day, I want to post this now.

Tomorrow will be my last day of radiation treatment (we've already finished the chemotherapy). I've noted this before, but I'll reiterate. I don't know how I would've made it this far (through five months of treatments) without Elaine Schock's constant vigilance, care and advocacy. Some of this medical process has been kinder than we expected, but some has also been scary. As Elaine said to me evening before last, she wasn't worried about the cancer as an immediate life threat to me so much as she was worried about the treatment's impact. There were a couple of nights when at least one, or both, of us may have doubted I would see the morning hours.

Every day I regret the worry that I put Elaine through. Without her help, I'd be dust scattered on the ocean. I also want to thank all of you, on behalf of both of us, for your many and daily kindnesses here. We've found that life on Facebook has been a blessing, and we wish that same blessing in multifold to our friends and acquaintances here as well.

I have one more thing to ask: please continue to extend your graces to Elaine and our family, no matter what develops. It's made a great difference, and I believe it will continue to do so.

**Elaine Schock**

**February 8, 2016**

Tomorrow is my husband, Mikal Gilmore's birthday. It is also the anniversary of The Beatles first appearance on *The Ed Sullivan Show*. That moment changed Mikal's life. I guess he is not the only one. The *Rolling Stone* cover stories written by Mikal often just have a two-week shelf life. That is the nature of writing for a magazine, but I intend to change that. These stories are too good not be shared– –and shared. And, he is too good a writer.

**Elaine Schock**

**February 9, 2016**

Happy birthday Mikal Gilmore. The radiation oncology department gave you a wonderful gift. Any ideas on how to make Mikal's radiation mask a piece of art? I think painting it may be the way to go. We will turn fear into something beautiful.

**Elaine Schock**

**February 9, 2016**

This is the gift bag Mikal Gilmore is giving to his fellow passengers to celebrate his last day of cancer treatment: Aquaphor for radiation burns, clementines, and some chocolate.

**Elaine Schock**

**February 13, 2016**

**"The Long and Winding Road"**

This was a huge week for us, but to be honest, it seems like every other week since we started this process. Yes, it is wonderful that Mikal finally ended his cancer treatments on his birthday last Tuesday. It is a relief to know he doesn't have to wake up and spend hours and hours in the hospital. He is still rail thin and weak, but that is to be expected. Things don't change overnight, in fact it could take weeks, even months, before he is back to normal. And I won't feel terribly comfortable until he has his port removed, but the doctors won't do that until he gets the all clear. So here we are. This is my last update until April 12, after the oncologist visit. It seems like forever since I started writing these posts.

I am not even sure how I got the nerve to write, but I did. And if I was going to write about Mikal's cancer, then I had to be completely honest, no matter the consequences, and I figured there would be some. This is a hard journey. There are no group therapy sessions for HPV-related stage 4 cancer (at least not here), which is different from any other stage 4 cancer.

When we told our friends on FB what Mikal was facing, we could never have imagined the many positive responses. Love, comfort, and just plain good advice from people who didn't have to take the time, and from those who knew first hand what cancer does to you or someone you love. It gave me a new faith in humanity. My family, and in particular my sister, rallied around us. We have never been closer. This thing, this diagnosis, hits you like a shot to the side. You are stunned and confused. What just happened? it must be a mistake, but of course, it is not.

And how do we deal with this news? How many doctors, tests, scans, drugs, side effects, and hospital visits can one take? But you do it all because you owe it not only to yourself to get well but to those who love you. It was Mikal's full time job. It was an ordeal. The worry part doesn't end. I suppose it will get easier over time, but there will always be a part of me that is acutely aware of mortality. I never thought that much about it before. It really is a long and winding road and we haven't quite gotten there yet, but we will.

I have decided a few things that will not change. If I learn anything new about HPV-related cancers, I will share them. That is the very least I can do. I am also going to share Mikal's work on a regular basis. The books aside, most of you are probably unaware of all Mikal has written. His work is lovely and profound. It is his legacy, and I am enormously proud of what he has accomplished.
In the next week I will launch an author's Facebook page that will feature Mikal's writings from the 70's to present day. The best news? He is writing everyday so there will be lots to read. Thank you all again for your kindness. You will never know how much you helped us in what was literally a life and death situation. With love and gratitude.

> **Mikal Gilmore:** Night before last Elaine and I had the most can-
> did conversation we've yet had on all this. We talked about our
> necessarily different perspectives and experiences during the last

many months. Elaine took on the management of all this while also taking care her of her family and home, as well as working a full-time job that often demands travel. Through it all, she has of course worried. The chemotherapy pretty much clobbered me in the first few weeks, back in October. Watching this was hard for Elaine and she went into a pro-active mode that expanded our treatments at the hospital. After that, I had only occasional bad hours, not days.

Now the treatment regimen is behind us and I want to see Elaine breathe again. I was so grateful to see the lovely smile on her face when she awoke this morning. For my part, it's now a matter of waiting things out. The radiation process didn't become rough until the last two weeks, when my throat started to burn and it started getting harder to eat. (I actually now agree with Elaine that I'm too thin—first time I've said that in my life.) I'm a little wobbly on my feet sometimes and my moods turn lower in the evenings, but my moods have been much worse in the past without the aid of chemotherapy and radiation.

I was surprised about the new Facebook author's page Elaine has started, and I'm gratified. Almost all the writing I've done is momentary—you write something for a magazine, it's there for a few weeks at best. Or, you write for a newspaper and it's gone in a day. That's the way it should be for the most part. There's no reason a review of Bananarama should survive the decades.

I feel quite differently about some things, though—especially some of my writing on jazz and early punk. I intend to comb through my *Down Beat* collection, as well as my newspaper writing (the Los Angeles County Library has the holdings for the *Los Angeles Herald Examiner*) and then determine what holds up, if anything. There are literally thousands of reviews, articles, and essays.

I'm moved and grateful that Elaine is taking this on. The Facebook page will be fun, a living and growing place, and hopefully we'll have many discussions there, as well as new stuff, much like what gets posted here. Elaine is the overseer there, and she is also the executor of my work.

I also want to echo what Elaine said. Facebook—that is, you good people—has given us kindness and encouragement every day. Thank you. We love you.

**Elaine Schock:** When we first met with the doctors, I asked what stage cancer and what was the survival rate, along with a dozen other questions. With HPV related tongue cancer, the survival rate was pretty good, even at stage 4. I did not think Mikal was going to die from cancer if he got the treatment he needed. There were times though, I was not entirely sure the treatment would not kill him. And, there is no way around it.

**Mikal Gilmore:** The recovery has been enervating this last week. Can't wait for that to pass.

**Elaine Schock:** All things must pass.

**Elaine Schock**
**February 16, 2016**
I have started an official Mikal Gilmore author page which will feature stories and commentary. Look for it at Facebook.com / MikalGilmoreAuthor.

**Mikal Gilmore**
**February 16, 2016**
In 1990 *Rolling Stone* ran a series of issues about the events and personalities that formed rock 'n' roll's impact in prior decades. I was asked to write about the rich period of the 1960s. I had a great time working on it, and when I was done, I realized that writing about historical lives and times—rather than chronicling the success or controversy arcs of contemporary pop and its current artists—was something I wanted to do more of. In the years after, that became primarily what I did. I owe the fine topic choices I covered to my editors at *Rolling Stone*. They picked great subjects, histories and personalities for me. Only occasionally did I suggest my own feature ideas.

Looking at this 1960s piece now I realize it became foundational to a main scope of what I've written since. My main regret is that I didn't credit 1960s music as much as I should have as a social and political force that changed values and possibilities; that I didn't make the case for the Beatles and the Rolling Stones as some of the most complex political influences on the world stage in those years. I also didn't own up enough to some of the darker results—there were some bad choices we made, and those too still reverberate.

I later made up for both of those shortcomings, especially in a 2007 article I wrote about San Francisco's Summer of Love—which was not a summer of love. Writing that was a sobering experience, and an interesting contrast to this article.

**Mikal Gilmore**
**February 17, 2016**
This is more to my liking than the last few days: rain.

**Mikal Gilmore**
**February 17, 2016**
Today is a milestone of sorts. My PICC line port is coming out in a few minutes.

**Elaine Schock**
**February 17, 2016**
Because Mikal Gilmore is getting his PICC line out, I am sure the dog days are over.

**Mikal Gilmore**
**February 17, 2016**
Last night Elaine and I were talking about the English rock band Joy Division, and she wondered why I seemed reluctant to see the films about them. The truth is, I already knew how the story ended and it scared me—I've learned to be careful about suicide triggers over the years. Indeed, the scenes from the dramatic film about singer-songwriter and band co-founder Ian Curtis still haunt me. Curtis suffered from epilepsy and depression, and committed suicide at age twenty-three on the eve of the band's first American tour.

Maybe all that had something to do with the difficulty I had in writing a review of Joy Division's albums. The music, and what Curtis went through to make those songs, was overpowering for me, but it was difficult to write about it in any way that seemed equitable to the man and the music. The article was scheduled to be a lead review in *Rolling Stone*, and I felt I'd failed it. I called Paul Nelson—the reviews editor and a good friend—and apologized. I told him I was thinking about quitting writing—which was true.

Paul said, "You've got your heart wrapped in this one, probably some fear, too. Maybe you should think of it as a story—the album's story, Ian Curtis's story, though it's probably your own story that scares you. See where that takes you."

Paul saved me in more ways than one in that conversation. I sat down alone in the *Rolling Stone* Century City offices after midnight, the skyscraper's floor-to-ceiling windows overlooking a bright, flat city that looked empty. I did in fact feel scared, and left the building a few hours later, the city looking even darker. I'd finished the review. It changed me forever, and I'm not altogether sure why. Thank you, Paul.

**Mikal Gilmore**
**February 17, 2016**
I have written in the past about my esteem for Frank Sinatra's voice as he aged. What Sinatra didn't do as well, with a very few exceptions, was age comparably in his studio recordings. Willie Nelson, remarkably, has done both. He performs live more frequently than most performers, traveling from show to show on his bus, and he has a matchless dedication to making new recordings.

I used to think the best way to age was as a blues or country or jazz artist, as a person who makes music because there's no other way that person knows how to get through the days and nights. Music can be both a living and a way of living, a bond of community, a language of communication. Several years ago I spent many nights aimlessly wandering the streets of Austin, Texas and Kansas City, Missouri, randomly picking bars or clubs where live music was played.

There, I saw older musicians who had been playing such places for decades, dreams of fame and fortune long past, but the meaning and purposes of music still drawing them into these venues or dives, still expressing their lives and souls. I also saw younger musicians who had similar dreams, and I have no doubt that if I went back to those places I'd still see some of them, playing music as meaning, as some nightly revelation that will draw them back the next night and the next, as far as mortality allows.

People like Duke Ellington, Louis Armstrong, Ella Fitzgerald, Alberta Hunter, Jimmy Scott, Ray Price, Muddy Waters exemplified that calling. Bob Dylan does too; he doesn't need to do what he does for any purposes of legend or reward. He loves music. Nobody, though, represents and lives this better than Willie Nelson. Do yourself a favor. If nothing else hear his renditions of "Somebody to Watch Over Me" and "But Not for Me." There's undeniably art and talent in every phrase and measure, but there's also the meanings that music carries, its love and humor and desire and pain, as well as its inner strengths, that gives the singer the ability to make these songs his own epiphanies as well as our own illumination and memory. Willie, thank you.

**Mikal Gilmore**
**February 20, 2016**
This is an additional update by my wife, Elaine Schock. Each week surprises us in ways big and small, and Elaine notices some of the ups and downs better than I.

**Elaine Schock**
**February 20, 2016**
**"Break on Through"**
I said I wasn't going to do an update until April but there are a few things I wanted to share. This week we turned a corner. Mikal's PICC line (a long thin hollow tube used to give chemo) was removed.

Mikal is eating well, and for the first time in a very long time, he looks quite healthy and his exhaustion is subsiding. He is writing everyday and has an assignment that is perfect for him. I will let you know when it is published. We are making plans for a romantic dinner, and will wait a week to see if Mikal's taste buds warrant an expensive meal, but I think it will happen. It seems like such a small thing, but it is huge to us. We talk about it like it is the biggest trip we have ever planned. And, we are hoping to plan a celebration party in July. Christmas in July, so to speak. You have been with us every step of the way and we appreciate it more than you will ever know.

This battle with cancer made me realize how important Mikal's legacy is, so in addition to Mikal's author page on Facebook being a place for his writings, musings, and commentary, it will give you a better idea of who he is. I hope you will stop in there regularly to read what is posted. I promise to make it a place for literature, friendship and peace. It will be a respite from all the negativity you see on the internet. If there is a favorite story Mikal has written, let me know so I can share it with everyone, or at least I will do my best.

> **Elaine Schock:** I do not fear Mikal's mortality (at least not now), nor am I angry. And for me it is not the same thing. I firmly believe that Mikal and I will be together for a long time. He is still experiencing side effects from the radiation that could take weeks or longer. The end of treatment brought on the worst of those. It makes him feel uncertain. The fatigue is common, but the emotions that come with that are not—at least not for him. Mikal worries about me but there is no getting around that. We worry about each other. We just need to walk through this and get to the other side; there is no express lane. I never know what tomorrow will bring but my hope is everyday it will get a little better until cancer is in our past.

## Mikal Gilmore
### February 22, 2016

I let Elaine use my Kindle account on her iPad. I have a lot of Civil War texts there for her interests, but she nonetheless comes away frustrated.

"Why would anybody have *so* many books by H.P. Lovecraft and about Joseph Smith in the same place?" she asks.

I whisper to myself, thank you, Lord, that she has no interest in looking in the garage.

## Mikal Gilmore
### February 23, 2016

It is two A.M. I am sitting up in bed as Elaine sleeps next to me. These last few late nights we've had are maybe the most meaningful conversations of our life together—about fears and hopes, shared and individual, about the life we both consciously and unconsciously shared before we loved together. As I've said before, Elaine is both stronger and braver than I. I barely mention the word cancer, even to her. Uttering it, I feel, makes me give some ground to it.

Elaine is fearless, yet that is a fearful undertaking of itself. I've seen it on her face at moments. When the doctor told us, back in September, that this is stage 4, Elaine recoiled so hard in her chair that I was afraid she would hit her head on the wall. I had never seen that vulnerable, wide-eyed look from her. That upset me more than the diagnosis itself. I didn't want my baby to go through that.

We've also talked about how at moments we each cry, but rarely in one another's presence. Sometimes when she comes home from work I'm sitting up here in bed (where I now live and work) and subdue myself the moment I hear the door open. I've put her through enough.

But of course there's more to go through. For me the unexpected twist has been, just as the treatment ended, I felt more mortally powerless than before. I lost a whole week there after my birthday, unable to work, falling asleep over and over, hating myself for doing so. Tonight Elaine came home and found me asleep, and she quietly and kindly retreated to the kitchen. I felt bad about doing that to her. This is a special person, a special woman. Without her, I might be gone by now, or in terrible shape. I told her the other night that I think the greatest thing anybody can do in life—whether it's in making art, or receiving what history and circumstance serves you—is to rise to the moment, to meet the occasion, engage with it, transform the outcome by recognizing that moment and what you can do in the face of its challenges and opportunities. Elaine has done that every day since mid-September. As I say, I'm afraid that's not over.

I was thinking about this tonight and I came to understand what my greatest fear is. It is not death. I might die of this. There are hours when I think maybe I feel the movement of that fate. If that happens, I fade and go, and I want Elaine to hold my hand. That's simply death. I won't know the worst part of what it inflicts. The worst part would be Elaine having to live with my going, and its aftermath. My greatest fear, I came to understand, is not being there when the persons I love most also need me the most. That's the cutting line I can't accept. Every day I do my best to avoid that, for Elaine, her children, and myself.

Elaine has said to me, more than once during all this, "I just want you back." I look forward to the look on her face when she feels we've retreated back to shore off this Styx and she can hold me, knowing I'm truly back. That day will come, baby.

## Mikal Gilmore
### February 23, 2016

I have no idea where these hand-painted Totoro sneakers came from! I mean, they came in a box from China, but I couldn't find a note or card. I actually jumped up and down (in my old shoes) when I saw these. Now I'm wearing them. Dear wonderful mystery stranger: please step forward. (There's always the possibility you sent me a Facebook message, but Messenger confuses me enough that I rarely check it.) Elaine just told me who sent them. Friends forever.

## Mikal Gilmore
### February 24, 2016

Elaine Schock and I were talking earlier in the week. I told her I miss her Saturday updates. The unexpected thing, for me anyway, was that everything became harder physically and mentally after the completion of radiation treatments. In some ways there has been as much—maybe more—to talk about since then. We've both seen how helpful and empathetic people here have been all along, and in the process we've all been mutually supportive—and good-humored—these last several months.

As result, Elaine will resume her Saturday posts of updates and commentaries. This is helpful to me—the stuff she writes is always surprising, and she says things about me and our relationship and our home that I have more trouble saying. I believe some friends here will welcome her words. Elaine is, as many here have noted, a terrific writer in her own right—certainly when it comes to these topics. Saturday, Elaine resumes.

**Mikal Gilmore**

**February 25, 2016**

I woke up at 5:38 this morning, unexpected fear and sadness taking hold. I didn't tell Elaine—she was already awake, working, answering mails on her iPhone. I knew I could handle this. I lay there, watching my wife for a time, looking for calm in her presence. Instead, I ended up remembering the worst night of my life. Elaine, Tessa, and I were leaving a restaurant when Elaine fell down. She hit her head badly, just above her eye. I rushed her to Cedars-Sinai Hospital and sat in emergency for hours. I learned the doctor wouldn't release Elaine until her blood pressure subsided a bit. I sat with her among the other patients and held her hand while an intern sewed up the wound. Later, I drove her home. Seeing her like that reaffirmed how I wanted to hold that hand forever.

This morning, knowing that hand was there helped. Things have been harder emotionally these last days—that's part of the recovery. Nothing helps me through this more than Elaine. We've been through a lot together. Most troubles have healed. Others take their time. Last night she told me she loved me more than she ever had before. My heart soared. Those were the words I heard in my mind as I fell back asleep in the dawn.

**Mikal Gilmore**

**February 26, 2016**

Elaine and I talked last night about documenting my history of cancer. I've been the reticent one, Elaine has been the more open one. I eventually come around to Elaine's way of thinking about many things. I know that I can't do this without her.

This is the time when I began to note trouble. In early 2014 I had written a feature for *Rolling Stone* on the occasion of the fiftieth anniversary of the Beatles coming to America. CNN was filming Tom Hanks' series, *The Sixties*, and asked me to sit for an interview about the Beatles' 1964 arrival in the American mind. I wore nice clothes; the interviewer thought my choices would look good on camera. If I remember right, I also wore one of my hats.

I felt a little unsettled on the way to the set. It wasn't anxiety—I've done other TV interviews. It felt as if something went off-center in my head. Still, I thought I'd be fine and get through this. It would only be an hour or so.

The crew made sound and light settings, and I sat down to talk. Midway through my first answer my eyes went almost blind and I felt feverish. I believe I answered that question sensibly—I can't imagine how—but as soon as I finished I asked if we could take a break. I was embarrassed, but I was also physically over-whelmed. I went and sat outside for a few minutes. I took off my hat and jacket to cool down. I had no idea what had happened to me. I'd never felt this way be-fore, even in my worst illness.

Eventually, I put my hat and coat back on and returned to the interview. This time I got through a few questions, but the scotoma and fever returned. I asked for another break, went into a bathroom, and was sick. I returned for a third round of questions, but knew I wasn't at my my best as an interview subject. Before long, I almost blacked out again. The crew felt concerned and got me a ride home immediately. As soon as I was in our bedroom I tore off my clothes and got into bed, shaking. I have never watched the CNN episode, and I never will. I don't want to see those moments when death might have crept inside me and sideswiped my consciousness.

Less than a month later I visited Santa Fe to interview author George R.R. Martin. As soon as I got off the plane in Albuquerque I felt terrible, but made the drive to Santa Fe. It was a nice, but cold, winter night. I met Martin at his film theater. We talked for a time—in part about a mutual friend, Neil Gaiman—then we sat for two hours of *Game of Thrones*. I knew the episodes well, but could barely focus. Walking back to my hotel in the cold I took off my jacket, scarf, and hat. I began to black out again, sat down on the sidewalk twice, and slowly crept back to my room, two blocks from Martin's theater. It was a long stretch.

Back at the hotel I took a sleeping pill, but I was restive throughout the night. The next morning, I tried to snap out of it, but couldn't. I cancelled the interview. For all I knew my problem might be communicable, and I didn't want to risk exposing Martin to it. Also, I wouldn't have lasted thirty minutes through the work of an interview, which requires constant attention. (A few weeks later I returned to Santa Fe to visit Martin again. We talked for twelve hours, amounting to a sixty-five-thousand-word interview that was edited for *Rolling Stone*.)

I managed to fly back to Los Angeles that night, where Elaine was waiting for me, a cappuccino and cookie in hand. I couldn't consume the food, but seeing Elaine when I got off that plane was like arriving at a sanctuary. I was home.

I'd learned during my night in Santa Fe that Pete Seeger had died. The next day *Rolling Stone* asked me to write a feature about him. That night back in Woodland Hills I started working. Not long after the Pete Seeger story, I wasn't working, and that made me feel lost and finished. Sometimes I was screaming inside the whole day, but tried not to show anything. In the afternoons I sometimes slept in a darkened room where I had played guitar in better days. I dreamed strange dreams, and spent hours in my office looking outside the door at our swimming pool. I can't swim.

Did my cancer begin during those weeks? I don't know. I'm not sure how cancer starts, if there's anything like a specific moment. Or, could people getting sick like I did be an early sign? Probably not. I do know that I never felt right after that, not for a day. I tried to keep it from Elaine, but some things got worse and it scared her. She worried she was looking at a man who was dying. I wasn't as thoughtful with her as she deserved, and my regret for that will last until my final thinking moments. After her son Preston's wedding, I went for an examination that, within a minute, yielded my diagnosis: HPV-related throat cancer.

**Mikal Gilmore:** Having quality time together, as an end nears, is one of the valuable possibilities of this cancer.

**Elaine Schock:** One of the things we discussed that was incredibly important to me is the fact that few people know about HPV related cancer in men. Not that much has ever been written about it, and there are many men who don't know it even exists. If we do not speak out, then people will suffer. What you don't know can kill you. And, being misdiagnosed is a major problem. There are better days for us but my hope is that somehow, you or someone you love will not have to go through this, that maybe what we know has changed you. I can only hope.

**Mikal Gilmore:** You're right. We men can be horribly stubborn. The compensation for me is that Elaine is even more stubborn. I don't fuck with her when she has decided something. She gives me a certain look and my ears go down like a puppy's.

**Elaine Schock**

**February 26, 2016**

I put up Mikal's Bruce Springsteen story on his author's page. It is lovely and I hope you enjoy the story here:

I met Bruce Springsteen a few times informally in the 1980s, and interviewed him formally once for a *Rolling Stone* Q&A. When the magazine ran a series of special issues about rock 'n' roll's decades, my editor asked me to work on a piece about Springsteen's development in the 1980s. This is that piece. Some of this is echoed in the liner notes I recently wrote for *The Ties That Bind* package, but this article covers a broader time and considers the artist's ongoing social and political, as well as musical, progress.

I mentioned the other day that I thought one of our most important callings in life is to meet our moment, our times, to respond to the challenges presented and, if possible, to also affect further progress. I've always thought of the Beatles as an ideal example of that in the 1960s. They started a certain change and had to meet the challenge of how their audience, as well as other artists, advanced what they did. That is, how fans (by then a community) and other musical thinkers upped the ante for everything, including for the Beatles. They also met the challenge of the times, as the world around us showed new possibilities, new dangers, and required new commitments. And, they revealed how the challenge of their own intellectual, musical, and personal growth proved ongoing. When the Beatles reached their zenith collectively, their dissolution also reflected the times.

Many movements or artists have done something similar over the years, but I think Springsteen's maturation from the 1970s through the 1980s was extraordinary. He responded to his times; he thought through the changes in the America around him and how those perilous changes might affect his audience; and he raised his voice, in his music, in interviews, and most important, in the long and thoughtful comments he made on stage night after night. I saw something like thirty-five of his 1980s shows, and though he made similar remarks on stage during that time, what he said also always changed, sometimes in heartbreaking or humorous ways. This revealed how his extensive reading and thinking about America's history illuminated him, and some of us in turn, as time went on. In fact, I've always thought the guy could write an enlightening history book if he ever wanted to take on the task.

I've said this before, in *The Ties That Bind* liner notes, but I want to repeat it here. I will always be grateful for living in the times that Springsteen saw and understood, and that he enhanced with his music. He is on tour again, in another volatile time, playing *The River*, the album that was his pivot point. It was an epic made up of short stories. Those songs still resonate now, perhaps in different ways. I'm glad Bruce Springsteen still meets his times.

## Mikal Gilmore
### February 26, 2016

This excerpt from a 1990s article I wrote—and a 1987 interview I did with Bruce Springsteen—appears in full context on the Facebook author's page Elaine has created for me. I'm singling it out because, in these crazy and sometimes awful times, as we witness the rise of demagoguery and blame and racism and hatred in our beautiful land, Springsteen's comments still resonate and are outstanding:

"The idea of America as a family is naive, maybe sentimental or simplistic," he told me in 1987, "but it's a good idea. And if people are sick and hurting and lost, I guess it falls on everybody to address those problems in some fashion. Because injustice, and the price of that injustice, falls on everyone's heads. The economic injustice falls on everybody's head and steals everyone's freedom. Your wife can't walk down the street at night. People keep guns in their homes. They live with a greater sense of apprehension, anxiety and fear than they would in a more just and open society. It's not an accident, and it's not simply that there are 'bad' people out there. It's an inbred part of the way that we are all living: It's a product of what we have accepted, what we have acceded to. And whether we mean it or not, our silence has spoken for us in some fashion."

## Mikal Gilmore
### February 27, 2016

As somebody noted here, fairly, I've been completely wrong about how well Trump would do in these primaries. I now doubt he can be stopped by the GOP, and I doubt there will be a brokered convention, though that would be fun. I certainly don't think he can muster a coalition that could win a national election, even with the white vote. That vote can be easily beat in the electoral vote, though Trump might sue.

**Elaine Schock**
**February 27, 2016**
**"Stay with Me"**
**"Let's Just Breathe"**

It has been a couple of weeks since I posted a real update on Mikal's cancer. I thought once we hit the landmark day of all days, the end of chemo / radiation, we might be home free. Back to normal. There would be no real news to report, just good times. But that wasn't the case, nor was it realistic. Just days before his medical care ended, the side effects hit hard. This was difficult not only because of the physical and mental pain, but we had such high hopes that maybe Mikal could escape the harsh punishment of his treatment. The fact he did not is hardly surprising, but disappointing nonetheless. His fatigue grew and although he was working, it impeded his work. His body was telling him to rest and he didn't want to. He wanted to be completely better.

Pressure to get writing done and to meet medical bills takes its toll. Mikal never missed a deadline. He was heroic. And as hard as these days are, they are better than the day before. The prognosis is good. But Mikal's depression deepens. He worries about what might happen next. And, I am not entirely sure when that will lift. This is not unusual for cancer patients, which goes to show just how horrid this disease is. You can say fuck cancer, but the truth is, it fucks you. But like everything else we have been through, this will pass. It just takes time. We have postponed our plans for a romantic dinner because it will be a while before that will be possible. Instead of big plans, we need to take it slow and just breathe.

It didn't take much to figure out that Facebook was a way for me to preserve Mikal's legacy. He doesn't really know how beautiful his writing is or how it gives voice to all of us in one way or another, but I do. I would like it if you liked it. I will also continue the weekly Saturday updates until there is no more to be said.

People have been so kind to us and have gifted us with actual gifts as well as good wishes and encouragement. We are so grateful and we know we are not the only ones facing this obstacle. Thank you for caring. With love and respect.

**Mikal Gilmore**
**February 27, 2016**
My greatest fear in recent years is that Elaine might stop loving me. I worried about it every day. It wasn't Elaine who caused that worry: it was my life of self-loathing, of self-destruction. As I told her, I didn't feel worthy, and I was afraid of losing her eyes upon me. She told me the other night, "I love you more now than I ever have." Please see Elaine's Saturday update from earlier today to understand why that fear of mine has gone away, and the solace that has replaced it.

**Elaine Schock**
**February 28, 2016**
Mikal Gilmore: "I remember hearing Hank Williams' music as long as I remember hearing anything. My mother played him around the house all the time. Sometimes she would take little dance steps to his more upbeat tones. Other times she sat and listened closely to the words, not moving her feet at all. In time, I understood why. Williams was one of America's greatest artists of any sort. His voice, poetry and mournful stories are eternal."

I love Hank Williams and I love Mikal's story.

**Elaine Schock**
**February 29, 2016**
For the racist perspective, ask Trump supporter Paul Noel, a research scientist from Madison, Alabama. "American blacks are unsophisticated in understanding that they need to make people earn their vote," he said. "We have had a batch of people who played like race was an issue. I don't see anybody here wanting to hurt a black person or cut their opportunities or anything."

You can see why these Trumpeters think the KKK thing is overblown or that it isn't a bad thing.

**Mikal Gilmore**
**February 29, 2016**
I used to think I'd take delight in the Republican Party's disintegration, but be careful what you wish for. There remain decent and reasonable voices in that party, whether I agree with them or not, and they deserve better than

this. The trouble is, the GOP made much of this possible with terrible views and polices that abetted the rise of Trump and his supporters. Also, they've waited too long to take on his threat.

I don't know if Trump can be stopped. If tomorrow turns out the way most of us suspect, then it's likely impossible. What happens either way? If Trump's denied and runs as a third party, fine. That rounds up a lot of malignant thinkers and racists into one group. If he wins the nomination, then it's soul-examination time for the entire Republican Party. Will its members do the right thing, and vote for the Democratic nominee, stay home, or just accept Trump and vote for him? I don't want to miss this drama, but I don't know if I want to witness its outcome. I still don't see how Trump can win the electoral vote but I've been wrong about his prevalence in recent months.

Something ugly and dangerous got unleashed in this country in the last few years, and Republicans, especially its Tea Party, certainly deserve much blame. Trump gives increasing permission to the ugliness, and one of the shameful aspects is he does it largely for ego and gratification of an undisguised power thirst. We all as Americans deserve better than this. Take this opportunity to resist the Trump wave.

## The Albums—Part 5
## Mikal Gilmore

Having a record player, I quickly realized, had other merits. I was sixteen in that summer of 1967, and along with the anticipation of every new cultural turn, there was also the anticipation of sex. I certainly didn't know all that sex was about, but I was getting a good idea. Nobody in my family had ever taken me aside and told me the first thing about it. I learned what I could by stealing a look at the occasional *Playboy*, and by reading the novels of Henry Miller, as well as John Cleland and Frank Harris's pornographic classics. I hid these things in the closet of my bedroom and read them late at night, when I was done with Franz Kafka and Herman Hesse.

On weekends I was going to the teen dance clubs in downtown Portland. One of them, the Headless Horseman, was located in the space of an old gangster's nightclub, where my brother Gary used to hang out. Now, it was full of teenagers all decked in the semi-mod fashion that preceded the soon-to-come hippie era. A male friend and I would go there in our wide-wale corduroys and polka dot or flower-print shirts with white collars and cuffs, and our knee-high boots. Inside the clubs, we would ask teenage women in short skirts and hoop earrings to dance to the club's regular bands—local groups like the Kingsmen (of "Louie, Louie" fame) and the Wailers. Maybe Paul Revere and the Raiders played there at some time, but if so I didn't see them.

Sometimes we'd talk the girls into leaving the club and going to hang out in the stairwell of a large parking structure a few blocks away. We would kiss for hours—we called it making out—and we'd try to run our hands over the young women's breasts or between their legs. I remember one girl telling me, "You sure have busy hands for a boy your age." I guess she was right.

This could only go on so long. I spent afternoons during that summer hanging out at Portland's Psychedelic Shop and Lair Hill Park—places where the longhairs and bikers congregated. In the evenings, my friends and I would go around the corner from The Psychedelic Shop to the Crystal Ballroom, an old upstairs dance hall that had been a popular place for big bands during the swing era.

The Crystal's main dance floor was built over ball bearings, and during that summer, when bands like the Grateful Dead and Quicksilver Messenger

Service played there, the hippies would dance and skip in circles on the floor, making the whole room bounce and shimmy, like the deck of a drunken ship. I met a young blond woman, Pamela, at one of these shows. Every day for weeks afterward, Pamela and I met at the psychedelic shop and sat on the floor, talking, holding hands, kissing. Sometimes, after midnight, when our parents were asleep, we had long, feverish phone conversations, talking about how much we loved each other, and whether we should have sex. We finally decided we should.

One day in late August we met at the psychedelic shop. Peter, Paul and Mary had released a new album, *Album 1700*, and we pooled our money and bought it. Then we took a bus to my home in Milwaukie. Nobody else was there. Pamela and I made a quick bed on the floor in an empty bedroom, and we put our new record on my portable stereo. "Leaving on a Jet Plane" was just starting to play when Pamela lay down, opened her legs, and guided me inside her. When I climaxed, "Leaving on a Jet Plane" was still playing.

Looking back, I see that 1967 imprinted me probably more than any other year in my life. In the fall, I started smoking marijuana. The first time I smoked enough to get high I was with two young men who, like myself, were members of the Mormon priesthood. We stayed up all night, talking about rock 'n' roll and girls and God. This was also the year that radicalized me. I read about the famous cases of Boston anarchists Nicola Sacco and Bartolomeo Vanzetti, and about union activist Joe Hill, who met his end in Salt Lake City. All these men were executed—at least officially—for the crime of murder. But they were also killed because they had challenged the nation's conventions of power and authority.

Learning the stories of these men, and reading the writings of Frantz Fanon and Upton Sinclair, forever changed something in me. It made me hate the people and the structures that used their power to keep others under their control. Plus, it made me understand that any state that had the power and the will to put a man to death was indeed a malevolent place. In addition, this was the year I first found deep, life-altering love. Not with Pamela (we ended when her parents discovered what was going on), but with a dark-haired, beautiful young woman who lived across the river from me, in the town of Lake Oswego, where girls were richer and more wicked. That relationship lasted a little over two years, and its ending transformed me in ways that didn't end until 2001, when Elaine became my love.

As all this developed, my record collection began to grow, and it began to signify both my own growth and the change of the world around me. In 1968, the politics of joy turned into a politics—an environment—of fear and rage. The music that illumined these times had to cope with this change, to decide where it stood. With *Beggar's Banquet* (1968) and *Let It Bleed* (1969), the Rolling Stones faced some of the paradoxes that these challenges presented to rock 'n' roll artists, and as a result made their most intelligent, committed and forcible music. These were records, in large measure, about social disorder and moral vacillation, and more than any other artists near the end of the 1960s, songwriters Mick Jagger and Keith Richards seemed to say something about the moods and idealism coming apart all around them.

The timing couldn't have been more apt. By this time, 1968, a year in which Robert Kennedy was murdered in Los Angeles; Dr. Martin Luther King, Jr. was shot to death in Memphis; and the broken hopes of millions of people erupted in costly, long-term violence (climaxing at the Chicago Democratic National Convention, at which police brutally bludgeoned American youth). Rock 'n' roll had become a field of hard options and opposing arguments.

The Beatles seemed especially dazed and wary in their role as youth leaders. On one hand, they recorded two versions of "Revolution," in which they opted in, and then out, of the notion of violent revolt. Then, on the flip side, they issued "Hey Jude," their greatest anthem of community and forbearance.

By contrast, the Stones faced the contradictions of their position more directly. In "Salt of the Earth" (from *Beggar's Banquet*), Mick Jagger extolled the working class masses only to admit his hopeless distance from any real involvement with such people (*When I search a faceless crowd / A swirling mass of gray and black and white / They don't look real to me / In fact they look so strange"*), and in "Street Fighting Man" (banned in several U.S. cities in the summer of 1968 for fear that it might incite further political riots), the Stones admitted to both a desire for violent confrontation and a longing for equivocation (*Hey! Think the time is right for a palace rev-oh-loo-tion / But where I live the game to play is compromise so-loo-tion*). For that matter, the Rolling Stones were asking some of the toughest questions around (*I shouted out, "Who killed the Kennedys?"* sang Jagger in "Sympathy for the Devil"), and they didn't hesitate to deliver hard answers. ("*Well after all, it was you and me.*")

From their earliest days, when they were viewed as scrutinizing young women rapaciously and were famously arrested for pissing in public, to the later brouhaha over their drug busts, the Rolling Stones epitomized rebellion and disrespect to both fans and detractors. They had long been the one band that many parents and authority figures hated most. Now, like the Doors, they flirted openly with questions about evil and violence, questions that aimed to reveal both themselves and their audience as accomplices in all the modern terror and chaos.

I never sided with the violent course, though I understood it. I sat in late night conversations with friends who wanted to blow up bridges and federal and city buildings in Portland, but I quarreled vehemently against those actions; real lives would be at risk. Later, I was a block away from Portland's city hall when a bomb detonated in the hours after midnight, and I was reminded of those arguments. I understood then how deeply crazy the war in Vietnam had driven us all, not just the young, but the entire nation, the times. It felt like a civil war was brewing. When push came to shove, I knew where I'd stand, though I wasn't sure how much good would come of it.

Meantime, in high school, I turned eighteen in 1969—the point at which I was required to register for the draft. I had been considering refusing to register. Joan Baez and her husband at the time, David Harris, had been waging a draft resistance campaign across the country, and I had even met and spoken with them during a visit they made to Reed College. Refusing to register, of course, would mean possible prison time, or leaving the country. In the end, I conceded to the requirement, though I felt ashamed. All my mother's other sons had ended up in prison or jail, and I found it too hard to subject her to another such experience.

As it turned out, I was never drafted. The lottery system was firmly in place by then, and my birth date fell at the far end of the list. I've never had a single doubt that I would have refused the draft, no matter the costs, but I've always felt guilt over registering for it in the midst of that deadly and wasteful war.

The period from the Beatles' *Ed Sullivan* shows in 1964 to 1969 spans my migration from the end of junior high school through the end of high school. These are often, of course, some of the most remarkable years in many young people's lives, and certainly for someone coming of age in the ferment of the 1960s, that span could prove both richer and riskier.

These were the years in which I moved from the ground of certainty to a knowledge of living without a net, in several ways. I lost any comfort in religion or in national virtue. I moved from uneasy patriotism to uneasy but committed radicalism. I also found drugs (by which I mean marijuana and psychedelics) and early blissful love. And, I soon enough found how both of those things could leave you feeling bereft in the world, unsure of existence's reasons and trusts.

The records I began to surround myself with, that I would carry with me through my life from then on, reflected my experiences, influenced my values, even gave direction to my ambitions. It wasn't yet a large collection at this point—maybe one or two hundred or albums—but it had already begun to realize the many purposes that I would attach to it. It was the place I'd turn to measure and test my beliefs, to seek accompaniment in times of pleasure and communion, to find some consolation or understanding in times of loss, even in the aftermath of deaths. More than once, I can say, my albums probably saved my saneness, maybe my life. That hadn't happened by the end of high school, but it wasn't long before it would.

MARCH
2016

**Mikal Gilmore**
**March 1, 2016**
Some kind people here—Kim Plant, Amélie Frank, Paul Slansky, my beautiful wife Elaine, and perhaps others—bought me an Apple Watch. Last year, after my diagnosis, I decided I would stop buying things, except for necessary books and music. I'd bought a lot of computer-related and hi-fi gear over the years, and then I'd have to turn around and replace some of it in a year or two. Sometimes it was more a headache than it was fun.

Back in September, when I thought I didn't know how long I'd live, I decided that unless it's a device I use hours every day—like an iPhone or iPad—I wouldn't consider any new gadgets. I looked at the Apple Watch with desire, tried it on more than once (funny how barren my wrist felt when the salesperson took it back), but decided I wouldn't add it to my apparatuses.

Then I got a surprise gift certificate. Elaine and I were finally able to go to the Apple Store a few nights ago. We settled on the larger face, 42cm (Elaine kept changing her mind every other minute), but when I put it on at home, I realized it was too overwhelming for my present one-inch wrist. So, Elaine exchanged it for the 38cm face. Now I don't even like to take it off when I sleep. It's quite a complex instrument with a steep learning curve, and it does far more than I realized. I've named it Chocker. Thank you, friends and Elaine. This is what I'd call a good and kind surprise.

**Elaine Schock**
**March 2, 2016**
From Mikal Gilmore's Facebook author page: In 1997 I wrote a review of Greil Marcus's *Invisible Republic* for *Rolling Stone* (the book was later retitled *The Old Weird America: The World of Bob Dylan's Basement Tapes*). My review never ran, though most of it appeared in another publication and I've since incorporated some of it in other materials.

*Invisible Republic* was about Bob Dylan full basement recordings with the Band in Woodstock, in 1967, as Dylan was in recuperation from an accident, or more likely in escape from a tempest that he created and no longer wanted part of. Marcus's book was many years before the release of much of the same material in 2014's *The Basement Tapes Complete: The Bootleg Series*

*Vol. 11.* (The recordings had been available in bootleg collections for some time.) I made a couple of date changes and other modifications in this review to avoid some confusion.

I also didn't address one of Marcus's main subjects in the book—Harry Smith's *Anthology of American Folk Music*—because the mysteries of the basement sessions were enough for me. Also, I have some doubts about viewing anything from the sessions in the context of community—an antecedent one or even a communion with the Band. Dylan wasn't about community, except in some early songs where he was singing about dissolving moral centers and dilemmas of democracy. Even his community with the Band didn't count for much past these recordings, until *Planet Waves* and their 1974 tour together, which was the end of that bonhomie. I'm not sure, to be honest, that even the Band was truly about community. Their fraternity lasted longer than the one with Dylan, but it ended in irreparable betrayals.

Just the same, Marcus's investigation into the Basement sessions' songs was utterly fascinating and full of new and rich insights, and it remains that way. But we'll never really crack the mysteries in those recordings, and I don't think Dylan ever wanted anything from them. They are his most abandoned body of work. Whatever he thinks of them—maybe they are reminders of mystifying seasons of repair and adjustments—he has never expressed affection for them or even interest. He left them to the shadows, and maybe he wouldn't have minded if they stayed there. However, once you go into their tales and matchless atmosphere—Bible parables and dirty stories enfolded in the country side, out of the reach of fame and American fire—you can't shake them. Only Dylan could do that.

## Elaine Schock
### March 2, 2016

The more I study cancer the more disgusted I am that smoking cigarettes is legal and cannabis is not. Smoking is a leading cause of cancer and death from cancer. It causes cancers of the lung, esophagus, larynx, mouth, throat, kidney, bladder, liver, pancreas, stomach, cervix, colon, and rectum, as well as acute myeloid leukemia. Now, the tobacco companies' propaganda is fair game and they lied to the public for decades and decades. There is no going back and we have flavored e-cigarettes now to look cool, but you should know the most important discovery in cancer was that cigarettes caused it. Cannabis, well, it is different. It won't kill you, but it is a Schedule 1 drug and can still get you jail time or your kids taken away, depending on the state. I don't understand crazy, but will be on the front lines trying to change it.

**Mikal Gilmore**
**March 4, 2016**
For Elaine: *Everyday seems a little longer / Every way, love's a little stronger / Come what may, do you ever long for / True love from me?* —"Everyday," by Buddy Holly

**Elaine Schock**
**March 5, 2016**
**"Beware of Darkness"**
We have been at this for six months now, and it hasn't gotten much easier. It is hard for Mikal to be sick month after month, day after day. He is worried about medical bills and that, too, causes stress and depression. It is all terribly difficult, but this has made Mikal's writing more profound. Perhaps facing mortality does that to a writer? He has an important voice and regardless of how he is feeling, he uses it.

I put up stories and new commentary every day on Mikal's author's page. And we are making progress gradually. I don't think Mikal is sick because of his cancer; I truly believe he is in remission now, and we will get that confirmed in April. I am sure it is the accumulation of chemo / radiation treatment and his mental state. Beware of darkness because it can hit you. It can hurt you.

There are days when Mikal can barely stand and other days that are better. And he looks good, if a bit gaunt. As a couple, we don't go out to dinner or shows. I have no idea how long it will be before we can have a social life. I miss those times. Yet for all of this, we are lucky. It will pass. Research is showing that Mikal's HPV related cancer has an excellent survival rate. They may even change the staging status system (meaning stage 1 thru 4 cancer), which determines the suggested treatment and prognosis. Mikal was diagnosed at stage 4 head and neck cancer, but they do not yet differentiate between HPV Negative (smoking) and HPV Positive (sexually transmitted virus). It *does* make a difference.

I was aware of this information before we ever started the aggressive chemo and radiation, but the research wasn't as conclusive as I wanted, and we discussed the options with Mikal's doctors. We did not want to take chances with the outcome. There is no regret, but the treatment is punishing. It was meant to be. It is supposed to kill cancer cells and save your life. The treatment for cancer hasn't progressed that much over the years, even though you hear about a new miracle drug or some crazy non-toxic cure that will eventually kill you, because there are no miracles. But on the flip side, we have had the most meaningful conversations of our lives during this adverse time. We have had to take a hard look at our marriage and what that means.

Maybe living for someone else is the ultimate test of love? We have come to this conclusion: no matter how this turns out, there is a happy ending. As tragic as this disease is, we realize how lucky we are to have each other, our family, and friends. Perhaps we took that for granted once but never will again. Mikal was so thrilled to get the gift card for his Apple Watch. He has wanted one since it came out, but because he has been so sick and the future uncertain, he didn't feel he should spend money on such a luxury item. So thank you for giving Mikal something that gives him such pleasure. That was an unexpected kindness. I also got a spa package which I certainly can use.

In our online community here, Mikal and I have been getting gifts, good thoughts, and encouragement since this ordeal began. We love you for that. You will never know what you have meant to us. Some day, some way soon, we will get beyond this. I can hardly wait.

**Mikal Gilmore**
**March 8, 2016**
On the death of George Martin: He was the best thing that happened to the Beatles, though they didn't always respect him as he deserved. His effect is forever, every time we hear the Beatles' studio work—anything other than the *Let It Be* album that Phil Spector fucked up.

**Elaine Schock**
**March 9, 2016**

Mitt Romney, unedited from Mikal's 2012 *Rolling Stone* story. It is just as relevant today as it was then. This is an excerpt:

"From age eleven to age fifteen I was an active member of the Mormon Church—the religion and people that my mother grew up with. I left that community at sixteen, knowing I could no longer belong to it. In 2012 I watched with great interest Mitt Romney's pursuit of the American presidency. He kept Mormonism in the shadows, but I knew the history of those shadows well."

After *Shot in the Heart* I wanted to write a volume about the visions and delusions and grand pursuits in Joseph Smith's mind, but it would have been a long project—years. Publishers usually want a finished book in eighteen months. Maybe if time allows I can still consider it. Until then, this article and some pages from *Shot in the Heart* embody some of my understanding of Mormon history, doctrine, society and politics. I should note that my outlook is not typical of most Mormons.

In recent years, due to the internet's ability to reveal and examine aspects of Mormon history that the church didn't want its members to decipher or question, many Mormons have left the fold. Similarly, the cruel treatment of same sex couples and their children has also inspired acts of flight. Here is an excerpt from that article:

It was a warm evening, summer of 1967. I was seated on the steps of my family's front porch in Milwaukie, Oregon, in conversation with a Mormon elder, a man I liked and respected. He was advising me, gently yet unambiguously, that perhaps I should not attend my church ward anymore.

"I've seen the way some of our younger people look at you," he said. "They respect you. I'm sorry, but I don't want that. I don't want you to mislead them, I don't want you to take them wayward."

As we talked, my mother waited in the living room, a few feet away, listening. She was a lifelong Mormon, from Provo, Utah. Her ancestors had experienced the persecution of Mormons in Missouri, in the late 1830s. One of them knew well the prophet Joseph Smith and his successor, Brigham Young, who in the 1840s led Mormons to a sanctuary in the Salt Lake Basin. Other forebears of hers had joined the last of the Mormons' handcart expeditions to Utah—they literally walked their way across America, pushing and carrying carts that held their possessions—after emigrating from Britain into a United States that would not tolerate them in its boundaries, for their differences with the rest of Christian America.

Now, my mother called me inside the house. She said, "This man is breaking my heart. I want to order him off my property."

I asked her not to do that. I still had regard for the elder, though I also knew I was nearing the end of something, as I'd been changing for some time. In the music and the politics of that time, I found beliefs and experiences the church couldn't match—ones that shaped character and morals just as decidedly. My parting from the Mormon community I'd known was now inevitable.

The elder left me with a caution I'd heard before from Mormon men: "We should be in the world, but not of the world." That counsel delineates the Mormon paradox, an illumination meant to define a people and their lifeline to redemption.

**Elaine Schock**
**March 12, 2016**
**"Getting Better"**

I started this journey when Mikal told me, "It is 100 percent cancer." It never crossed my mind that could actually be the diagnosis. Now what? I had to travel for work the next day. All I could do was study, on the plane, on the bus, in the hotel room. The only thing I could control was my knowledge, and I had to start from scratch.

There are hundreds of different cancers, I knew nothing about any of them, and I still research. I even have "HPV-related cancer" on Google alert. There is not all that much that comes up that is new, and I think that is probably the same for other cancers. I get angry we haven't gotten farther with a cure or a way to manage the disease.

And, I worry. Did Mikal eat today? Because eating is going to determine his well-being, and without taste buds that can be chore. He might forget or decide there is something he wants at the last minute that I have to pick up for him after work. Truth is, sometimes I just don't want to think about it. I have to work, take care of family and run a home. It can be exhausting, and one more thing is sometimes one more thing too many.

When people said at the beginning that I was a caretaker, I bristled. Me? Caretaker? I just had no idea what that meant. The truth is, I am. It was even suggested that I had to take care of myself. Well, they knew a lot more than I did. Of course I had to be okay, because I was my family's lifeline. That is an enormous responsibility. Worry is part of my life. What is going to happen next? How is Mikal's illness affecting the children? They love him. It can be a little overwhelming. You go to sleep and wake up with the same heavy heart. That is cancer.

But it is getting better. A little better all the time. The grueling five months of chemo / radiation are over. Recovery isn't immediate, but it is slowly happening. The gaunt look works for Mikal, but ten pounds more would be great. He is getting out more. His depression seems to be lifting and even the fatigue, though still an issue, is getting to be less of one. Mikal is helping more with chores and writing every day.

This week was a good one. I'm cautiously optimistic the next few weeks will be significant ones. We have an important doctor's appointment coming up on the 22nd, as well as in April. I know we are not the only people going through this. Our thoughts and prayers go out to the families who lose their loved ones, and we see it daily. We hurt for them, and to be honest, it makes us a little more fearful of what can happen. And when cancer happens to children, we are just gutted. It is hard enough for an adult. There is no making sense of this disease. Although Mikal's treatment was brutal, he did pretty well considering, and has an excellent chance of remission. Plus, we have the support of so many. You can get consumed and discouraged by the political hate rhetoric. It is easy to forgot how wonderful people are.

I travel next week. I will be in Nashville for the Kris Kristofferson tribute. It will be lovely to see him and his wife, and then to Willie's ranch for the Luck Reunion Banquet and Festival. My daughter will be there with me. Good food and music, and I will be with people I love. But I am always of two minds when I leave. It is never easy these days. A part of me wants to be here, but this is my job. As always our deepest gratitude. We feel your presence every day.

**Mikal Gilmore:** Elaine has always carried a lot of the pressure in our household, and it's been manifold since my cancer diagnosis. It may seem that, because of my magazine writing, I'm able to contribute significantly to our expenses, but unfortunately that's not the case. I write two or three times a year for quite decent fees, but it adds up to moderate annual income at best. Since Elaine and I started to live together she has always supported us, her children, her business, and our house. That's a tremendous amount of burden and it certainly takes a toll (which is why I'm glad to see her enjoy boxing and exercise, and to see her travel to interesting events and places in good company).

Since the diagnosis the weight of all this has increased for her—not so much financially, but in emotional terms: worry, stress, sleeplessness, fear. I suppose caretaker is the right word, though to me Elaine seems our family's provider and my advocate. She has studied the specifics of my disease and she has helped direct my treatment in our medical consultations. At home, she tells me when I need to eat and finds palatable food for me. Too many occasions she has had to take trips out after work or at night to get something necessary for me. At times I guess there was no other option—some days I was shaky about driving, even walking. But as things improve, I try to do as much as possible for myself, though I know I can still wear on her energy.

The weeks since my birthday have been the hardest, because of recovery from radiation. I have had all sorts of unexpected reactions. Elaine is better prepared and informed, and she explains to me what is happening. That helps immeasurably—it gives a better perspective to my worry, and I don't feel as upset or sideswiped. Gradually, most things have improved. As Elaine says, it's getting better.

My main encumbrances are an inability to taste foods—which makes many things feel like unbearable cardboard—and the fatigue, worse on some days than others. I don't know why, but that latter one leads to embarrassment and self-loathing, as well as worry when I'm working. I've started drinking cappuccino again, hoping the caffeine might help me stay awake. Maybe it does, but the fatigue persists.

All this will pass. Elaine gets me through every day in many ways, and I look forward to nothing more than being with her every night, talking, and watching her unfortunate tastes in television. Not only do I expect my health to improve, but I hope the strain on her lessens. She has been kind to me throughout all this, and that has made the biggest difference of all.

And in the not remote future, we have a romantic date dinner planned. I even bought a new fedora for the event.

### Mikal Gilmore
### March 13, 2016

The Ramones' first four albums—*Ramones, Leave Home, Rocket to Russia* and *Road to Ruin*, recorded between 1976 and 1978—are among the best sequence in rock 'n' roll history: an inventive mix of old and new; radical, perplexing, ridiculous and liberating. The band changed our world, and in return they were hated.

After that, something broke. Their label didn't know what to do with the group's sound and image; as a result, the magic got obscured, damaged. The Ramones never again made a great album until *Too Tough to Die* (with their original creative team, including former drummer Tommy Ramone, on production), in 1985—but this one proved to be their greatest of all. It was easy to overlook—they had broken faith too many times, and were no longer cutting edge. Plus, there's no liberating fun in *Too Tough to Die*. By this time the Ramones fucking hated each other (they never overcame that). The album is a world of real rage and hurt and the kind of heartbreak that is irreparable—it's about striking out, maybe dangerously.

This was also the album on which the Ramones out-Sex Pistoled the Sex Pistols, spitting back at their copyists. *Too Tough to Die* was vengeance on all those who had shunned the Ramones, including each other. They couldn't be killed easily, and they couldn't be healed. In time, the four original Ramones all died in miserable ways.

*It was glowing, glowing, glowing / Glowing in the dark / It was sparkling, sparkling, sparkling / Sparkling in the night / I took the law and threw it away / Cause there's nothing wrong / It's just for play / There's no law, no law anymore / I want to steal from the rich and / Give to the poor.*
—Dee Dee Ramone, "Howling at the Moon"

## Mikal Gilmore
### March 13, 2016
From Dee Dee Ramone's devastating autobiography, *Lobotomy*:

"Hey, guys, can you lower the music?"

Tommy said, "I am tripping on LSD. Those Stooges songs are freaking me out. You don't want to run me off the road."

That was like the signal for things to get worse. "What's the matter, Tommy? You don't like the Stooges?"

Ho, ho, ho. I lit up a joint of Chiba Chiba Colombian Gold. I was having a good time until I noticed a burning rubber smell. It was the car, not the marijuana. The car was on fire. The electric system had gone, and smoke was pouring out of the engine, which, in a Volkswagen, is in the back. Everybody started shouting with glee. In two more minutes, the car stopped running completely. Since the rest of the 59th Street Bridge is on a downward angle, we were able to coast into Manhattan anyway. We left the car on the sidewalk, where it smashed into one of Bloomingdales' windows on 59th and Third, crushing the dummies in the store window to death.

## Mikal Gilmore
### March 14, 2016
"Dedicated to the One I Love" was written by Lowman Pauling and Ralph Bass and was a hit for the "5" Royales, the Shirelles and the Mamas & the Papas (Pauling was the guitarist of The "5" Royales, the group that recorded the original version of the song). The song has been a loving testament between Elaine and me for years, even before we were married. She leaves tomorrow for Nashville and Austin for a week. I will miss her terribly, every minute. In

the last few months she has taken on tremendous worry and advocacy for me. This prayer goes both ways. I will be fine, baby, while you are gone; please be fine for me and for your children. And though the Shirelles' version is matchless and haunting, I also like the big harmonies here—and I've always liked the Mamas & Papas.

**Mikal Gilmore**
**March 14, 2016**
Johnny Ramone (who was no angel) on Phil Spector: "So here's this little guy with lifts in his shoes, a wig on his head, four guns—two in his boots and one on each side of his chest—and two bodyguards. After he shot that girl, I thought, 'I'm surprised that he didn't shoot someone every year.'" Excerpt from Johnny Ramone, *Commando*.

**Mikal Gilmore**
**March 14, 2016**
A few weeks ago I posted some songs, mid to late 1970s, that formed something of a continuum in the rise of punk. Listening to the Ramones it's always plain how strong they were melodically. Despite their blaring sheets of sound, they were writing and playing pop songs. That started me thinking today about what was once called "power pop" (a phrase I never liked), and made me revisit some music that was largely contemporaneous with punk, and that to some degree interacted with it (though some of my picks actually predated punk). There's no continuum here, there are just some connections, some associations, that bounced around for me, and there's a couple that were new to me. In fact, there's a ton of this stuff, and perhaps too much of it got slighted due to all the excitement that met new punk bands. The Ramones showed how punk and pop coexisted. These songs are testament to a lot of tuneful and clever bands and music that still deserve hearing. Association 1: "Come Out and Play," by the the Paley Brothers, who were friends and label mates with the Ramones, and appeared with them in "Rock 'n' roll High School."

**Mikal Gilmore**

**March 16, 2016**

Elaine is spending time on Willie's bus tonight. I told her she should challenge him to a game of poker.

**Mikal Gilmore**

**March 18, 2016**

I'm forever surprised at how low Trump can go and still win applause. "Do I love the Mormons? I have many friends that live in Salt Lake City—and by the way, Mitt Romney is not one of them," Trump said to applause. "Are you sure he's a Mormon? Are we sure?"

Sure, Trump loves "the Mormons"—same as he loves "the blacks." Just another populace to condescend to, and to dominate or use. For the record, I'm a residual Mormon, but I strongly resent their social views and actions of recent decades—particularly against same-sex marriage. During the last election I wrote critically at length about Romney and his ancestral history, and Mormonism's wayward political development. Elaine recently posted that writing on the author's page she has created for me. Still, I'm just residual enough that when I see this sort of statement my blood can boil.

**Elaine Schock**

**March 19, 2016**

**"Dedicated to the One I Love"**

I've been far away from home this last week. I travel a lot for business—that's nothing new—but for the first time in six months I feel one less burden. Mikal is not completely healed but he is doing better, and my worries have eased a bit. I'm having a good time. I didn't stay awake most nights because of stress. I slept. In my heart I know it's OK at home, at least for now. The reassuring texts and plans about the future are so encouraging. Yes, get the leather jacket that you want, Mikal. It will look great on you. Recovery starts from within and the belief it will happen. I guess you call it hope.

Mikal is finishing up an important and compelling story for *Rolling Stone*. He is handling the home front responsibilities, maybe not with ease, but it is all getting done. At the Kris Kristofferson tribute, a good friend I haven't seen in

awhile grabbed me, gave me a big hug and said, "You have been through so much."
It was the first time it hit me how true that was. It was an emotional moment and
caught me off guard. I had to stop myself from just weeping. But there is no crying
in the music business. On the road, I'm with an extended family. There is comfort
in that.

As we get closer to seeing the doctors about the success of Mikal's treatment
I get scared, even though logically I know the results will be positive. But, I have
the next steps planned, just in case. I would rather be prepared than blindsided.
That would be too great a disappointment. This is cancer.

This post is dedicated to the one I love. Every night while I'm away I whisper
a little prayer for my family, because I know it's hard for them. It is hard for me
too. This is not a religious thing, it is about truth and love. Thank you for being
there, and for all your good thoughts and words of encouragement for Mikal and
me. We are grateful beyond words.

> **Mikal Gilmore:** Elaine has indeed been through a great deal in
> recent months. She has done her best to sustain her family and
> me, and to keep me healthy and in good spirits, during both my
> treatment and more recently in my (surprisingly more difficult)
> recovery. She has informed herself expertly about cancer and my
> particular strain of it—HPV-related throat cancer—and she has
> been with me at every important medical appointment. Her
> knowledge on the matter and her determination to keep me alive
> have had a great and beneficial effect during this whole ordeal.
>
> I am always glad to see Elaine enjoy herself and her friends
> during her trips out of town—I think it can be of help to both of
> us. She deserves every smile and relief she can get, even though I
> missed her more this time than ever before. In part that's because
> it was a long trip. Also we've grown so close through this that she
> is a key part of my balance; I would lose my mind and intent with-
> out her. We are fast approaching an appointment that may clarify
> the success of the treatment, and we are both understandably anx-
> ious. I want to see my baby breathe more easily and sleep better. I
> hope those days and nights are coming.

## Mikal Gilmore
## March 21, 2016

Elaine arrived back Saturday from Luck, Texas, where she got to visit with Willie Nelson and several good friends. She had a great time—she was accompanied by her daughter, Samantha—and she even got to see a big and scary thunderstorm (I was envious). Plus, the day before she attended a tribute to Kris Kristofferson, in Nashville, where several artists performed songs from his remarkable body of work. We are both hard at work this week—I'm on a deadline—and we are attending a medical appointment in Hollywood tomorrow. The best news of all, though, is that I get to see her lovely face every day.

## Elaine Schock
## March 22, 2016
## "Alright"

I normally post my updates on Saturday but decided to do one today (Tuesday) as well. We went to Radiology Oncology in Hollywood this morning to see if Mikal's cancer was still present now that treatment ended. The scopes and probing are tough and take time but the doctor said to Mikal, he better get used to it since he will have to do this again in July, and then regularly for years to come. Today we got great news: *There is no trace of cancer!*

The truth is with Mikal's HPV-related stage 4 cancer, recurrence is more likely within the next six months, but he will have to be monitored his entire life. Still, those words sounded just wonderful to us. Mikal's throat is healing nicely, no soreness inside or out. His voice is clear. They said he is doing really well and the worst is over. We won't notice the daily progress much, but during the three- to six-month period we will see some real recovery, and taste should come back within a year. Salt is the first flavor that returns, and that has already started to happen.

Mikal will also have to gain weight and exercise. He is still suffering from fatigue but they said exercise will help change that. Of course, the problem with being exhausted is that you don't want to work out. Mikal needs to build on his health now. Time to get those muscles toned up. It sounds so normal, a doctor telling his patient to diet and exercise. We still have the PET scan, which will now take place in May. The last one came up clear, so there is a good chance this one will as well. I know Mikal didn't sleep more than a few hours last night, although he has been working full time. But, I have a feeling he will be able to rest better now. I know I will.

This was a big day, and although I believed the check-up would go well, there is always that worry in the back of your mind. What if? It looks like Mikal is going to have to put up with me for a lot longer than he thought. We are going to be all right. Thank you for your prayers and encouragement. Your support helped us through our darkest times. We still have a way to go and uncertainty will linger, but this is a new day and I will take it.

> **Mikal Gilmore** I was apprehensive today. I haven't been sleeping much lately—in part because I'm working long hours, but also because this appointment was coming up. Since I've been weak lately, and have an eye infection, I was worried that my report might be less than what was hoped for. Elaine, though, has always had hope, and it has helped me every minute. In fact, it's given me hope. There was a moment during our consultation when, after one of the doctors gave us the results, I looked at Elaine, and she had a happy smile on her face. That not only made my day, but it made all the days since September rewarding. Seeing my baby smile is what I was really hoping for today. She's been through a lot. She earned that smile.

## Mikal Gilmore
### March 22, 2016

Leukemia is, to me, one of the most frightening fates. Once, years ago, a doctor took a blood test and told me I appeared to have leukemia. I thought about that in the days that followed and decided some things had hurt in my life but that I also had a good life. I felt the same after this diagnosis. I went back to that doctor a week later for a follow-up on the leukemia and he said, "I'm sorry, we were looking at the wrong test." I don't know if I've ever told Elaine about that.

**Elaine Schock**

**March 23, 2016**

HPV cancer is related to sexual activity. That is a fact, and embarrassing or not, we have to deal with it. Ignoring it won't make it go away. The vaccine is one thing and important but embarrassment can also mean not speaking to your doctor if you have concerns. It is a relatively new cancer and it may be misdiagnosed. It often is by a GP.

Mikal Gilmore was misdiagnosed for a year. When he was finally diagnosed by a head and neck specialist, he was stage 4 base of the tongue and neck cancer. We didn't know anything about this sort of cancer. Michael Douglas had it and after that initial publicity died down, it was the last I heard about anyone getting HPV related cancer. People ridiculed Mr. Douglas, and his wives were none too happy he disclosed his illness. He walked back a bit, but his honesty in his interviews about the disease was so helpful to me and I will be forever grateful to him. I have tried to be totally forthright in my posts so it can help the next person. The fact is, my not being aware didn't prevent it from happening to my husband. It never entered my mind he would get it. Who but one celebrity ever got the disease? Now, I know.

**Mikal Gilmore**

**March 24, 2016**

Swell. I'm sitting here in the bedroom, working, when Fubar comes running in with something in his mouth. Doesn't look right to me. Turns out it's a lizard. He drops it and the lizard scurries behind the dressers. I've been trying to find it, but it's impossible. Fubar is bereft. I can't imagine how Elaine will react if she steps on the damn thing in the middle of the night.

**Elaine Schock**

**March 26, 2016**

**"The Healing Game"**

On Tuesday we went to the most important doctor visit yet. There were tubes and scopes and it looked pretty uncomfortable. I watched while the doctors looked for a healthy throat. Then we waited anxiously for the results. And they were good. No trace of cancer to be found. The truth is, this is the second good result. They probed before and Mikal had a clear PET scan (he has another scheduled in May). Still, treatment, which was sometimes brutal, continued. But we didn't stop. Nope, couldn't take that chance, even though it would have been easier. Mikal completed his last round of chemo and radiation on his birthday, February 9th. With cancer, there is no easy way out. Recurrence is a threat.

It is a new day. Everything seems to be getting better, attitude, appetite, and energy. We needed this. These last weeks were probably the hardest physically and emotionally since the diagnosis. I had read they might be, but everyone is different and you always hope you will beat the odds. It will take a few more months to feel the full benefits of recovery, but Mikal is working full time now and that is a pretty good start. The oncology department at Kaiser has been incredible. I had done my research but don't pretend to be an expert. They were willing to hear me out and so was Mikal. We learned there are ways to ease some of the side effects, and they were great at making sure Mikal received treatment that was perhaps beyond what they normally prescribed.

Maybe it was my charm, or that I would say, "He has stage 4 cancer; can you just do it?" As a publicist, I know a hook. I had about a thousand questions and needed to speak to a real person. No one in oncology would have time for that, so, I often called the National Cancer Institute. They sent books on nutrition, chemo and radiation, and had an oncology nurse on the phone with me when I needed one. I asked some crazy-ass questions, too. They also put me in touch with several yoga instructors and nutritionists who specialize in cancer patients. None of which I ever used because the truth is Mikal was going to end up eating what he could with as much protein and vitamins as possible.

And, the nurses in infusion were so helpful with their food suggestions. They are a remarkable source of knowledge, as well as being a great comfort. A feeding tube was never an option we wanted to consider, and we were able to avoid that. The yoga classes sounded good but it was just too much after hours and hours of treatment. The group counseling sessions didn't work out either for stage 4; the mortality rate is too high.

HPV-related head and neck cancer is a different thing. The survival rate is very good. Things I worried about mostly didn't happen, and the things I didn't think about did. It is all a learning process. And finally, after over six long, arduous months, we are happily in the healing game.

In all these posts on Mikal's cancer there is something about medical and psychological care in the message. I know I am talking to those who may have cancer or have loved ones that do. This is a journey we are on together. It is where we trade information as well as love and encouragement. We have come to rely on your support and hope that we give back. For all of you that are suffering, we are hoping for a speedy recovery and are with you in this fight. What a terrible disease. It will fuck you up and all you can do is battle on to survival and to put it behind you. Thank you all for caring.

> **Mikal Gilmore:** Elaine's knowledge and determination kept me alive. I have no doubt about it. She wasn't going to accept me going into an irretrievable dark. Without her tenacity, I might well have been there by now.
>
> This passage has been brutal and scary to us both—yet we seem to be fortunate in many ways. The greatest fortune for me is this: this ordeal has made our love unremitting in this lifetime. The other night Elaine said something that meant the world to me. I won't repeat it here—it wasn't anything intimate, though it was private. It amounted to an assurance to me that our marriage is unshakeable; we made the right choice all those years ago. As Elaine has said before, no matter what happens, this will have a happy ending.

## Mikal Gilmore
### March 31, 2016

I just finished watching the current season of *House of Cards*. This is a good example of life imitating art as I've ever seen; it's as if somebody gave the show's makers a crystal ball to gaze into our present madness. The last few episodes, though—thrilling and frightening—are about as brutal as political drama can get. Holy hell. You have to steel yourself for what everybody has done to everybody else, for what comes at the end, "We don't submit to terror. We make the terror." And you have to steel yourself for whatever comes next. This, more than any coverage or commentary that our enfeebled news media has offered, delivers to us the present moment of American horror.

## Elaine Schock
### March 31, 2016

Everyone I know appreciates the passion of Bernie Sanders supporters, but this is too important a race to pretend it is OK to take your marbles and go home if he doesn't get the nomination. People's lives are at stake. Women's rights, being punished for having an abortion depending on the day and state, banning Muslims, the systematic deportation of 11 million Mexicans through a gorgeous door, plus—above all else—the Supreme Court. The ignorance that Trump or Cruz could be good for this country in any way literally takes my breath away. This isn't up for debate. Sure, Bernie first, absolutely. But then don't let your ideology ruin this country. Enough is enough. You can say what you like about Hillary, but the GOP is running on a war against immigrants, women, and religious freedom. They declared that. That is what your vote or non-vote will go toward.

**The Albums - Part 6**

By the end of 1969, I was out of high school, into college, not doing well. I was going through one of my periodic funks, following one of my periodic failed love affairs, though this one counted for much, since it was my first real love. (The woman overnight became a born again Christian and married the man who impregnated her. Later we would come back together, which was a mistake on my part.)

In this period, the late winter of 1969 and the early winter of 1970, I was taking a lot of drugs, learning how to drink and staying up all night until the sun rose, then I'd hit the bed (actually, the floor, which was my bed at the time), and finally find sleep. It was in this time that I began to find the deeper purposes of having a record collection: In those long and alone dark hours I turned to music that resounded the emptiness I was both feeling and making for myself.

In the dissolute scenarios of the Rolling Stones' *Let it Bleed*, in the lower depths marked out in *The Velvet Underground & Nico*, I found an awareness that somehow helped me: Stories of dissolution lay out a more compassionate scope than pledges of love. That is, it's easy to live with love, but by learning to live in the shadows of its absence, you find a better understanding of others who live with loss, as well as an inner resolve that can sustain you when there's nothing or nobody else to hold you. I couldn't stay in this place for long, nor did I, but then neither did I leave it quickly or easily, and never entirely.

This seemed, even to me then, to go together with the times. The 1960s had not only come to an end; they had come undone. Rock's consensus of joy and opportunity was finished, and its most significant components fell apart quickly. At the end of their 1969 American tour, the Rolling Stones played a free concert in Altamont, outside San Francisco, and took the Grateful Dead's terrible advice to hire the Hell's Angels as a security force. It was a day of legendary violence. The Angels pummeled scores of people, for little or no provocation, and in the evening, as the Stones performed "Under My Thumb," the bikers beat and stabbed a young black man to death in front of the stage, in full view of the band, audience members, and a camera crew.

Altamont was rock culture's ugliest moment; for years, it deflated the music's sense of its own idealism. Darkness was all around at the end of the

1960s and the beginning of the 1970s—after the hippie dream had turned into cynicism and exploitation; after the Students for a Democratic Society imploded and the crazy and scary Weathermen (who took their name from a Bob Dylan lyric) finished what remained of the New Left; after American police had disrupted the Black Panther movement by jailing and killing several of its key members; after the murderous horror wrought by the Charles Manson Family in Los Angeles; after the Vietnam War continued to make a callous sacrifice of thousands and thousands American and Southeast Asian lives, and as the menacing years of Richard Nixon were on the rise.

And, perhaps more markedly than anything, all this happened as the Beatles ended as bitter, mutually unbelieving strangers who regarded one another as creations of undeserved hype. Their deterioration, in effect, became a metaphor for a larger breakdown, the failed hope of a social community we longed for, but never achieved. It all turned dark. As one of rock's most honest voices soon announced, the dream—which is to say, revolution—was over.

By this time, something called the "rock press" had developed with magazines like *Cheetah*, *Crawdaddy!* and *Rolling Stone*, where one could read passionate and informed opinions and arguments about current music and, better yet, also learn about earlier musicians who had helped make the late 1960s and early 1970s innovations possible. This included everyone from Robert Johnson, Louis Armstrong, Bessie Smith, Billie Holiday and Duke Ellington to the Carter Family, Lotte Lenya, Miles Davis, Charles Mingus, Thelonious Monk, and Ornette Coleman (some of whom were still alive, making essential music), and countless more.

As a result, the journalism—that is, the essays, rants, profiles, interviews and historical perspectives—of such writers as Ralph J. Gleason, Paul Williams, Greil Marcus, Jon Landau, Dave Marsh, Langdon Winner, Jonathan Cott, Lester Bangs, Paul Nelson, Nick Tosches, Robert Christgau, and Ellen Willis came to seem as exciting and meaningful to me as much of the music they were writing about. Although, too damn few of them for my liking were willing to stand up for the Velvet Underground and Lou Reed (Nelson, Christgau, and Willis being notable and important exceptions).

Reading these writers, who were inventing new ways to comprehend the meanings of 20th Century music, fueled my desire for records perhaps more than any other inspiration ever has. These critics in effect were opening up catalogs, directories that helped link the undercurrents of blues, jazz and folk music with the emerging purposes of rock 'n' roll. This in turn opened up the histories of people, places, social realities and the attempts to contain or even refuse all these developments.

Rock 'n' roll, or any thriving popular music, is made from and for the moment, aiming mainly to satisfy that immediacy. But people who best loved this music understood there were valuable histories and experiences that had made that moment possible, and that today's moments were tomorrow's history. It felt like whole new vistas, a whole new world—a secret, vibrant world that told the true stories and nature of our times—had opened up to me.

This meant spending more money, of course, but I was working in that time as a drug counselor for the State of Oregon. It paid about two hundred dollars a month. Rent was never more than seventy-five dollars a month then, and albums were about five or six dollars, so I made do the best I could.

Of course, it wasn't only critics who had a line on music's meanings. In 1970, I made a new lifelong friend, Michael Sugg. When we met, he was managing one of Portland's primary independent record stores, Long Hair Music. I visited that store many times every week—and eventually I'd work there myself. It was a good place to stay informed about interesting new—and old—recordings.

I'd overheard Michael as he talked with customers in the stores about their tastes and interests, and could tell he was well informed about a wide range of music history—including jazz. We first struck up a rapport one day when I was trying to describe to him a haunting piece of solo piano jazz I'd heard late one night on a car radio. I mentioned this story briefly in my seven days challenge. Heading home from a rock festival somebody dropped LSD into a water jug several friends and I were sharing—without telling us about it. I was having a rough time with the acid (it was cut with something else, something harsh and a bit scary, maybe speed) and my friend driving was trying to find some music on the radio that might help me feel better about the experience I was having.

He came across this piano piece on an after-midnight jazz show. It began with restful chord phrasing and carried you along—and then it pulled apart gradually into dissonant melodic jags that seemed to match my mental state. After a few minutes, it settled back into its lovely harmonic straits, and as it did, I knew I was over the worst of my bad passage with the drug. It felt like the music had mended my mind.

The disc jockey never announced who had played the piano on that recording, but I felt I needed to know. I owed something to that bit of music––and to the musician who had played it. I dropped into Long Hair Music and started to describe the track to Michael Sugg, and within seconds he told me, "It's 'Peace Piece,' by Bill Evans. It's from his 1958 album, *Everybody Digs Bill Evans*."

I knew who Evans was—he had played piano on Miles Davis's landmark *Kind of Blue* album (Davis's and John Coltrane's recordings reconfigured my own aesthetics). But I'd never heard the albums Evans recorded on his own and with his trios. That would now change, and from then on his music mattered enormously to me.

I was living in a large house in southeast Portland at the time, with several other friends—an informal hippie commune, full of people who shared almost no collective values or tastes beyond drugs and ill-advised sex. I went home that afternoon with my new Bill Evans album and played it for the person in the house who I thought possessed the most adventurous musical tastes, a woman named Cameron, who had once been a classical violinist.

She liked "Peace Piece," and after we played it a couple of times, she said, "You should come out with me tonight, over to my friend's place. He has a lot of albums, just like you, and he's pretty sophisticated about music." So, I tagged along with Cameron, and it turned out her boyfriend was Michael Sugg. We spent the night smoking dope, and I had a great time poring over Michael's impressive record collection. He clearly knew his jazz history.

Michael played me some solo recordings by pianist Art Tatum that astounded me. Since Michael also worked at a record store, he had a large pile of free promotional records that he hadn't yet listened to. I thumbed through one of them and came across an interesting cover. It showed a young man with long blond hair; he was looking upward, as if he saw something inescapable above him, and he was pulling his hair back with both hands. The record was *Hunky Dory* and it was by David Bowie—somebody I'd never heard of. I asked Michael about it and he said he hadn't yet played it, so we put it on the turntable—and we all immediately fell in love with it.

That night was the real beginning of my friendship with Michael. I didn't have other friends I could share that many different musical tastes with. Though the 1960s had precipitated some new attitudes of openness, it also fostered much generational clannishness. Either one liked the Grateful Dead or the Rolling Stones or country-rock. Many of my friends and I found little to agree on. None of them could much abide Miles Davis or John Coltrane––but Sugg not only liked that music, he knew it well and was happy to share his knowledge with me. Michael and Cameron didn't last long—nobody lasted long with Cameron—but Sugg and I started hanging out a lot, drinking, smoking marijuana, listening to music and talking about our quest for the perfect girlfriend.

Michael became what I would call my best friend. We heard and saw a lot of music together and shared confidences about romances and heartbreaks. He invited me to live in a nice large house in southeast Portland (dubbed Locust House), in the company of another renter. Then I did something wrong that was hurtful to Michael, and it damaged our friendship. I left the house we shared, and found myself without my best friend through my own damn fault.

Michael and I didn't speak to one another for over a year. He was bitter. I was mortified. During the same period of our lives, each of us decided to become a music journalist—for different local publications. Also, I took a job at the record store that Michael had once managed. He still had an occasional relationship to the store and came in now and then, and eventually we began talking about music again. I think that it seemed like a safer, less personal topic area for us to try to rebuild a relationship on, though as I look back, I realize that in many ways music was as personal between us—and as essential to the bond of our friendship—as anything else ever had been.

It took time, but we repaired our comradeship. We even collaborated on writing. As the years went along, as I watched my mother's health decline and as I went through the horror of my brother's drama, Michael was one of those people who helped me most, without judgment or qualification. Around the time that *Night Beat* was being published, a journalist in Portland asked me who had been the biggest influences on my writing—which authors and journalists and which musicians helped shape me or gave me models to emulate.

I realized—and said—that maybe my biggest influence had been Michael Sugg. He had taught me new ways to hear music, and he had opened up worlds of pop and jazz for me that even my favorite rock critics rarely gave me insight into. In the many years since I've met Michael, I hardly ever sat down to listen seriously to a recording or concert, or to do my best to write accurately and effectively about music, without employing something that I learned from him. Without his influence, I'm not sure I would have appreciated many of the details and nuances of sound as well as I have come to. Sometimes your friends or family are your greatest influences—and that has been both one of the best and toughest lessons I've had to learn. For that matter, I derived *Night Beat*'s title from the Sam Cooke album of the same name—a record introduced to me by Michael Sugg.

This isn't to say we've shared common views and responses on all matters. When the punk revolt happened in the late 1970s, Michael wasn't persuaded by much of it. I think I actually drove him out of his Northwest Portland house one night while playing the Sex Pistols' "Anarchy in the U.K.," full roar, on his mammoth speakers.

APRIL
2016

**Elaine Schock**
**April 2, 2016**
**"You Don't Miss Your Water"**

The song "The Times They Are A-Changing" just came into my head. I thought back to December when I had my doubts that Mikal would see another Christmas, making the best of what might be our last. It was all so heavy. That sounds kind of hipster but it's a real feeling of dread on your entire being.

Now it seems clear that Mikal is in recovery. I don't worry about the future or recurrence. I don't see the point. I used to hedge all my bets in these posts, but not today. That weight has been lifted. The time after treatment is tough, and Mikal gets frustrated with how long it takes to get over the fatigue and other side effects. Since I feel things are so positive, I hope I don't forget to be a sympathetic ear because he still feels badly and worries every new pain is cancer-related. It's just below the surface. He doesn't say it but I know that is what he is thinking. Certainly his concern is quite understandable. Three months of aggressive chemo, and then immediately more chemo and thirty-five rounds of targeted radiation, is brutal. The fear of reliving that experience is something you don't get over easily, if ever.

The odd thing is that when Mikal works, he doesn't feel the fatigue as much. He has been focused on writing a cover story for *Rolling Stone* on the Ramones. It is an important story and the fact that all the original Ramones members have died is not something you can ignore. Three of the four died from cancer. Writing about tragedy is what Mikal does best. And for whatever reason that lessens his own problems with the disease, or maybe he is slowly getting better and doesn't notice just yet.

Mikal is getting used to the hearing loss, but it is no fun. In the next few months, we will buy the best hearing aids for his problem; you are supposed to wait six months after the end of chemo. It is an investment in a sound mind and quality of life. Every step of the way, I needed to make sure when this was over he would not suffer the consequences of treatment for years to come. The aim was for a good life.

Mikal just bought shoes and a hat. For a long time, he wouldn't buy anything other than books or music. I guess he didn't want to waste money on things he was not going to use. We even discussed going to a movie. This is the first time in over six months that we have seriously thought about going out. Maybe this weekend.

People ask me if I am all right, and I can honestly say I am fine. I don't get angry at the things I used to. I let the little things go and laugh. A lot. Even if things turned out differently, I would still have felt this time as a change for the better in my own attitude, and as a compassionate human being, to rise up to the occasion no matter what that is. I now appreciate things I used to take for granted. And, I have a marriage I wanted instead of one I had hoped to have. There is this saying that you don't miss your water till the well runs dry. Well, I got to feel that way about the people I love before it was too late. I don't believe this happened for a reason. It wasn't a blessing, but I did change in ways I'm grateful for. As always, you are in our thoughts.

> **Mikal Gilmore:** I've never had a greater learning experience than our marriage. It was a slow and belated way for me to grow up, and I still have much more of that to do, fates willing. I see better now some of the ways I was unkind and selfish, and how I didn't appreciate Elaine's depth of love and patience. Through cancer, we've found new levels of kindness and hope. Sometimes we realize that from long, late night conversations. Other times, a touch, or a smile we share when we first see each other in the morning or evening. Yes, there are moments that the side-effects are a considerable drag, but when I see Elaine's face and hear her reassurances, everything is better. It always will be.

## Elaine Schock
## April 2, 2016

On April 1, 1984, we were celebrating my second marriage at my apartment in New York City. A number of staffers from *Rolling Stone* were there. The phone rang and it was Mikal Gilmore and I thought it was so nice he was calling to congratulate me. I said so before he had the time to explain that he was calling because Marvin Gaye had just been murdered by his father, and he needed to speak to his editor. It was April Fool's Day but I could tell by the sound of Mikal's voice, this was no joke. I was at Columbia Records at that time and it had been less than a year before when we had those big shows at Radio City Music Hall with Marvin. Marvin had been killed the day before his birthday.

### Mikal Gilmore
### April 3, 2016
Just finished watching the second season of the unusual British police drama *Happy Valley* on Netflix. It has all the merits of the first season; in some ways it's more complex, with intriguing and gripping lines that all come together. It's also less brutal—that is, until we see what the final seconds imply. This season is all about the dark inheritance of families, the sins of the fathers, and the prices children—and others—pay. At the very end, the lead character, a policewoman, watches her innocent grandson as he runs ahead of her, playing, and you know what it is she's thinking. Her mind has connected all those lines. She's looking ahead at where the child's heritage is headed, and at the possible blood on her own hands. It fucks you up.

### Mikal Gilmore
### April 5, 2016
Bob Dylan changed the world more than he ever wanted to, and recognized the worth and price of chaos. Then, not bearing it any longer, he retreated and came back with this in "I Threw it All Away": *Love is all there is, it makes the world go 'round / Love and only love, it can't be denied / No matter what you think about it / You just won't be able to do without it / Take a tip from one who's tried.*

For years now, Bob Dylan has spoken to both fear and love.

### Elaine Schock
### April 7, 2016
Mikal Gilmore's *Rolling Stone* cover story on The Ramones is out now. Perhaps they are more famous dead than when they were alive. I'm not really sure that is a bad thing. Our legacy lives on far longer than we do. All four original members died relatively young men, three of the four of cancer. That is something. That wolf knocks down everyone's door.

**Elaine Schock**
**April 7, 2016**
Mikal Gilmore wrote a booklet for the soundtrack for the HBO movie, *Shot in the Heart* based on the book about his family and the tragedies they endured. I will post the text from booklet soon but here are his words about Merle Haggard:

**"Sing Me Back Home," Merle Haggard (From Collector's Series)**
In the same conversation in which [my brother] Gary told me he had received a call from Johnny Cash, I asked him if had heard from any other singers or celebrities.

He said, "Yeah. I heard from Merle Haggard."

This got my interest, since Haggard—despite his apparent politics—had made a lot of music that mattered to me over the years.

"What did he say?" I asked.

"He said, 'Don't let the bastards do it to you. They've killed too many of us already.'"

I was moved by what Haggard had said. I asked Gary what he said in reply.

"I told him it was too late. I was just making them finish the job."

Haggard was indeed right: They had killed too many. They were just getting started. It matters whom we elect as president, because that president will name justices and Supreme Court judges that will affect us, our society, and our children—for a century or more.

**Elaine Schock**
**April 7, 2016**
Cancer is getting so many these days. Maybe it was always like this and I just didn't notice.

**Mikal Gilmore**
**April 8, 2016**
Merle Haggard to *Rolling Stone*'s Jason Fine in 2009, after recovery from lung surgery, at the outset of a new tour: "It was a bit surprising to find that the outcome of the surgery was as good as it was. It's kind of like finding out there's more time on the show and you've played your best songs. I was probably

ready to go, you know. I'd done about everything I knew how to do. But to get an extension is always nice. God was kind. But now he expects some work out of it." Merle Haggard passed away on April 6, from complications due to cancer.

### Elaine Schock
### April 9, 2016

Let me be honest here, I have used restrooms pretty much all my life. I would not know if a transgendered person was in the stall next me. If you go into one of these bathrooms, they are not open, and have doors and locks. So you don't get to peek. Being transgendered doesn't make you a potential rapist, and these new "bathroom laws" assume that is the case, and that women and girls need protection. If they truly cared, take guns away from domestic violence abusers. That is a real problem. Lots of proof there. This is just outright bigotry, based on nothing but pure ignorance and hate. It is disgusting. And, North Carolina looks insane. But so does any state that passes these laws. Birth certificate proof? You have got to be kidding me.

### Mikal Gilmore
### April 9, 2016

It's hard to find a link for the song "In the Arms of Love," from *Live in Muskogee, Oklahoma / 1969* by Merle Haggard. It comes from one of the most interesting live albums—because of its imperfections—that Haggard made. Haggard doesn't sing it; his bassist Gene Pride does. It goes by quick, and I don't know if it ever had another life. But it's a pleasure to hear and feel.

### Mikal Gilmore
### April 9, 2016

Haggard was a complex man, with complicated and contradictory political and social views. On the same album that he sang the anti-hippie "Okie from Muskogee," he also delivered the Jimmie Rodgers lament to America's unwanted men, "Hobo Bill." Haggard's delivery of both is remarkable. The only person who sang Rodgers better was Rodgers.

**Elaine Schock**

**April 9, 2016**

**"One Way Out"**

Mikal's cover story for *Rolling Stone* on the Ramones is on the stands. It is a brilliantly written tragic story. Exactly what Mikal does best.

The Ramones are more famous and appreciated now than before most of them succumbed to cancer. I don't know why I never noticed the disease at the door before it knocked it down. Was it always like this? It is the defining illness of our time. We will either get cancer or someone we love will get it. Many never tell anyone other than their closest confidants that they have the disease. It was even strange for me to say, "My husband has cancer."

Going public is not the norm unless you need a gofundme page. Financial needs have to be met. How do you pay the mortgage or electricity if you can't work? Medical insurance only covers so much. It is clear that cancer can make friends and spouses run for the hills. The treatment is not pretty. For some there is an element of shame. And it is so frightening. No one wants to face their own mortality. Your own needs are not usually met and your partner's are all encompassing. Your workload will be overwhelming. Hell, your everyday chores just doubled and that is nothing compared to everything else that will hit you. And, women are much more likely to be abandoned compared with men. But if you love someone, how can you just let them fall behind? I can't wrap my head around that. The emotional support is what helps you survive. I am never going to leave. There is only one way out for us.

Got my annual checkup. I passed the HPV exam last Friday, and all is good. It is important to get tested. There is no cure for HPV, but it is essential to know if you have it. I don't know why it becomes cancerous in some people and disappears in others. There is a lot I don't know, but what I do know is that soon they will conclude that HPV-related head and neck cancer will not be treated the same way as cancer caused by tobacco.

Here we are, on the verge of that discovery—not soon enough for Mikal to benefit, though his prognosis will help researchers. One size does not fit all. The survival rate is too high for this cancer. The recurrence rate too low. It will be treated differently, still toxic but not as toxic. Mikal's recovery is worse than the treatment. He needs to gain weight and exercise. That is not easy, given he is fatigued and can't taste a lot of food. It is a kind of a Catch-22. He is too exhausted to work out but if he doesn't he will suffer fatigue longer.

This week is a good one; he is much better although we have a good six weeks or longer of recovery ahead of us. Mikal is handing in another assignment. He is in demand and works a lot. That is good for him and for me. I love reading his pieces, and there was a time not too long ago that he was not confident that anyone cared. Thanks to all of you for changing that.

These posts have been helpful to us in many ways, but the appreciation for Mikal's writing was most gratifying. He is still depressed about his hearing loss and other lingering side effects, plus the fact we have a new normal and liked the old normal better. I am sick and tired of Mikal being sick and tired. But there are no short cuts, we just have to move forward. Thank you all again for being with us. We are with you, too.

> **Mikal Gilmore:** Cancer, plus recovery from treatments, can be overwhelming for relationships. Each person has a burden. The sick person has to weather sickness and treatment and do the best to improve. The person who cares for the sick one has to watch that sickness, understand it, care for the ill or recovering person, and through it all still try to care for others, work, and to look after him- or herself. Elaine has her own concerns that I need to pay attention to, because I love her and I put her welfare at least equal to mine.
>
> Last week I went with her when she got her medical examination. I was relieved that we were doing it, and I breathed much easier when the results came back fine. But my care for my wife has to go beyond that. Every time I see her face when she arrives home, every time I see her smile, it helps to heal me. And I have become better aware in recent days that I'm indeed healing—I'm adapting to the new normal—even the hearing loss. Also, the fatigue is gradually ebbing and eating is becoming easier.
>
> None of this would have been possible without the love and care Elaine has given me. If I ever need to do the same for

her, I'll do so without hesitation; I would rise to meet that task. But I pray that never develops. Elaine is my wife—I want long, healthful and happy days for her, times that aren't consumed by worry and work and strain. I want her to feel loved, to be happy, and to enjoy her strength and her days and nights.

When I first learned about my diagnosis, I didn't know if there would be only one way out or not. I didn't know if this could be endured and beat. My first goal was to have a happy Christmas with my wife and family. Soon, I will have a happy summer with them. That's because of Elaine—she gave me the hopeful and loving way forward. I need to find ways to better show her that her well-being is central to my own heart and well-being. My future wouldn't mean much without her feeling loved, happy and healthy. I never really thought anything as good as Elaine could happen to me. I bless the day I found her.

**Mikal Gilmore**
**April 10, 2016**
The light is the last thing you convince yourself of before the night.

**Mikal Gilmore**
**April 10, 2016**
One of my favorite songs, "It's All in the Game," was a 1958 hit for Tommy Edwards. Carl Sigman composed the lyrics in 1951 to a wordless 1911 composition entitled "Melody in A Major," written by Charles Dawes, later vice president of the United States under Calvin Coolidge. According to Wikipedia, it is the only number 1 pop single to have been co-written by a U.S. vice president or winner of the Nobel Peace Prize.

**Elaine Schock**
**April 11, 2016**
This is all about education. That difference is equivalent to how much national life expectancies would rise if we eliminated cancer. "If you think about the cancer comparison, having cancer is not just about having a shorter life. It's

also about having an unhealthier life, a much lower quality of life," this from Harvard (and former Stanford) economist Raj Chetty, the lead author of a study about how income and geography shape life expectancies that was published in the *Journal of the American Medical Association.*

Doomed from the start, depending on where you live.

**Mikal Gilmore**

**April 12, 2016**

Elaine and I have had a good couple of days We had welcome news (I'll let Elaine share it when she's ready), plus we finalized future plans we've wanted to make for some time. I also finished a story I care a lot about. April has so far been kind. The best part, as always, is I get to sleep next to my meaning for living. This time, I'll even do it before sunrise.

**Mikal Gilmore**

**April 13, 2016**

Whenever Fubar and Tuffy get into a fight, Foofie rushes for the popcorn so she can watch. "The intensity of the fight has sparked another round of caustic rhetoric—including allegations from party leaders that Trump supporters are making death threats." (Ed O'Keefe, *The Washington Post*)

**Mikal Gilmore**

**April 15, 2016**

Last night, after Elaine went to sleep, I was watching *Skinwalkers*, a TV movie based on Tony Hillerman's Navajo reservation murder novels. At one point the lead detective learns that his wife's cancer has recurred, and before I knew it I was weeping. I was surprised and embarrassed at first, but then I realized I was weeping for the spouse who was learning of his wife's illness, which meant I was weeping for Elaine. I thought about all she has had to go through because of this, and how she kept me alive when my first reaction was acceptance. I waited a long time for somebody to love me enough to keep me. Without Elaine, by now I wouldn't even be a shadow on this planet anymore.

Elaine Schock
April 16, 2016
"The Turning Point"

This is the news Mikal mentioned. On Monday we went to the doctor for Mikal's check up and a Q&A. Mikal asked about the occasional pain where the tumor was radiated. The doctor said it was scar tissue and that scars change with time. It can be uncomfortable. OK, good answer. Now the big one: was Mikal cancer free?

The doctor said yes. I knew it, but it was good to hear. We practically danced out of there so excited that the oncology department looked different. It is still a place of pain and confusion, but not for us, not today. We made it to the other side. What a long and winding road. Mikal will be monitored closely. His health will be reviewed every two months, at least for a while. These are crucial times but the success rate for his HPV-related cancer is very high. I never doubted this would happen—well, maybe a few times.

These last months have been tough and became harder after treatment ended. It seemed like Mikal would never be anything but sick. Recovery is so drawn out and painful, it is hard to imagine life without cancer. And truth be told we never will, but this is a turning point. Mikal is feeling much better. He is eating and his taste buds are slow to return but he has some. His fatigue is not gone yet, but it doesn't hang over everything. And, his depression is lifting. Maybe it is because he is so focused on writing, or maybe he is just healthier. He even tried pushups, which to be honest, I don't recall him ever doing.

Mikal just spent a few all-nighters working on the Merle Haggard cover for *Rolling Stone*. It was worth it. The read is incredible. Mikal related to Merle for a number of reasons, not least because of his brother Gary, who, like Merle, also went to prison at a young age. Merle spent three years in San Quentin. He knew about death row. He saw it first-hand and it must have haunted him. It certainly influenced his songwriting. All of this insight on such a complicated, talented man makes the piece so compelling. His passing is a big loss and reading this article helps, at least for me.

I am leaving for New York on business soon and emailed Mikal my itinerary. He replied that he would drive me to the airport. You could have knocked me over with a feather. I missed those drives terribly. I knew it made

Mikal happy to be able to tell me that. He is always an hour early waiting for me at LAX to return, just because. We will be taking a short vacation to Portland in July. We are planning things that we used to only hope for after the diagnosis. It is funny, one day you have nothing but dread and the next you have a life again.

We also cannot forget that the ups and downs of the disease happen to the whole family. Tessa takes great delight in telling me that Mikal ate a banana with his hot fudge sundae. She can feel he is getting better and it eases her young mind. No one wants to see her parent struggle. Mikal has to buy razor blades because his face is no longer smooth. His hair also needs to be cut; it is darker than it was before, too. Last week I couldn't imagine all of this. It isn't just about hoping it will happen. It is happening. I feel good again. Slow and steady. Thank you for being there for us. Your support has been so wonderful. It helped more than you will ever know.

**Mikal Gilmore**
**April 16, 2016**

I hope you've had a chance to read Elaine's post about the state of things from earlier today. I wanted to add this:

Elaine and I had some hard days and weeks in the last couple of seasons. Visiting oncology was always sobering—as much for the suffering we saw others—especially children—go through. There was one day Elaine almost had to drag me out of Kaiser or I'd have ended up in tears after seeing an eight-year-old boy. Seemed unfathomable.

This last week was the week we had waited for, the news of remission. Elaine's beautiful smile as we left oncology almost made me cry as well, for all the right reasons. Before these last months, I'd never say the word cancer. I doubt if Elaine noticed—we'd had little immediate reason to use the term—but after losing my father to it when I was eleven, it haunted me in ways I couldn't describe. I still dream about what he went through during his nights.

After my diagnosis I wasn't sure what my future held, but I quickly learned. My wife wasn't going to let this go down without a disciplined and informed fight. She saved me. There's no doubt about it. On my own, I wouldn't have done half the things she persuaded me to do, and they added up to all the difference. This woman is the best thing that has happened to me in my life. Even if the news had been different this week, I'd feel the same. We learned to be much more honest with each other, and we learned to let the small grievances go. That's a big help, letting the small things go.

Also, one of the things that has surprised me most is my ability to write again—I really thought those days were over, maybe even for posting—plus I've found that I was now doing some of the writing I've cared the most about.

Regarding Merle Haggard: While working on that article I'd tell Elaine about all the ways his story reminded me of my brother, though I didn't note any of them in the article; it wouldn't have been relevant there. I'll note here, though, that both men were incarcerated while still children, and the treatment and cruelty they saw hardened them, and deepened their identity with criminal life. Both, as very young men, saw other men die, and both were always haunted by death row.

Gary went further with his law breaking—he took the ultimate path, and paid the ultimate price. Haggard wouldn't go further after San Quentin. He respected his talent and it lifted him and others. Gary also had talent as an artist—as a painter and drawer—that might have saved him, but he refused to let that happen.

What saved Merle is also what condemned Gary. Each was looking to come to terms with his lost father. Merle wanted to touch, to behold, and honor his. Gary, though, wanted to defeat our father. He wanted to pay back all the rejection and brutality.

Gary's last words were, "There will always be a father."

I think Merle would have understood.

**Elaine Schock:** We had a great team work with us. From the oncologists from chemo and radiation as well as the nurses and the people who helped schedule intravenous infusion on a daily basis when I knew it was tough for them to do. They did it. And, the oncology pharmacist who dealt with every possible side effect so Mikal suffered as little as possible. There were literally a dozen or so people who helped Mikal Gilmore go through this to survive.

**Elaine Schock**
**April 18, 2016**
Mikal Gilmore's cover story on the Ramones is out now. In addition, the Merle Haggard cover story will be out in the next couple of weeks. Both are great.

**Mikal Gilmore**
**April 18, 2016**
The soundtrack music to the movie, *Shot in the Heart* is exquisite. The liner notes are almost as good. They are a long but a great read:

When I began the writing of *Shot in the Heart*, I decided I would not linger much on the musical moments in my family's history—that is, how certain voices and songs fit into the events in our lives. As it turned out, I provided a fair amount of detail along those lines—information about what we liked and why we liked it. But I didn't want to overplay this element, because I have been a music critic and historian for many years, I thought I already ran a certain risk by dragging musical memories into the mix. I did it a bit here and there, but I didn't intend *Shot in the Heart* to be a music historian's tale, but rather, a tale of a family. Looking back, that was clearly the right choice. Music was indeed a part of our story, and I gave it representation when it seemed vital. But I couldn't afford to let it outweigh the story's other elements.

As I became more closely involved in the preparations for the film production of *Shot in the Heart*, various people sometimes asked me what songs would fit best into this story, and why? I began to stir my memories again—music has a way of attaching itself to certain moments and becoming an indelible addition to your memory—and I began to keep a list or two. What I am offering here is that list. Elaine might later post links on Spotify, iTunes, Facebook, or elsewhere.

**"Gloria," Patti Smith (from *Horses*)**
We start off in high territory, with one of the greatest blasts of invention and vision that 1970s rock 'n' roll brought us. This song is here in part due to its opening lyrics: *Jesus died for somebody's sins but not mine / meltin' in a pot of thieves / wild card up my sleeve / thick heart of stone / my sins my own / they belong to me, me / people say "beware!" / but I don't care / the words are just / rules and regulations to me, me*

It's also here because it was part of the vibe in my world just before all the bad news in Gary's story came down. It should be remembered that Smith was very controversial when *Horses* was released. Some of us saw her as an innovator in the tradition blazed open by Bob Dylan. With improvisatory-style lyrics and images that added up to meanings that sealed off one world and opened up another, she all the while made timeless truths more fathomable—and deeper—than ever before. Others saw her as a charlatan. It's safe to say she proved the naysayers to be sightless.

I recall the day this album came out. There had been a good deal of advance word about it, and accordingly, there were high expectations for it. Smith's earlier independent label single, "Piss Factory," had shown lyrical range and real daring, but it didn't adequately prepare us for her inventive vocals and gifted musicality. Moments into the album you knew we were headed into new sonic and poetic regions.

Patti Smith's music is here because it was there, at that time, in my life—a high mark of the music I loved and was writing about. That's who I was just before going to Utah: a young man full of excitement at the prospects of new frontiers, aware that the most meaningful frontiers would necessarily encompass unexplored prospects and unpredictable consequences. But not as aware as he would be by the time the story closes.

### "Drive Back," Neil Young (from *Zuma*)

I think Neil Young's best albums are *Tonight's the Night* (not to be confused, really not at all, with that Rod Stewart song of the same title), *On the Beach*, and *Zuma*. All are from the mid 1970s. The first two albums are about dissolution, death, and fucked-upness, and *Zuma* is about rebirth, but it's quiet a fierce form of rebirth.

This is a tough and dynamic performance, but while critics liked *Zuma*, many of them dismissed the song "Drive Back." Some saw it as too superficial. I always saw it as the song that best defined the album. I can't see the words, combined with the music . . . reading it as anything other than an expression of both threat and release, and a wish for an escape to some distant spot in the night that is appealing because, in its bleakness, it promises to save you from memories that you can't bear.

I think of Gary driving in his white truck that night, after the murder of Ben Bushnell, on his way to the airport, to head back to his old town, Portland, where I lived. I think of what might have been in his head, and in his heart. I think these words might have captured his reflections on that dark drive. Or maybe it's just the insane impetus that propels Neil Young's amazing guitar solo. Maybe that's meaning enough. Maybe that's warning enough.

The song hasn't lost any of its intensity over the years. I guess Neil Young hasn't either. He was able to withstand what he comprehended in the heart of his darkest songs, and didn't get consumed along the way. I'm glad we have artists like that. Their darkness and violence goes into their work, and then their work helps free the rest of us.

I guess I always thought Gary could have become that kind of artist. I guess I was always wrong about that.

### "Folsom Prison Blues," Johnny Cash (from *At Folsom Prison*)

Johnny Cash was my family's patron saint. This song is here as a marker for Gary. There will be more Cash songs to come.

In the late 1960s, this live version was a huge hit on Top 40 radio. It was kind of startling, a turning point of some sort. Cash was singing to prisoners about shooting a man "just to watch him die," and the audience erupted in applause, recognition, celebration. I've never heard anything quite like it in a radio hit before, even in Eminem's songs.

Listening to Eminem (or Notorious B.I.G., or any number of others), critics suspect that the audience has been either badly defiled by the songs or somehow complicit in the ugliness that the singer sings about. In this performance, Cash sang a song about murder and imprisonment to an audience of imprisoned men, some of whom had committed real murders, and there's no question about whether they're damaged or complicit. There's also no question that the song is rich and humane. Even killers need somebody to sing to them now and then.

### "Ode to Billie Joe," Bobbie Gentry (from *Ode to Billie Joe*)

I've always liked the rhythmic riff that begins this song and propels the music's motif. It's choppy and funky and churns throughout like a riddle that can't resolve itself—which is precisely what the song is about.

"Ode to Billie Joe" is about what's buried in our secret hearts and secret lives, when a family gathers in the most supposedly familiar and intimate of settings, the nightly dinner table. Nothing much happens in the words and dialogue in this song, but everything, especially something quite horrible, happens between those words. Or, to be more accurate, outside them, in the events the song alludes to but refuses to explain or illuminate.

This song was probably the greatest mystery tale that ever became an enduring Top 40 hit. To this day, nobody can really say for sure what was thrown off that bridge, though we all have an idea.

I think that my father, had he lived long enough, would have liked this song. I think he would have understood the singer's secret, and he would have approved of burying that secret. I think he would have felt contempt for Billie Joe himself, for his inability to live with the effect of having done what it was that was done. My father, I bet, could live with what Billie Joe McAllister could not live with, and I think my family was the living proof of my bet.

Did I say "living"? You know what I mean. It's just a phrase.

### "Old Shep," Elvis Presley (from *Elvis*)

My mother used to sing this on the piano. Gary used to sing it now and then. And my Uncle Vernon made it an a capella specialty (although I think any dog probably ran from the sound).

In the song, the singer must put his dog to death, but he can't bring himself to do it. "I wish they would shoot me instead."

The dog loves the master, so the dog helps his master in this hardest of tasks. It's a wonderful song, and Elvis's version is among the best recordings of his brilliant early career. It might seem a bit sentimental, compared to some of the songs here, but in its own way it's just as brutal. Certainly, it has a heavier heart. Besides, my family—like many families—could be brutal in one moment and sentimental in the next, so there's a kind of sense to this juxtaposition. My family unanimously agreed on only three musical touchstones: Elvis, Johnny Cash and Hank Williams (though Gary, like me, enjoyed Miles Davis, and as you'll see, we shared a few other odd tastes here and there). All those touchstones appear on these CDs.

Unfortunately, it's very hard (and likely quite expensive) to get the rights to any Elvis recording for a soundtrack. I've rarely seen it happen. But for your own reference, here is the true story of "Old Shep," and when Elvis sings it, you believe he means every word of it.

Also, the song in part resonated for my family because my mother and Gary had owned a dog, Queen, that had been "put to sleep." It was a vicious dog who loved and protected my mother and brothers and nobody else. My mother got rid of it—that is, gave it to a neighbor—when I was born, because she feared it might have torn me apart out of jealousy over a newborn. When the dog nearly killed the neighbor, that was the end of the dog.

So I guess that in a way I'm to blame for the dog's death. It's true what they say: you're born into this life knowing you're guilty.

### "You're Gonna Make Me Lonesome When You Go," Bob Dylan (from *Blood on the Tracks*)

One of my favorite Dylan recordings, a lovely song about realizing you're going to have to live with the knowledge that you've lost the one person you can't afford to live without. Dylan, of course, is a main touchstone.

I like the fact that song has the phrase "shooting in the dark" in it. As often as not when I was on my book tour, people introduced me as the author of *Shot in the Dark*, which of course is the title of the Blake Edwards / Peter Sellers movie, but which is not the title of my book. But since the title of my book wasn't at first going be the title of the movie, it was a little joke on my part to have a song here that pays passing reference to the title that everybody mistook *Shot in the Heart* for.

### "Kill Your Sons," Lou Reed (from *Sally Can't Dance*)

I was listening to songs like "Kicks," "Gloria," and "Drive Back" around the time that Gary was freed from prison in Utah and committed his awful acts. I've always listened to Lou Reed's music a lot.

Gary and I shared a taste for what a curious person might find in the shadows, but while I appreciated violence in the arts, I didn't want it anywhere near my life. It certainly didn't drive my own motivations. I noted in *Shot in the Heart* that in the darkest music of the 1960s and 1970s—for example, the music of the Rolling Stones or Doors or Velvet Underground—I could participate in darkness without submitting to it, which is something my brothers had been unable to do. The music of somebody like Lou Reed gave me a chance to contemplate some fairly dark stuff without making easy or comforting moral judgments.

But Gary couldn't turn his darkness into art in any way that helped him. In fact, it's almost like he was an artist only when he was in prison. Outside of prison, he was a dangerous man—not as cruel, perhaps, as the man that Reed envisions in this song, but every bit as deadly. Art didn't do anything to free Gary, to give him an outlet for his moods and anger and hurt. Art didn't make him a better man. He wasn't the sort to try to translate his worst thoughts and feelings into a work of expression when he was in the outside world. In the outside world, he could only act impulsively and without concern for consequences. Contemplation was something that he did in prison. And in time, both his contemplations and his actions brought him to the same conclusion: that he should force himself out of the world, that he was better off without this life, and this life was better off without him.

We see a character like that in the arts—in a movie, a song, or a book—and we might think they're attractive, emboldening. I know I can certainly have that reaction. We see a character like that on the nightly news, and we might feel something quite different: that we too are better off with such a person dead.

What we're not prepared for is for that person to say, as Gary did, "Kill me. Right now. Let's do it." That determination only made Gary seem more dangerous to people, more deserving of hate. With somebody like Gary, you couldn't win. You could kill him, but you couldn't force his death on him, and that took the sense of vindication out of killing him. And because he turned the tables on America in that way, some people only hated him more.

Maybe that was Gary's real (and horrid) art: to own his death, to determine it in a way that would rob the world of any virtue of retribution. I guess that's a good trick in an entirely awful way, but it only works once.

Anyway, in 1979, when I first met my greatest pop hero, Lou Reed, Reed's first words to me were, "You were Gary Gilmore's brother. What was it like, being his brother?"

I didn't yet know how to answer that question. If I'd answered honestly, I would have said, "It was horrible. It was heartbreaking. It tore away my future. It left me with regret and hatred in all directions. It was the worse loss you could imagine, because the loss spread so far beyond my own life, and because Gary got to make me a partner in that ruin—and he was able to do so because I had also been part of what had ruined his own heart."

But I didn't say that. I was caught off guard. I replied, in a faltering way, "It was . . . odd."

Reed said, "Odd? That's an . . . odd way to put it."

I said, "Maybe I can better explain it at another time."

Reed never brought the subject up again, though we communicated off and on for years.

In all the years I've interviewed people for publication, Lou Reed is the only artist who ever asked me that question. But I could tell that the question lingered unspoken on plenty of other occasions. Reed had the candor and the honor simply to put it on the table. His way of saying, "You want to know about my life and heart? You want to tell me about yours first?"

### "Howlin' Wind," Graham Parker (from *Howlin' Wind*)

Graham Parker was one of the great breakthrough artists of the 1970s, though, unfortunately, his breakthrough didn't last that long. What I mean is, his first two albums were full of terror and wit and invention and singular rage—traits that anticipated the punk revolt that was about to sweep a lot of things away, including Parker's own claim to an edge. He had two great early albums, *Howlin' Wind* and *Heat Treatment*, then a couple years later the nearly as great *Squeezing Out Sparks*, then a series of respectable albums that just never mattered in the same way.

Still, the guy was special, sort of what might have emerged had you fused Bruce Springsteen's energy and formalism with Elvis Costello's early wry sharpness. Maybe the sort of vision that Parker saw and spoke about in songs like this one, a vision of an end, sure to come and sure to raze everything in its path for one outcome or another, was just too difficult or frightening to sustain.

I've often thought it bore some comparison to what Dylan went through and accomplished in the mid 1960s. He walked right up to the edge of an abyss, gazed into it, reported back to us, then reeled away from the vision before it consumed him altogether. There's one school of thought that says it's worth dying for vision and brilliance. There's another that says it's worth living to sing again another day. My bet is that Parker, like Dylan, will have that day again effectively sometime in his future.

Around the time that Gary was close to committing his murders, I visited San Francisco to meet Parker and do a story on him. A few months later, on the night after my first visit with Gary at Draper Prison's death row, I had drinks with Bill Moyers, President Johnson's former White House Press Secretary. Moyers had worked for years as a press correspondent and commentator, and he was in Utah for a CBS special about my brother and the return of the death penalty. Later that same night I met Lawrence Schiller at the Salt Lake Hilton for our one and only get-together during the whole episode. Schiller was a photographer, film producer and entrepreneur and had purchased the rights to Gary's life story after my brother became national news.

I was at odds with Schiller about how he'd maneuvered the whole deal, and he knew it. As we talked, I could occasionally hear music playing from somewhere, maybe from a radio behind the reception desk, many feet away. I'm not sure where the music came from, to be honest. But I am sure that during the hour or so while Larry Schiller and I talked, I remember hearing two songs among the other songs that played. One was Bobbie Gentry's "Ode to Billie Joe." The other was Graham Parker's "Howlin' Wind."

I thought, "What the fuck is this song doing, playing here, in this place and time?" I was truly startled. I wanted to tell Schiller: "Stop asking me questions and listen to this song. It has something in it you need to hear." Of course I didn't say that. I just kept a note in my head that the song had played on a night when I badly needed to hear a voice of courage.

Having music like that to turn to in those days helped a little, and a little was a lot at that time. It always has been. I'm convinced that hearing the right music at the right time in your life can be a blessing. In my case I think it's helped keep me alive. It's been my best friend, something you can turn to that will never refuse you, desert you, or lie to you. Sometimes it feels like music can hear us and respond to us as just as much as we can hear and respond to it—and of course, it can. That's because music is a way in which people can give one of the best parts of themselves to others, even if it's a sad or dark or angry part, and by doing so, embolden our hearts in personal and transforming ways, even though we may never meet or know the people who made the music. Even though they may still speak to us long after they're dead.

**"Family Affair," Sly Stone (from *There's a Riot Goin' On*)**

Maybe the grimmest funk hit single of the 1970s. It was just so fucking weird and mesmerizing to hear this thing playing every hour or so on the car radio. It's obvious why this is here. The first verse: *One child grows up to be / Somebody that just loves to learn / And another child grows up to be / Somebody you'd just love to burn / Mom loves the both of them / You see it's in the blood / Both kids are good to Mom / "Blood's thicker than mud" / It's a family affair, it's a family affair. . .*

**"One Way Out," The Allman Brothers (from *Eat a Peach*)**

There's a little story about this one. In the fall of 1972, Gary was released from Oregon State Penitentiary in Salem on a school leave, to study art in Eugene. A few minutes into his leave, he left the school and hitched a ride to Portland to visit first my mother, then me. This story is in *Shot in the Heart*.

A small part of what follows here was not in the book. When Gary visited me that day, and took me to "lunch" at a strip joint (that served no food, as I recall), there was this lovely woman dancing topless on the stage. She was the only one on the shift that afternoon, and she was dancing and dancing and dancing.

There was only a handful of men in the bar, and none of them were tipping much. Finally, she sat down on the stage, spread her legs, and glared around the room. "You know, guys," she said, "I'm not doing this just for my health."

Gary smiled at her, got up, walked to the stage, and handed her a few dollars. Looking back, it must have been almost all the money he had for that day (though he had other ways of making money in a pinch).

The woman smiled at him and said, "What would you like me to dance to?"

Gary replied, "Dance to whatever you like."

She played an Allman Brothers single, "One Way Out"—a song originally recorded by blues artist Sonny Boy Williamson in the early 1960s. She danced fine to it. I can still remember how she moved. The only time I took my eyes off her was to study Gary's face as he watched her. He was smarter than I was. He never took his eyes off her to study me.

After the song finished, Gary turned to me and asked me to get him a gun, ostensibly to free a fellow prisoner friend, but I read it as a promise of murder, probably the murder of a guard. I wouldn't help him. I said I would never have anything to do with something like that.

"I'd do it for *my* brother," he said, and I'm sure he meant it.

"Gary did not forgive me for my refusal until the last few days of his life," I told Schiller, "in the conversations that your film will depict."

Anyway, I think of that afternoon every time I hear this song.

A few years ago I wrote a feature about the Allman Brothers for *Rolling Stone*. It began: "Some say there was a ghost." There are always ghosts, whether you believe in them or not, and of course, I don't.

The song says there's one way out when you've fucked up too much. The ghost I have in mind as I write these words became a ghost because in life, he believed the same thing: there's one way out.

**"Valley of Tears," Fats Domino (from *They Call Me the Fat Man*)**

At the end of my third visit with Gary at Draper's death row, the visit in which we began to find each other, Gary asked for a favor. "Would you call this radio station in Salt Lake and ask them to play this Fats Domino song? Tell them to play it to Nicole, from Gary." It was a way Gary figured he might be able to say something to Nicole—his girlfriend, whom he'd attempted a suicide pact with before he died—since he was no longer allowed to communicate with her. The station played the song the way it was requested, and the fact that the request had come from Gary's brother made the next day's news. Nicole later told me that she and Gary had considered the song "their song."

It's a great song, with remarkable and laconic lyrics:
*I want you to take me/ Where I belong / Where hearts has been broken / With a kiss and a song / Spend the rest of my days / Without any cares / Everyone understand me / In the valley of tears / Soft words has been spoken / So sweet and low / But my mind has made up / Love has got to go / Spend the rest of my day / Without any care / Everyone understand me / In the valley of tears* .

I think Gary liked the song because he'd always loved Fats Domino's music. Despite his racism, Gary loved black music (which is true of quite a few racists). But I think the song also worked so well for Gary and Nicole because of where they lived and loved when they listened to it.

A few years ago, when I was in Utah, every time I drove between Provo and Salt Lake, I passed Draper Prison, where Gary died. It lies at the end point of a long mountain range (the place is, in fact, named Point of the Mountain), in a valley so lovely it's a cruelty that a prison was ever built there. Not a cruelty to the land, but to the men who must live behind bars amid such a beauty that they will never get to roam or touch.

I'd play the radio as I drove past the prison, time and again. I'd scan the stations, hoping maybe I'd stumble across that song, beaming out over some ghostly airwaves. I never did, but that was okay. Like Gary and Nicole, I learned to carry the song in my heart.

**Charlie Rich "Feel Like Going Home" (from *Demos*)**
**"Gary Gilmore's Eyes," The Adverts (from *Crossing the Red Sea*)**
The first song is the moment in this soundtrack when Gary walks to his death. The second begins what would follow soon enough: the aftermath.

I was showing this song list to somebody a few days ago, and a friend asked me what the Adverts' "Gary Gilmore's Eyes" meant to me. I replied that I didn't want to answer just yet. Truth is, the question scared the hell out of me, because more than any other song here, this song hurts to hear. It's always scared me. It's just too damn close to some godawful truths.

In the course of preparing for his death, my brother Gary determined that various parts of his body should be donated to people who might need them to improve or prolong their lives. The one decision along these lines that drew the most media attention and curiosity was about who would receive Gary's eyes for a possible transplant.

Now, to be honest, I'm not sure whether or not eyes can in fact be transplanted with the result of providing or improving vision, but that was Gary's wish just the same, and in time he decided the recipient should be a young man whose doctor contacted the prison. Gary had also considered the request of an older man, but decided on the younger person because a youthful man supposedly had a longer life of vision ahead of him. I know who the man was whom Gary bequeathed his eyes to, and at one time I thought of trying to learn something about that man's life. Since the request and decision had been conducted privately, there was never any news about the recipient, but I found his name among some of Gary's prison records.

In the end, I decided not to try to find the man. I thought some things are better left alone. Besides, what if I were to meet him? What if he were still alive?

What if he now saw the world through Gary's eyes? Would those eyes know me? I'm pretty sure I'd know them, and I couldn't bear to see them again under these circumstances, even though by leaving his eyes to someone Gary tried, for once, to do something to leave the world a better place.

The song asks the questions: What would it be like to awaken and see the world through Gary Gilmore's eyes? Would the world look different? More maddened? Bloodier? How would you look at your own brother? Would the eyes hold memories? Would they take over a man like the transplanted hands of a murderer had supposedly done to a disfigured musician in *Mad Love*, or like the relocated brain of a killer had done to the lifeless corpse of Frankenstein's monster? What if you knew you had Gary Gilmore's eyes? Worse, what if you didn't?

There's more to my reaction to the song than that.

The British punk band The Adverts recorded "Gary Gilmore's Eyes" in 1977, shortly after my brother's execution. The song was a hit in the U.K., but since the mass media and mainstream U.S. audiences reviled punk, not to mention how they felt about Gary Gilmore, the song never found much of a market here. I hadn't even known it had been recorded until one night when I was shopping at the Tower Record Store on Sunset Boulevard. (I had moved to Los Angeles from Portland, Oregon, a few months after Gary's death.) I was flipping through the latest import punk singles, and there it was. I was repelled but I had to hear it.

So, I took it home, played it, and instantly hated it. I took it off my turntable. The song felt like a curse, in fact, part of a larger curse: the malediction of living with the knowledge that I was now, more than ever before, Gary Gilmore's little brother. And, I would always be that. I would never be known for anything as much as my relationship to a killer. I write about this a bit in *Shot in the Heart*, how for my first few seasons in Los Angeles, new friends would want to know about my brother, about my life with him.

To some people, it made me seem a bit cool. To others, it made me seem like somebody they didn't want to get too close to. That's never changed much over the years. Even to this day, people sometimes introduce me to others as Gary Gilmore. What they're really saying is that I can never be anything other than Gary's brother, that's all they see me as.

I went back to this song a few times after that first hearing. Over time, I came to respect it, and I came to like The Adverts other music quite a bit (though there wasn't all that much of it). But I've never been comfortable with the song. It still disturbs me; it still scares me. Even now, I often skip past it as I've listened to these CDs, trying to find a final sequence for the songs.

I know what it's like to live with Gary Gilmore's eyes. Those eyes have followed me for all these years. Night after night, I see them in my dreams. If you had ever been in the same room with them, you too wouldn't easily forget them.

### "I Can't Help Wondering," Kitty Wells (from Kitty Wells *Greatest Hits*)

This is one of my mother, Bessie's, songs. In fact, this is one of Bessie's major songs. She used to sing this song to us all in an a cappella voice, and she taught me to sing along with her.

I remember how she did an interesting little waltz-pattern step with her feet as she sang the song. She'd sing, and she'd study her feet, and she'd look at me to see if I could equal her moves. I couldn't.

### "Blue Moon Revisited," The Cowboy Junkies (from *The Trinity Session*)

Nicole, Gary's girlfriend, hasn't had any representation in the music in these sets, and she doesn't appear much more than as a name and photo and a longed-for dream in the script, but as we all know, Nicole is at the core of this story. Gary, in part, killed for her, and he also in part died for her. Nicole and I have been friends off and on over the years, but we're both hard people to keep track of, and I now find she has moved again, with no new phone number.

But, she deserves a voice here. "You see," Margo Timmins sings, "I was afraid / To let my baby stray / I kept him too tightly by my side / And then one sad day / He went away and died." Then she delivers us to the sublimely haunted Rodgers and Hart masterpiece, "Blue Moon." It's like one ghost, a living one, singing to another ghost, one that has crossed the threshold.

### "I Won't Back Down," Johnny Cash (from *American III: Solitary Man*)

Johnny Cash's version of a Tom Petty song, from Cash's most recent, and best album.

At sixty-nine years of age, Johnny Cash remained one of America's greatest voices. My family fucked up a lot of things, but we got one thing just right: our pick of a modern-day patron saint.

**"Mama Tried," "Sing Me Back Home," "I Wonder if I Care as Much," The Everly Brothers (from *Roots*)**

*Roots* has always been one of my two favorite Everly Brothers albums (the other is the restrained but magnificent *Songs Our Daddy Taught Us*). *Roots* is luminous and novel, but true to the traditions it reveres. Maybe it's that combination of virtues that condemned the album to an unjustified obscurity.

I played parts of this record a lot around the time Gary died. I mean, a lot. I played "Sing Me Back Home"—the Everlys' cover of a famous Merle Haggard song—the morning Gary died, in the minutes before I left my home to be with my mother at the time of his shooting. That night, I played the Everlys' version of Haggard's "Mama Tried."

I acknowledge that this was maudlin. But in the face of such an enormous and public death in one's own family, a maudlin moment deepened the pain just enough to allow me to find something bearable in it all. Sometimes a good sad song helps you cry, and sometimes, crying is all that you can do.

My mother and brothers loved the music of the Everlys. There are a few songs in this collection that reflect what was bad in my family. By contrast, here's a song that reflected some of what we had in common, and how we could find strong bonds of love in some of our shared pleasures. Every time an Everly Brothers song played on the radio and we were in the same room, you could see we liked being around each other in those moments.

Some music can take on a special grace when you share it with people you love—maybe even more so if you actually don't love those people so much. A good song at the right time has the effect of a heralding forgiveness entering your premises. It's as if a prayer has caught and held everybody's hearts in the same moment. It's only a moment here and there. But that's what so much of life is anyway: moments here and there that matter, for better and worse.

Hearing the Everlys . . . those were moments that mattered for us, for the better. I hear their recordings now, and remember how much I could love my family, how much I miss the chance to sit with them all in the same room, to talk and laugh and be silly and funny. That was the other (equally important and dimensional) side of us, and I'm afraid I didn't show that enough in my book.

We were a real family. We could hurt each other, but we could also love each other. Indeed, if we hadn't loved each other so much, this story wouldn't have hurt or mattered as much. I told myself for years that I didn't love Gary anymore. And I believe he told himself the same thing about me. And then, in that last week, when we realized we did still love each other, after everything horrible we both had done—the occasion he had tried to pressure me to get him a pistol so he could free a friend from a prison guard and I had refused; and the many times—years—I'd failed to visit or write him in prison. Strange as it may seem, these last days of his contained some of the best moments of my life.

That's also why they also contained the worst moments: we both recognized all the love we had let go to waste and that we were both now about to lose, within hours, for eternity.

I've sometimes told people very close to me that nobody broke my heart more than Gary. A few have tried, but they wouldn't know how to come close. And I suspect, at the end, I broke his heart too, by finally giving him the love I'd withheld from him so long. Sometimes, receiving love can hurt even more than not receiving it. You learn how to live with the latter condition, without the love you so badly crave and need. You get used to it and you expect it. It gives you the steel and energy to hate and oppose. But then if you wind up getting the love . . . that upends everything. It makes even plainer how much you had originally lost, because it gives you a taste of what you had lived without.

That's a miracle and a curse, in the same motion. But that's largely what this story is all about: two men finding a way to recognize each other for nearly a week, replete with blessings and curses that cannot ever again be separated from one another, even by death.

I miss Gary. I miss my family. More by the day. I'll never have their presence again. They were often horrible. But I also never felt safer, more comfortable, or closer to shelter anywhere else in my life. After all, they were my family. I also never felt more strongly the need of shelter than I did within my own family.

"Blood is our only permanent history," wrote author Harry Crews, "and blood history does not admit of revision." To which I would simply add: blood history also does not admit any easy escape.

"I Wonder If I Care as Much," written by Don Everly first appeared on the Everly Brothers debut album. This version has an odd construction. It rides in on sustained guitar notes, then settles into doleful harmonies. A repeating one-note bass passage then carries it to doleful harmonies and inconsolable words:

*Last night I cried myself to sleep / For the one that makes me weep / I dried my eyes to greet the day / I wondered why I had to pay / Tears that I have shed by day / Give relief and wash away / The memory of the night before / I wonder if I'll suffer more*

Then, another swell of sustained guitar notes, and a slight shift in sound and pace. Instruments start dropping away, one by one. A bass pounds, and the voices return to say: *I wonder if I care as much / As I did before*

That's all that happens, except for what the bass does in the last minute.

Again, I listened repeatedly to this album a lot around the time Gary died. I knew what this song meant to me, and I knew that the feel of its music matched the feel of my spirit.

It wasn't until a year or so ago, when I actually first started to think about some musical possibilities for *Shot in the Heart*, did I understand why the song had so much power for me: it's that bass line at the end. It beats steady, until it doesn't beat anymore, and then there's the small cry of a guitar. Listening to it one night in 1998, I realized the bass is the heart line. What we're hearing is the fading of a heart, as it beats out the last of if its life.

This is an obscure song, but a remarkable one—a matchless construction of sound, words, space, meaning and emotion that creates a sonic rendering of a once-full heart that now exists solely because it has learned to hold emptiness.

## "My Father's House," Bruce Springsteen (from *Nebraska*)

Some people don't like this song much. They feel it meanders, that it takes too long to make its point, that Springsteen's phrasing is too odd, his cadence too illogical. Maybe the fools are right about that. Either you find those qualities to the detriment of the song, or they intensify its melancholy and longing for you. You can guess which way it works for me. This is a dream song, and I value dreams. Without them I would not be able to stay in regular touch with my family.

*My father's house shines hard and bright / it stands like a beacon calling me in the night / Calling and calling so cold and lone / Shining cross this dark highway where our sins lie unatoned*

As it pertains to my father's house, if you ever like, I can show you where it once stood. I can show you the highway. Of course, I don't need to show you the sins.

## EXTRAS
### "Campaigner," Neil Young (from *Decade*)

Of any new song I heard around the time of Gary's death, I attached feelings about my brother to "Campaigner" more than to anything else. I know it was in part the wordplay I went through in my head over Neil Young's album title: *Decay. Decayed. Decade.* Also, it was because Young had written so powerfully about dissolution in *Tonight's the Night* and *On the Beach*—albums I mentioned earlier.

In those days, I felt as if I were to call up Johnny Cash or Neil Young and try to talk to them about my brother, they might be able to understand what I would say. Many years later, after Young became a big supporter of Ronald Reagan, I wondered if maybe I'd been wrong about that. Then, even more years later, after he'd made *Eldorado* (another of his best records, released only in Japan) and the out of-the-blue wondrous *Freedom*, and after he wrote some pretty affecting songs about Kurt Cobain, I figured I'd been right in the first place and that I shouldn't write him off because of some fitful political sidetrack on his part.

"Campaigner" might also seem like it has something to do with politics. Maybe it does. In the song, Young seemingly ponders the disgraced American president, Richard Nixon, whom the singer had measured and condemned so soundly in the song "Ohio," following the killing of young American students at Kent State University by young American civil guardsmen. But this particular consideration of Nixon is more sympathetic—surprisingly so, given the tenor of those times.

Young's song says the following: As awful as we thought Richard Nixon to be, he was still a man with a soul. Even his betrayals couldn't rob him of that truth. If Richard Nixon, who betrayed his office and country and who sent thousands of young Americans and hundreds of thousands of Vietnamese soldiers and citizens to unnecessary deaths, had a soul . . . if Richard Nixon was a man to feel a certain sympathy for, as well as a certain abhorrence . . . then how could I sit and listen to this song and feel compassion for this awful fucking president but not for my brother?

Hearing this song, combined with my dream of Gary being bayoneted to death, started to turn my heart around about my brother. I decided to go see him, to face him before he died, or before I caused his death by forcing him to a suicide. If Richard Nixon had a soul, Gary Gilmore had a soul too. I had no idea what would become of that soul when it passed into death, whether it would face judgment or rehabilitation or eventual forgiveness, or if it would simply evaporate—that is, simply not exist. Either we have souls, each and every one of us, or we don't. Our sins might change what becomes of our souls, but our sins don't arise because we are soulless. Nobody is soulless, or everybody is soulless. And after that, your soul is up for whatever it's up for, or your non-soul—which would never have existed in the first place. Then, it fades like a myth, with your last breath.

I guess that's what I got from the song. I had to respect Gary's soul, no matter what he had done. I wasn't fit to be his judge, even though, on the night I realized this, I also wasn't yet fit to be his brother; we had never really formed that closeness. That would come during the week that *Shot in the Heart* depicts.

But, I didn't exactly escape all my own judgments. I remember that many years later, when Kurt Cobain died of his own hand, I felt that there was something deeply wrong about a world in which Richard Nixon got to outlive Kurt Cobain.

If there's a God, then final judgments belong to God. If anybody can afford final judgments, it's God, right? I'm glad final judgments don't belong to me—and that, too, is something I learned from that last week I spent with Gary.

Just the same, I wish Cobain had been able to outlive Nixon, even if the fault belonged more to Cobain than Nixon. I wish because at some point I guess I made another judgment, whether I was entitled to or not: namely, that fucked-up powerless kids like Cobain were better for the world than embittered powerful men like Nixon.

But what kind of judge am I? Either I know as much as I'm ever going to know in this life, or maybe, if the myths and traditions are to be believed, I'll know more when I'm dead. This, and only this, is certain: I'm far past knowing which outcome would be the better one.

## "Spanish is the Loving Tongue," Bob Dylan (from the Japanese album, *Masterpieces*, unreleased in the U.S.)

There's a bit in Schiller's script about how Gary used to taunt me because I liked Bob Dylan. To be more accurate, Gary taunted me because Dylan had written anthems about civil rights, and Gary—an avowed and proud racist—hated Dylan for that.

Gary was in and out of many prisons throughout his life, some with better security than others. During his escape from prison in 1972, when he visited me at my dormitory room a few times, he always wanted to hear music. He'd ask me to play Johnny Cash songs (Cash was one of the few tastes we shared).

One night I played for him the only duet Dylan had yet officially released, his recording with Johnny Cash of "Girl from the North Country," from *Nashville Skyline*. Dylan and Cash had been friends for years, and at the same time they worked on this track, they also recorded an entire unreleased album—and it's pretty damn good.

Gary listened to "Girl from the North Country" and said. "I'd heard that Johnny Cash and Bob Dylan were friends, but it never made sense to me. But that right there, that's pretty good. What else you got from Dylan that's not about civil rights?"

I played him this track, the obscure B-Side of a Dylan single. Gary said, "There's kind of Mexican thing there, eh? I like that piano. I like that line about 'I can't cross the line no more.' Maybe there's some hope for the guy after all."

That's why the song is here. It's one of the last moments Gary and I ever got to agree on much of anything, a moment in which Gary extended himself to me. It's also here because I've always loved this recording. As Gary noted, Dylan's piano playing is notable—weird, but notable. And his singing soars. He gets to the heart of the man who will never see his lover again because he committed an impulsive and unwise act of violence. Dylan was kind of singing about Gary's future. I guess if I'd known that, I might have kept the song to myself.

### "Never Let Me Go," Johnny Ace (from *Memorial Album*)

Johnny Ace was an accomplished and respected R&B and jazz balladeer of the early 1950s, but he enjoyed special favor with my brothers for the same reason he enjoyed special favor with much of American youth in that time. This was because he died as the result of a tragic game of Russian Roulette, sort of the accidental Kurt Cobain of the pre-Elvis set. Following his death, Ace had his biggest hit with the exquisite-sounding "Pledging My Love."

But, for me and for a few others, the song, "Never Let Me Go," was his paramount recording. It was unadulterated in its yearning, and there was a spectral quality to Ace's voice. But that had been cleaned out of "Pledging My Love."

In the early 1970s, when my brother Gaylen used to show up at my house in Portland around three A.M., reeling drunk, we'd play Johnny Cash songs, as I would later with Gary. One morning, about four A.M., he asked if I had any Johnny Ace recordings. I had the one album: *Memorial Album*. I put it on my turntable. Gaylen reclined on my sofa, draping an arm over his head. He muttered something I didn't understand, so I asked him to repeat it. He said, in the sort of drunken, smeary manner that, if we know life well enough we all fall subject to at one time or another, "I would like to die like Johnny Ace."

Gaylen passed out within moments. I put a blanket over him and went back to my own bedroom, to sleep.

The next morning, Gaylen was gone. We never discussed that night.

Time gave Gaylen what he wanted, but in the process, time took its own sweet time. Not all more-or-less self-inflicted wounds result in swift ends. Gaylen died something like Johnny Ace—his alcoholism was a Russian Roulette—but I'm not sure he got to understand that pitiable truth.

**"Alone and Forsaken," Hank Williams (from *I Ain't Got Nothing but Time*)**
Hank, another of my family's patron saints. This is the best representation I could give him, and the song speaks for itself. I can't add anything to its fear and integrity.

The performance is a prayer, and like the best prayers, it is born of fear and the painful need for deliverance, even if your deliverance comes by way of death.

**"Seven Shells," Fred Eaglesmith (from *Lipstick Lies & Gasoline*)**
Another gun song from Eaglesmith (actually, his only other gun song). I like the song, I like Eaglesmith. Plus, I'd add like to add this certain point:

When I visited Utah in the early 1990s with my brother Frank, to see our remaining family there, my Uncle Vernon (my mother's brother-in-law, and a witness to Gary's execution, as well as a brief character in both *The Executioner's Song* and *Shot in the Heart*), took me aside and said, "I have Gary's clothes here in the house with me, the ones he was wearing when he was shot. There's something about them I want to show you. Would you like to see them?"

I said I would be willing to see them another time, but didn't think it would be appropriate to do it in front of Frank. I went back another night and sat at

Vern's kitchen table as he brought me a large plastic bag. From the bag he pulled out a sleeveless black sweatshirt, white pants, and tennis shoes with red, white and blue shoestrings, and spread them before me. These were the clothes that Gary was wearing when he was executed. I had expected them to be bloodied and ravaged, but they weren't. All the blood had since been washed out. I sat there and ran my hands over the clothes. They felt soft to me, and for some reason it did not make me sad to touch them. There was almost something comforting about it.

Vern picked up the shirt and pointed out the pattern of perforations that the bullets had made, as they pierced the cloth and ripped through Gary's heart. Four neat holes, each about the size you could put your finger through.

"Look at this," Vern said, and pointed out another hole, a little farther apart from the others. "That, too," he said, "is a bullet hole."

According to Utah's tradition, and its law as well, there are five men on a firing squad, but only four of them have loaded rifles. One has a gun with a blank in it. This is done so that if any man is bothered by his conscience, he can always entertain a reasonable doubt that he never actually fired a bullet into the condemned man.

There should have been four holes in the shirt. Instead, there were five. The State of Utah, apparently, had taken no chances on the morning that it put my brother to death.

This song sort of says, in its own way, the same awful thing that Gary and his executioners said, at different points in time: don't waste a single shot.

**"An American Trilogy," Mickey Newberry (from *Frisco Mabel Joy*)**
The story behind my choice of this song can best be told in a passage from *Shot in the Heart*, about the death of my brother Gaylen:

On October 8, 1971, Gaylen and his girlfriend Janet were married in a simple civil ceremony, across the Columbia River from Portland, in Vancouver, Washington. My mother and my brother Frank and I attended the wedding, and then we all went out to a restaurant and had dinner afterward. My mother was happy to make it her treat. She had never had a son get married before.

Gaylen looked happier that evening than I had ever seen him . He had come back to Milwaukie after fleeing years before on a bad check charge, and settled the matter with the court. But he seemed changed—rail thin and physically shaky, though he still had his razor-sharp wit and charm. He was, it turned out, weak and infected, but I'd known nothing about it. I'd also known nothing about the night a friend, Grace McGinnis, drove him all over town, seeking medical care, nor did I know about any of his other hospital visits. For the first time since he had returned home, I thought Gaylen might have a second chance after all.

A few nights later, Janet showed up at my door. She was drunk, and she was crying. "I'm through with that lousy bastard," she said. "He's yelled at me for the last time. I'm going back to my friends in Chicago as soon as I can raise the money. Until then, can I stay here with you for a day or two?"

I knew exactly what Janet was asking, and the thought scared the hell out of me. Just then, the phone rang. It was Gaylen.

"Have you seen Janet?" he asked.

"Yes," I said. "She's here right now. The two of you should have a talk."

Gaylen showed up a short time later, and he and Janet were in each other's arms right away, crying, promising to be better to one another. Soon, the three of us were laughing and playing Johnny Cash records. As they were leaving, Gaylen paused at the doorway and turned to me. "I want to thank you for helping us tonight," he said. "I also want to thank you for coming to my wedding. It meant a lot to me."

I was unprepared for this moment of sincerity, so I made a dumb joke, "Oh, you're welcome. Hell, I'll even go to your funeral if you like."

It was one of those things you say that you can't retract, that you later never forget, and never forgive yourself for. Still, we both laughed. Brothers could laugh about anything.

Gaylen leaned over and gave me a kiss on the cheek. "Goodbye," he said, and turned and walked down the stairs.

I could already feel winter emerging from the fall. The air was turning cold.

A couple of weeks later, I got a call from my mother. "I thought you should know," she said. "Gaylen went into the hospital today. It looks like he's going to need a little surgery."

"What's wrong?" I asked.

"It's his stomach. He's been having some trouble lately, and the doctor thought he should go in and have the problem taken care of."

"What sort of trouble is it? An ulcer?"

"It's some kind of perforation. That's all I really know."

I asked for the name of the hospital.

"He's at Oregon City Hospital, but I think you should wait a few days before going to see him. It might be a little while before he's ready for visitors."

That didn't sound good to me, but my mother insisted. I hate to admit it, but it wasn't that hard to convince me. I despised going to hospitals, even more than I despised visiting prisons. Both places scared and depressed me.

Next I heard, the surgery got delayed for a few days. Gaylen was improving, and the doctor didn't want to operate unless it was necessary. It all seemed less urgent, and I let that suffice as my excuse for not going to see him.

Then, a week after he went into the hospital, my mother called again, at nighttime. "Gaylen had his surgery late this afternoon," she told me. "He's still unconscious, but the doctor thinks he'll be fine."

I told her to keep me informed.

For the next few days, the reports were good. Gaylen was doing a little better each day. Meantime, I always found some reason not to visit. He would be out soon, I told myself. I would see him then.

Two o'clock in the morning, one of my roommates knocked on my bedroom door. I was sitting up in bed, reading, listening to the radio. "There's a woman on the phone for you," he said. "She says it's important."

I was used to friends and girlfriends calling me at odd hours. I lived during odd hours.

I picked up the phone.

"Mikal, it's Janet. Gaylen's dead."

"What? Are you sure?"

"He just died on the operating table. He had to go back into emergency surgery."

I was stunned. There was no reprieve for news like this. When you hear such a thing, you have to find a way to accept it, and still be able to breathe in the next moment. Otherwise, you might fall into a pit of such deep fear and pain you could never climb out.

"Janet," I said, "stay where you are. I'm going to call a cab and come out to get you."

"No," Janet said, "I don't want to stay here. One of Gaylen's friends, John, is here. He'll bring me over to you. We have to go tell your mother."

I hung up the phone and went back into my bedroom. A song by folk and country singer Mickey Newbury was playing on the radio, "An American Trilogy."

"Hush little baby, don't you cry," sang Newbury, in his mournful, brandy-tone voice. "You know your daddy's bound to die / And all my trials, Lord, will soon be over."

Many years later, Elvis Presley adopted this tune as one of his signature songs. Elvis was the American artist that Gaylen loved above all other singers or poets, and a half decade later, when Elvis died—only a few months after Gary was executed—I thought of my brothers, leaving behind so many fragmented, incomplete hearts to ache over them and all their terrible deeds. It wouldn't be until many years later—in the early 1990s, when I was writing *Shot in the Heart*—that I learned Gaylen had been in the hospital for an icepick stabbing wound he'd received in Chicago, when Janet's husband caught Gaylen and Janet together. The wound never truly healed and Gaylen just kept on drinking, night after night, into the dark.

I put on my coat and went out on my front porch to wait for Janet. I sat there in the night, and began to shake. Death had come very close this night. It had swooped in, with its unerring scythe, and taken my brother. It could have taken me; it was just a matter of death making the choice. I wondered what it was like to pass into whatever realm or place of non-being that Gaylen had passed into, only minutes before. I looked around me, at the silent streets, and then above me at the darkness, and its few stars. I thought I saw something moving up there. I thought it was death. I felt it hover, and felt it regard me. If I tell it to take me instead, I thought, and return Gaylen to Janet and my family, death will do that. But I could not bring myself to make death this offer, and then death moved on.

I am glad it was not me who died, I thought, and a chilly wind kicked up around me, as if in reprimand to my ugly and selfish thought.

Most people know Elvis's version of this song. Newbury's is better because it's less grand. It's a brokenhearted story about divided and sad people living in a dark land in uncertain times. Not all make it through the experience alive.

**Elaine Schock**

**April 20, 2016**

Congratulations Mikal Gilmore on some of your best writing and back-to-back *Rolling Stone* covers

> **Mikal Gilmore:** Thank you, baby. Friends, I wouldn't have made my way though all this, including the work, without Elaine's encouragement. She is the best sounding board I've ever known when I work, and she is the reason I thrive.

**Elaine Schock**

**April 20, 2016**

You probably know how proud I am of Mikal Gilmore's *Rolling Stone* cover story on Merle Haggard. This makes three cover stories (two back-to-back) in three months. David Bowie, the Ramones, and Merle Haggard. But it is more than just professional pride. It is about courage. Most of these men died from cancer. That is no small factor since Mikal was either in the throes of cancer treatment or recovering from that treatment (which was even worse). He still is. There were days he could barely get out of bed or eat, but damn he sure could write. And emotionally, he had to see his own mortality in each story. This is a huge victory for us. I will go into this more on Saturday with my weekly update but there is no doubt it was heroic. I think this is some of Mikal's finest writing and I hope you will read it. It is hard to see someone you love suffer but it is gratifying to watch them thrive.

**Mikal Gilmore**

**April 21, 2016**

There are days that shock and clobber you. I woke up this morning to the news that Prince had been found dead at his home, Paisley Park, in Chanhassen, Minnesota. Prince gave us a tremendous amount to cherish, and for me seeing him was like seeing Miles Davis—there was new stuff going on in intricate and tricky places, irrepressible invention that reflected life and mind. I'm grateful for the many opportunities to see him live, to listen over and over to his recordings and concerts. It was good to live during his days.

## Mikal Gilmore
### April 22, 2016

I recently read a fine reflection on Prince's most paradigmatic work, 1980's *Dirty Mind*—an album not romping with the deserved wild pride in the regal and taut inventions that fast followed, but concise, artistic, sexy, full of hurt and rage and come-on. I've never figured out why, but in listening to early Prince, I sometimes felt I was listening to Robert Johnson, or a private dream of Miles Davis. In short, a work of secrets and intimations, and odd and surprising connections. It got under my skin and never left. Arguably, greater moments would come but none that stole into the heart deeper, and certainly none that said, as this one did, "Just you wait—just you wait—a year or two or ten. Just you wait." We waited, and he made good on the implied promise.

## Elaine Schock
### April 23, 2016
### "Running Up That Hill"

Mikal is writing about men whose lives were ended by cancer. His third *Rolling Stone* cover story in as many months is out, the latest being Merle Haggard. The Ramones is still on our newsstand. They have both issues on display. Made me proud. I bought five copies of the latest issue and another of the Ramones. The guy at the newsstand asked if I was a collector. Yes, I told him. I've been there first thing Wednesday morning when Mikal's features came out.

Even at the end, no matter how sick Merle was, he showed up. That was hero stuff. Mikal too. When he wrote about David Bowie, it was sheer determination. He was in the throes of chemo and radiation. Mikal was getting treatment for hours every day. It was painful to watch. More than anything I hated to see him type with his PICC line in his arm. It is a constant visual reminder of hell, and I never got used to seeing it. Mikal would still be working when I went to sleep. But it was important to us both that he succeed. I worried constantly but this was the beginning of a new chapter of our lives; I had to be supportive. Mikal was writing again, which was something he doubted he could do after his diagnosis. As it turned out, he is writing better than ever.

Not only did he write these cover stories but he wrote the liner notes for Bruce Springsteen's *The River* box set, *The Ties that Bind*; The Highwaymen's

CDs / DVD; and Kris Kristofferson's Legacy release. The appreciation for Mikal's writing helped so much. Maybe having cancer made him a better writer. It certainly made him a better man and husband. No, it wasn't worth it, but we take the good with the bad. Life is fragile and can turn on a dime. Once that happens, you are painfully aware you can be blindsided again.

Mikal came down with a stomach virus a few days ago. The first thing I thought of was, cancer again? My heart stopped. What does this mean? What do we do? But it wasn't life and death this time; it was just an ordinary illness that I caught as well. Mikal is doing fine. Me, I'm still a little shaky. The ironic thing is he is having to take care of me. How do you like that? I don't know when we will stop panicking, but I figure it will be a while. I'm already anxious about May's PET Scan. I know perfectly well the odds are in our favor and that being fearful doesn't change a thing but I can't help it.

Fighting cancer is like running up a hill. We can see the top and are still running, but it is tough to get there with snags along the way. Mikal is better day by day. Fatigue and weight are issues, but not as much as they used to be. His voice is clear and smooth, but he will probably have to carry water with him for the rest of his life. Radiation for head and neck affects the salivary glands and Mikal needs to drink more than he used to. Having water on him at all times will become a habit just as much as carrying his wallet when he heads out.

We can live with these little inconveniences. Every accomplishment is so joyful. It took a long time to get here and it is only the beginning. This is my truth about cancer. Thank you for your support, love and encouragement. It has gotten us through some dark days.

> **Mikal Gilmore:** Reading the part of how seeing the PICC line was disturbing to Elaine came as painful news. I'd worried that it might bother her or Tessa. She covered it well. Wearing it didn't bother me much at first, but it sure did after a few months.
>
> In the late 1990s, into 2001, I was a heavy drinker, and it did damage. After I quit, though, I didn't continue to see myself as an alcoholic. I realize you're supposed to do that, especially

if you've been through AA. But I didn't use AA and I didn't retain the consciousness that I'm an alcoholic. Cancer has been different. In some ways the disease has been more gripping since treatment. It's certainly part of my identity and awareness now.

Physical problems are more alarming because—as Elaine noted—a commonplace ailment, like a virus, might not seem that different than symptoms of something much worse. I try to keep most of those occasional worries to myself, but I couldn't with this recent bout of nausea and headaches—it was too much to ignore or pretend about, and that made it troubling. Perhaps it will always be like this. I found that with depression I was always on the lookout for its return; it was like it was lurking at the window and I worried it would find me. I think that's somewhat the case now, but perhaps with time that will improve.

I don't want to be the cause of more bad news and worry for Elaine. That has been the worst part of it. She talked about how this experience has made me a better man and husband. I believe that's true. If it's not, then these seasons of treatment and improvement would've been partly a waste. I don't think they were. I became aware early on that I felt kinder, and that much of my anger had dissipated. There were moments of exception, but not that many. That worked the same for us both. We are much closer now and more immediately concerned about one another.

I believe this is the marriage we envisioned since 2001—an empathetic and romantic partnership that makes us pretty joyful every moment we're together. We are now planning a trip to Portland and we're both looking forward to it. I hardly ever travel, and truth is, haven't much liked vacations since the 1990s. I traveled a lot in that time, and something about it was exhausting and sometimes depressing. Elaine, of course, travels all the time. She has great adventures, but she misses home, we miss her, and fun as it is for her, I know she's happy when she returns. We've rarely traveled together—maybe a couple of times per year for brief periods.

This trip to Portland is exciting to us. It represents new adventures to cherish together, as we see people that, for the most part, are people Elaine hasn't yet met in person. I sometimes fall asleep thinking about what our room will be like, the long green parkways, the roses I can show Elaine, and the areas I grew up and lived in. I can't wait.

I'm grateful in many ways for what the last few months have given me: a better perspective about time, about what matters and what can be set aside, and about love. If I fall down tomorrow, I will fall into knowledge of a love I never knew or thought possible, and that I waited for my whole life. I want decades more of that, but regardless, this is a blessed story.

## Elaine Schock
### April 23, 2016

My sister and I were discussing the episode of *Mad Men*, which had a story line about Chicago mass-murderer Richard Speck. We lived on the south side of Chicago at that time. I was young and my parents were hearing impaired, so I always picked up the phone. It was early in the morning when my grandfather called and, by the sound of his voice, I knew he was panicked.

I remember distinctly that he said something terrible had happened down the street (we lived about three blocks away), and to make sure none of us kids went out. It was summer so we always went out as soon as we could. I was a pretty fearless kid even then, but I remember being completely terrified. I thought I even recognized Speck, which wouldn't have been impossible since the Merchant Marines were directly across from my school, as was the townhouse where some of the murders took place. The candy store was there too. But I don't know for sure. Speck's pockmarked murderous-looking face was on the news constantly. He was eventually caught, but not soon enough. I wouldn't say it was the end of innocence, but it was the realization that nightmares can come true.

**Elaine Schock** shared **Mikal Gilmore**'s post.

**April 26, 2016**

"This Be the Verse," by Philip Larkin:

*They fuck you up, your mum and dad / They may not mean to, but they do / They fill you with the faults they had / And add some extra, just for you.*

**Elaine Schock**

**April 26, 2016**

The magazine *Granta* published Mikal's proposal for *Shot in the Heart*. This, along with other authors' stories, is great reading. The piece is in *Granta* 37, and titled "The Family: They Fuck You Up."

**Mikal Gilmore**  .

**April 26, 2016**

Like many of you, I've been listening to the music of iconic pop star Prince these last few nights. There's a lot to listen to, especially if you take in some of the bootlegs over the years, including the *21 Nights* series. I still need to re-consider some works, but I've come to enjoy his (rather uniformly low-rated) his 1994 album, *Come*, as one of his best. It has an uncommon mood and jazz-funk experimentalism. I can see why some haven't been patient with it, but it's one I've been playing again and again. I find it transfixing.

**Elaine Schock**

**April 28, 2016**

Tomorrow is Willie Nelson's eighty-third birthday. There is always some con-fusion on the date because he was born close to midnight and the doctor signed the birth certificate the next day. But if you ask Willie, he usually says, it is the 29th, and he should know because he was there. That always makes me laugh. We are lucky to have Willie Nelson in the world.

**Elaine Schock**

**April 29, 2016**

In honor of Willie Nelson's birthday today, I am going to share the three rules he has for his family, which should extend to all of us:

The first rule: don't be an asshole.

Second rule: don't be an asshole.

Third rule: don't be a fucking asshole.

I believe we will all do much better if we follow Willie's rules.

**Elaine Schock**
**April 30, 2016**
**"Survival"**

For seven months, we didn't quarrel about anything. It would have been too difficult for both of us. You don't argue with someone whose health is extremely precarious and the treatment so brutal. The only thing you focus on is survival. Don't sweat the small stuff and ignore the big stuff. But that doesn't mean all your grievances disappear. You just put them aside. You don't even notice when they come sneaking back. And since we are slowly resuming the life we had before this devastating illness, we are more or less on stable ground. It is just a natural progression, if you will.

Mikal's book, *Shot in the Heart* was not a fairy tale, and even small disagreements are a big deal in our home. Still, we work to make it better. Our history may make that a little more complicated, but who doesn't carry some baggage? Just throw in stage 4 HPV-related cancer for the cherry on top. But we are a family, for better, for worse, in sickness and health and in annoying-as-hell. We get through it all somehow.

Mikal can eat what he likes now, which is mostly chicken tacos, pasta, eggs, and root beer floats. There is a medicine called Magic Mouthwash—they really call it that. It relieves the burning that chemo and radiation cause in his mouth and throat. It makes swallowing easier so he can get nutrition. As I have said, a feeding tube was never an option we would consider.

Mikal's pharmacy oncologist suggested the medicine, and the other patients on the bus who rode with Mikal to radiation treatments swore by it and made sure he knew how useful it was to head and neck patients. The thing about the communal cancer ride is that he got tips on enduring this disease. Some people there were second timers, so they knew. This diet will probably go on for weeks until more taste returns. Weight is still an issue—he needs to add more Ensure Plus—and the fatigue is harder.

When Mikal is on deadline he is just focused on the story and being tired doesn't fit into the schedule. Still, he is more energetic than before. Mikal looks better too. When I was at the grocery store with him a month or so ago, I ran into someone I knew. She asked me quietly if Mikal had cancer. Truth is, she could tell. He doesn't look that way any longer, or at least not to me. Next step will be to go out and socialize again. We will get there soon.

I will be working all weekend at Fox's *American Country Countdown Show*. My client Toby Keith is doing a tribute to Merle Haggard. I am looking forward to it. Another musical milestone for me to witness. Then I immediately head to NYC for Willie's son and his band, Lukas Nelson and his band, The Promise of The Real, who are booked on *The Late Show with Stephen Colbert*. Mikal will have to handle our world on his own and will be fine. My sister won't have to lend a helping hand, although I doubt she will be able to stop herself. It will be a lot easier for me to have a good time when I travel to New York City in May. It is a lovely time to be there.

Every week is different and a new challenge. We rise to the occasion or we sink. There isn't any middle ground here. And, I have no idea what tomorrow will bring. It could go either way. This is my truth about cancer. I try to put in the good, bad, and medically informative in each of these posts. I know that others go through this but don't necessarily discuss it. Or maybe it really is just us. I don't know, to be honest. But this I do know: I appreciate each and every one of you. Thank you for your support and encourage.

With love,
Elaine


**Mikal Gilmore:** It is true that we've done the best we ever have after we learned the diagnosis. I don't think it was forced—it just came naturally. Something irritating comes along and you realize, without thinking, that it's insignificant in comparison to the time, long or short, you spend with people you love.

But we're nonetheless human, sometimes painfully so. I recently did something that Elaine felt hurt by, and she let me know. It was rough for us both. It was also, I trust, an anomaly. I'm not built for argument any longer, and I don't think I will be again. At the same time, I can't ask Elaine to sublimate all her grievances. I have to be more careful, plus be willing to understand why she might be upset; it's hardly illegitimate. Lifetime partnership is still a learning process, but now—after seasons in cancer—learning is more vital than ever.

What I'm about to say isn't exactly related to that, but I still want to share it. Fear of death is debilitating for self, family, and everybody in the vicinity. I was at moments frozen by that fear in earlier years—I mean frozen by the knowledge of inevitability, as swell as by the deaths of everybody in the family I grew up in, one after another, starting when I was eleven. It felt like I slept in a house with death. Maybe that's changed.

Obviously, in the case of knowing a violent or accidental or especially painful death is upon you, then that would be terrifying. If it's a long fade, as I expected when I first heard my diagnosis, that might leave more time for adjustment. I wasn't in fear after that diagnosis. I'm presently in fear of a recurrence because the prospect of going through treatment and recovery again seems too daunting. I'm down to 120 pounds.

But I learned something this last week or so. I've been having bad recurring dreams. They are essentially dreams about Elaine dealing with my death after the fact. I'm always there with her when she learns it, since it's a dream, but I can't console her. Her reaction in the dream is painful to see. More than once, or even twice, in recent days I've awakened from that dream, panicked and depressed. That lasts a long time—hours. Happened yesterday morning just after dawn, in fact. I lay in bed, trying to get back to sleep, but it was hard to do. Sometimes I have to wait until Elaine has risen for the day, or I take something to help me sleep. But the dread lingers anyway.

Fear of death isn't simply a fear of what becomes of you after your own end. It's also a fear of what will become of the people you love when you can no longer touch them. I'm afraid that's a fear that can't go away.

## The Albums - Part 7

By 1974, I had the foundations for a collection that would become more exhaustive, more complete, from then on. When I began buying albums in the summer of 1967, I had not set out to be in any sense a collector, and in some ways I never have been. I was just gathering the music I liked and wanted to hear. As time went along, my listening grew better informed and became invested as much in the history of popular music, traditional music, and jazz as in the flux of the moment. My collection reflected my growing interests, but it was far from archival status.

I never set out to collect rare records (in fact I've only done that in narrow areas recently), though plenty of what I did accumulate became rare of natural course, especially when CDs later replaced vinyl albums as listening currency. In any event, by 1974 I had enough albums that they could fill a wall where I lived. I was proud of this growing asset and was aware by then that it reflected something central about myself. More and more I was thinking how to expand my collection effectively, so that it might begin to hold a better history of musical forms, like jazz and blues, and take on the purposes of a personal library.

That was also the year I began to write about popular music. What made this possible was Bob Dylan's "comeback" tour (his first such American trek in eight years) with the Band. This was also a time, I should note, when in addition to my night work at the record store, I spent my days working as a counselor at a Portland, Oregon, drug abuse clinic (though I still smoked marijuana regularly—maybe even more than before). Then I saw Dylan in early 1974 (again, on the occasion of my birthday, ten years after the Beatles' debut on *The Ed Sullivan Show*). Before the show, a friend suggested to an editor at a local underground newspaper that I'd be fit to write about the event. After doing so, I never looked back.

The piece, of course, was awful (at least to my eyes today), but that hardly mattered. I'd managed to put together my two greatest dreams and pleasures: writing (as a result of a love of reading) and music criticism (as a result of listening to music). When I finished that article, I knew what I wanted to do. I wanted to write about popular music—it was pretty much all I cared about as a vocation. Within a season I had quit my drug-counseling job (also had cut way back on my drug intake—a connection?) and started writing for a number of local publications.

I also began writing jazz reviews for *Down Beat* (jazz, by this time, had come to mean as much to me as rock 'n' roll), and along with the help of some good friends, I was soon editing a Portland-based magazine, *Musical Notes*. I found that when I began writing about music, I also began receiving regular shipments of new album releases from most record labels, which not only had a kind effect on my budget, but which exposed me further to new music that I could now delve into. This felt like an arrival for me, like a peak of sorts.

At night, a few dreams were active in my life. Then those dreams turned to nightmares, to the worst horror I could imagine. In 1976, when I was twenty-five, I began to write for *Rolling Stone*. When the magazine came along in 1967, it announced itself as a voice that might prove as fervent and intelligent as the brave new music that it dared to champion. From the time I began to read the magazine, I held a dream of someday writing for its pages. To me, that would be a way of participating in the development of the music I had come to love so much.

It was in the autumn of that year when I first learned that the magazine had accepted an article of mine—about an overlooked band, Artful Dodger—for publication. I was elated. Then, about a week later I learned something horrible, something that killed my elation. My older brother, Gary Gilmore, was going to be put to death by a firing squad in Utah. It didn't look like there was much that could stop it—and I didn't know if I could live with it.

A few months before, in April 1976, Gary—ten years my senior—had been paroled from the U.S. Penitentiary at Marion, Illinois, to Provo, Utah, following a fifteen-year period of often brutal incarceration, largely at Oregon State Prison. Unfortunately, Gary's new life as a free man shortly grew troubled and violent, and on a hot and desperate July night, my brother crossed a line that no man should ever come to cross. In a moment born from a life of anger and ruin, Gary murdered an innocent man—a young Mormon named Max Jensen—during a service station robbery.

The next night, he murdered another innocent man—another young Mormon, Ben Bushnell, who was working as a Provo motel manager—during a second robbery. Within hours, Gary was arrested, and within days he had confessed. The trial was pretty much an open-and-shut affair. Gary was convicted of first degree murder in the shooting of Ben Bushnell, and sentenced to death. Given the choice of being hung or shot, Gary elected to be shot.

All this happened, as I say, in 1976, before I began writing for *Rolling Stone*. A few months later, when my work had been accepted at the magazine for publication, I never mentioned anything about my brother or his crimes to any of my editors or fellow journalists. Only a handful of my friends knew about my strained relationship with my troubled brother. The truth is, I had put myself at a distance from the realities of Gary's life for many years; I told myself that I feared him, that I resented his violent and self-ruinous choices, that he and I did not really share the same bloodline.

After Gary's killings and his subsequent death sentence, I felt grief and rage over his acts, and I also felt deep and painful humiliation. I could not believe that my brother had left his family with so much horror and shame to live with, and I could not forgive him for what he had done to the families of Max Jensen and Ben Bushnell. In a way, the whole episode seemed more like a culmination of horror rather than its new beginning—though it proved to be both. Part of me believed that Gary would never be executed—after all, there had not been any executions in America in a decade—and that he instead would simply rot away the rest of his life in the bitter nothingness of a Utah prison. At the same time, I think another, deeper part of me always understood that Gary had been born (or at least raised) to die the death he would die.

Shortly after I heard about Gary's wish to be executed, I told my editor at *Rolling Stone*, Ben Fong-Torres, about my relationship with Gary. By this time, Gary Gilmore was a daily name in nationwide headlines, and I felt that the magazine had a right to know that I was his brother. Fong-Torres, who had lost a brother of his own through violence, was extremely sympathetic and supportive during the period that followed, and eventually gave me the opportunity to write about my experience of Gary's execution for the magazine. To be honest, not everybody at *Rolling Stone* back in early 1977 thought it was such a great idea to run that article ("A Death in the Family," March 10, 1977), and I could understand their misgivings. After all, what would be the point of publishing what might appear to be one man's apology for his murderous and suicidal brother?

Still, following the turmoil of Gary's death, I needed to find a way to express the devastation that I had gone through, or else I might never be able to climb out of that devastation. With the help of Fong-Torres and fellow editors Barbara Downey and Sarah Lazin, a fairly decent and honest piece of first-person journalism was created, and in the process a significant portion of my sanity and hope were salvaged. More important, perhaps the people who read it got a glimpse into the reality of living at the center of an unstoppable national nightmare.

I've spoken to this experience, and its antecedent history, at length in *Shot in the Heart*, published in 1994. For my purposes here, I should say that with my brother's execution in early 1977, I felt that any hope for serenity in my life appeared to been destroyed—though years later my wife, Elaine Schock, changed that for me. I still wanted to be a writer back then—in particular to write about the music that still meant so much to me, that still gave me guidance.

In the season that followed Gary's death, I went to work for *Rolling Stone* full-time in Los Angeles. It wasn't an easy period for me—I felt displaced, and (once again) was drinking too much and taking too many pills—but the magazine gave me plenty of slack; maybe more than I deserved. As time went along, I began to find some of my strength and purpose again as a music writer, and *Rolling Stone* gave me the opportunity to meet and write about some of the people whose music and words had mattered most in my life. I wrote about a lot of R&B and jazz. Also, about disco.

It was also a season in which I spent many nights lost in the dark and brilliant splendor of punk. I liked the way the music confronted its listeners with the reality of our merciless age. Punk, as much as anything, saved my soul in those years, and gave me cause for hope—which is perhaps a funny thing to say about a movement (or experiment) that's first premise was: there are no simple hopes that are not false or at least suspect.

MAY
2016

**Mikal Gilmore**
**May 2, 2016**
Because Elaine is flying today: *Silver wings shining in the sunlight / Roaring engines headed somewhere in flight / They're taking you away, leaving me lonely / Silver wings slowly fading out of sight.*
—Merle Haggard, "Silver Wings"

**Mikal Gilmore**
**May 3, 2016 at 4:45pm PDT**
Heard on the way from the hospital: *Last night I heard your voice / You were crying, crying, you were so alone / You said your love had never died / You were waiting for me at home / Put on my jacket, I ran through the woods / I ran till I thought my chest would explode / There in the clearing, beyond the highway / In the moonlight, our wedding house shone / I rushed through the yard, I burst through the front door / My head pounding hard, up the stairs I climbed / The room was dark, our bed was empty / Then I heard that long whistle whine / And I dropped to my knees, hung my head and cried.*
—Bruce Springsteen, "Downbound Train"

**Elaine Schock**
**May 7, 2016**
**"Thing Called Love"**
I have been in NYC this week. It was very successful and fun. I get asked if Mikal resents my traveling so frequently while he has been battling cancer and does it put a strain on the marriage? I have not changed my work schedule throughout this entire ordeal. When Mikal initially told me the news of his cancer, I was heading out of town. I may have been shell-shocked, but I had a job to do. I also railed against being called a caregiver, but I was wrong there.

Truth is when I wasn't at work, I was working on getting Mikal well. As much as I have supported Mikal, he has supported me in what I need to do, which includes leaving him and my family regularly. As sick as he was, he would make sure I left easy. And he was, and is, always a part of my trips—maybe not physically, but he was with me. I document it all for him. And he sends me photos daily. This week it was food pics and selfies in restaurants and other places so I knew he was eating and getting out. Tessa is usually Mikal's companion at dinner. She gives him advice and sympathy when he can't taste his food and needs to drink water just to swallow. It is frustrating for him, but it his job to gain weight.

Mikal doesn't want me to worry. His biggest concern is always me. I motivate his recuperation, work and nightmares. He dreams of leaving me alone if he doesn't survive this. It is a thing called love.

Getting back to normal is hard. The worry is still there. The upcoming PET scan is looming. I have been told this dread will subside with time. I look forward to that. This is a positive time for us. Mikal is getting his energy back and has even done a lot of spring cleaning. He put his fancy turntable next to our bed and is all about the vinyl and his extensive collection. He will be putting up an original piece on that collection in the next few days. It will be as heartrending as you think. We have lived through some incredible adventures together including saving that collection when it was stolen.

Thank you for the many gifts, support and words of encouragement. People say how much these posts mean to them. I love hearing that but the truth is, I get back so much more than I could ever have given. I never thought there was an unworldly reason for Mikal's suffering, and it sure wasn't a blessing, but seeing the sheer goodness of people is definitely an upside. I would have preferred to have come to that realization another way. This is my truth about cancer. We love you.

**Mikal Gilmore:** Elaine summarized well what the first many months were like for us after the news and during treatment. Her travel has never caused strain for us. I do the stuff at home that needs to be done, and Elaine's youngest daughter, Tessa, and I keep each other company. The two of us often have a lot of fun; Tessa is so easy to tease it's like shooting ducks in a barrel. In the last several months I missed driving Elaine to and from the airport. It certainly makes life easier for her when I do, and I like that it affords us time to say goodbye and to reconnect. I'm grateful I can do it again. I noticed on these last trips that, no matter what we talked about, there was an air in our conversation. We simply liked being with each other, talking and laughing. We do anyway, but for some reason these drives focused it more, maybe because there would be days when we couldn't do that.

I have a new therapist and a new psychiatrist at Kaiser. I could tell right away the therapist was going to be good. Her initial questions got to the core of a lot my history and depression. I told her I'd been depressed since I was a child, and I've accepted that I always will be, that when it hits hard now it hits especially hard, face-down time. Yet, as I told her, I also didn't feel depression or fear when I received my diagnosis in September. I wasn't sure why—in the first minutes I felt resignation, as if the illness was a clear consequence for my life. In my mind at the time, I also retired as a writer. I hadn't been able to do much in that way for a year or more, and I accepted that it was over, though I was grateful for all it gave me. In fact, what caught me completely off-guard was that the recovery process has been at times deeply depressing—loss of taste, unpredictable hours of fatigue, bad dreams every damn night. All that is improving, except the very odd dreams.

It wasn't until I talked to Elaine, an hour after my diagnosis, that I realized I'd be doing my best to fight this. As I've said many, many times before, I wouldn't be in good condition, might not be alive, without Elaine's advocacy and love. I know it has been hard for her, the worry, the work, the sleeplessness, living with being viewed as a caregiver. My prayer is that she has overcome that toll as much as possible. I think we are doing pretty good now.

As I type, I'm in a coffee shop nearby a place that gives massages and facials—I think it's called a spa. Those places give me the heebie-jeebies, but to be fair, going into an audio or CD store does the same to Elaine. Anyway, I'm sitting here with a cappuccino and even a cookie with a sense of well-being (though there are some extraordinarily loud Girl Scouts in here). I love my marriage and family, I love the home that Elaine—and Elaine alone—has provided us, and I love being able to work. I've been more productive than any year in many, and I'm presently finishing a story that has been in the works for about five years now, about one of the best subjects possible. Then I move on to another, about one of the best subjects possible. In January, after David Bowie's death, I realized I hadn't retired after all, though I sure rue all these deaths this year.

As Elaine mentioned, next week we are putting up something I've written about my life with my vinyl collection. I've collected notes and passages about this for years and assembled it in the last several days into something twenty-five thousand words long (it will run over the period of a week or two). I'm not sure it's worth that length, but one nice thing about Facebook is that these aren't real pages—they're infinity.

**Mikal Gilmore**

**May 7, 2016**

I never used to appreciate holidays like Mother's Day and Father's Day—I had no children of my own, until Elaine gave me the incredible opportunity to be a stepfather. I've come around about a lot of stuff. Now, when this holiday occurs, the only thing that frustrates me is that I never feel I can give Elaine enough of what she deserves. Happy Mother's Day, baby: thank you for everything, including saving my life these last few months.

*Tell Mama all about it / Tell Mama what you need / Tell Mama / And I'll make everything alright.*

—"Tell Mama," Etta James

**Mikal Gilmore**

**May 8, 2016**

I've been working on assembling a table top stereo in our bedroom. The other night I brought in a couple handfuls of some of my better audio interconnects. I said to Elaine, "Look, here are the good cables."

"What makes then better than regular cables?" she asked.

I stared in disbelief at this woman who is my wife. "Because they said they're better! And I paid more for them!"

She didn't seem properly impressed.

## Elaine Schock
### May 14, 2016
### "As Time Goes By"

Time heals all wounds. OK, that may not be completely true but when it comes to cancer, it does get better. The fear subsides a little. Even though I have no real control of the future, I'm confident that I have done as much as I can for now with numerous options and doctors in my back pocket just in case. That is my nature, I need that plan B. I haven't forgotten how earth shattering the last eight months were or how the diagnosis stunned me. But life is getting back to normal. I look back to where we have been and I can't believe it. Damn, that was hard. I now worry less about the disease killing Mikal and more about my own well-being. There is good and bad to that.

As time goes by, I have given myself permission to feel anger or disappointment as well as success. This is a shock for our relationship. I went from all caring to "Hmm, you did that?" And, although it came back naturally to me, it hit Mikal pretty hard. Because of his family history, arguing has always been a very difficult thing for us. It is almost never worth it and we don't do it that much but there are times when he just pisses me off. We are not the perfect couple.

I was well aware of Mikal's past and how it effects his moods and reactions. I read the book *Shot in the Heart* and I saw the movie. None of this is news to me. And being married to me didn't change that although I hoped it would have made a bigger difference. I didn't figure in the cancer part though. That magnifies everything. When the person I love has stage 4 cancer, my only thought is to make sure he lives and gets through the treatment with as much ease as possible.

The stage of the specific cancer determines how aggressive treatment will be. There is no Stage 5. Both of us were geared toward saving one person's life. That is how a marriage works in sickness, but not in health. And, I am not exactly the passive type. I box for sport. That is my history. We both came with baggage. Every week is different. One problem solved and then another hits. This is all part of cancer—fighting and recovery. We are both working hard these days and keep different hours. We don't see each other as much as we used to. Mikal has to be completely independent. He is writing so prolifically that he put up an original story on Facebook, which is completely brilliant and a long read.

Mikal is still very thin but eating and adding new things to his diet regularly. I came home last night and he was in bed eating a frozen blueberry waffle that he toasted. He is not good with any sort of cooking, including using a microwave or toaster. I'm pretty sure he doesn't know how to turn on the stove. He burned two of the three waffles. Not my idea of a meal or snack, but let's face it, his diet has remained remarkably consistent for most of his life. Mikal's eyes tell the story of his health. They are clear and sky blue. I always look hard at them to see how he is doing.

Marriage is difficult with jealousy, passion and worry, which is why the divorce rate is understandably high, but then there is that lifetime love and commitment that makes it all worth it. I have learned a lot about that lately. After Mikal's deadline for his next story, I have decided we are finally going on that expensive and romantic dinner. Mikal may not be able to eat everything on the menu, but he will find something. It will be just the two of us. I am definitely getting a well-deserved dirty martini. Thank you all for caring, listening and encouraging. Slow and steady, we are making progress even if we take a step or two backwards. We are still going forward.

> **Mikal Gilmore:** The biggest miracles in my life are that Elaine kept me, and then that she saved me. I don't believe I deserved her, and so I am forever grateful. I'm also regretful of careless things I've done and said over the years. I had a lot to learn, through pain and humility, and of course I still do. She has done a tremendous amount for me recently, and I see how exhausting that has been for her, both physically and emotionally.
>
> I understand that Elaine may feel resentment from the past, but I hope that cures with time. Unremitting resentment

can create a mutual wound that that eats away and worsens. Because of how I grew up—in a home where the vocal fights between my parents were vicious, and scared me in ways I've never recovered from, and never will—I don't like anger, mine or anybody else's. It's basic human instinct but that's the problem: Instinct can become reflexive, disproportionate and ruinous. I thought I had rid myself of that when I was dying. Maybe I was wrong.

May Elaine's be the last face I ever see and the last hand I ever touch. Touch in love. I can't bear the thought that either of us might resent the other when that moment comes. Some things are mysteries saved for the last moment, but for now, Elaine and I will savor all that we have, for as long as we have it.

THE END

# ACKNOWLEDGEMENTS

I want to thank all the people who helped me live through these times and not go crazy. First and foremost, my children: Samantha, Preston, Tessa, and Claudia. They are my heart. My sister, Linda Ifri, whose care I left Mikal in when I had to travel. Mikal will never forget the adventure of driving with her. It kept his heart rate up. My brother, Rick Cooper. My mother Adrienne Cooper. Willie Nelson, Annie Nelson, Toby Keith. TK Kimbrell, Meredith Louie, Chip Schutzma, and Teresa Arias: thank you.

I also have to thank the oncology nurses at Kaiser who spent hours on a daily basis with Mikal and gave us the best advice: don't eat strawberries or lettuce when your immune system is compromised by chemo. Thank you also to Dr. Lok, Mikal's oncologist who listened to every question I had and acted on it. Much appreciation must go to Fubar, Muffy, Tuffy, Fluffy, and Foofie (our feline family), and Indie, our rescue dog who died at our lowest point. A big welcome to our newest edition, Ruby.

Obamacare. What can I say? Mikal would have died without it. The cost of treatment for his cancer would have been to great too handle. Timing is everything.

Thank you to Paul Slanskey for his encouragement and brilliant editing to get our posts into something resembling a readable manuscript. To Liz Dubelman, John E. Williams, and every single person who commented on the posts when I started the blog: my best advice was from you. Facebook, regardless of it sins, gave me a platform in which to write and share my thoughts and feelings.

My ever patient book editors, Lisa Wysocky and Cindy Johnson, worked so very hard on our behalf. And our co-publishers, Cindy and Neville Johnson, saw something in my posts they wanted to publish. The American Cancer Society advised me when I had no idea where to turn and was an invaluable help, especially as Mikal's diagnosis of HPV-related cancer was a blindside from a disease I had not known about.

With all my love and respect,
Elaine

I concur with Elaine's acknowledgments of all the good people she mentions. In particular, her family. They were there for me through my treatment, recovery, and beyond. It is obvious that I grew up in a family that, as I once said, should never have existed. I used to dream of having a family of my own—wife, children, home, hearth, pets—to compensate for the abject model I grew up in. In late, 2001 I became romantically involved with Elaine. One night in October of that year, I sat out on the patio of Elaine's home with her—and her children. Elaine casually draped her arm on my knee. It was a gesture to us all, meaning here was a new love and union. Her children had never seen her do that with anybody other than their father. I wondered: Could this be a new family for me? Since then we have been weather- and psyche-tested and are still standing, learning, loving, hurting, and occasionally frightened. We presently look forward to the future more than ever.

As *Stay With Me* was in its final editing, Elaine's mother, Adrienne Cooper, died in her sleep at age eighty-four. Adrienne was always kind and gracious to me, and always made sure to have bottled coke ready for me every time we visited her home. I was grateful. I worried about Adrienne's health in recent years, and she worried about mine. When I was well enough to visit her again, I think it was a genuine surprise. She embraced me with a big smile and loving arms. As Elaine and I were taking our leave that day, I bent over to give a goodbye kiss on her cheek. She said to me, in a quiet voice, "I'm your mother, too." That was not a sentence I'd ever expected to hear again, and it made for a new bloodline to my heart. I replied, "I know. Thank you." Thank you, Adrienne Cooper, as well, for the wonderful family you produced. I will miss you in ways I'm not even prepared for.

I also want to mention Teresa Lynn Pusheck, MD, at Kaiser Permanente in Woodland Hills, California. Dr. Pusheck's specialty is otolaryngology, or head and neck surgery, and she first diagnosed my tumor. My primary physician during treatment was Dr. Lok, whom Elaine also thanked. Doctors Pusheck and Lok, and Elaine, saved my life. They, and President Barack Obama. His pursuit of the Patient Protection and Affordable Care Act—more commonly known as Obamacare—made health insurance accessible and affordable. It was a godsend for me, as well as for millions of other Americans.

I saw many people who benefited from the ACA. One young woman who rode the radiation bus had one of the rarest forms of cancer. She often seemed in deep pain and worry, but also wore goofy hats. On her last day of treatment she met her husband at the hospital. He wore a loving smile and handed his wife a bouquet of flowers, then shook my hand warmly. The woman turned to me and said, "I want to thank you for your kindness. Can I give you a hug?" I often wonder how she fared, and want to express gratitude to all the people I encountered during treatment—and their families, friends, and medical teams.

Thanks also to my Milwaukie High School teachers George Bouthilet in English and humanities, and Grace McGinnis in creative writing. Bouthilet introduced me to a diverse syllabus of literature that has served me throughout my life. McGinnis looked after my mother and brothers at times when I did not. Both are now dead, but I am grateful to have spent meaningful time with each of them.

Music critic Ralph J. Gleason wrote for the San Francisco Chronicle, where he championed—like a prophet—the emerging San Francisco psychedelic music scene. He was an early and crucial proponent of the Jefferson Airplane and Grateful Dead. With Jann Wenner, Gleason founded Rolling Stone in 1967, and contributed to it until his death in 1975. He was the writer who set a path I dreamed of following. He was able to move from Frank Sinatra to Woody Guthrie, from John Coltrane to Bob Dylan, in sentences that demonstrated the connectedness.

The music writer I grew closest to, though, was Paul Nelson. Paul was important in supporting the careers of Dylan, Leonard Cohen, Willie Nelson, Bruce Springsteen, Jackson Browne, Neil Young, the Ramones, the Sex Pistols and Warren Zevon. He also worked at the A&R department of Mercury Records from 1970 to 1975, and briefly served as David Bowie's publicist. I'm not sure why Paul befriended me. Maybe it was our attachment not only to certain music artists, but to the work of Ross Macdonald. Macdonald wrote about buried pasts that never quite stayed buried. Macdonald's writings about family, history and transgression in modern California helped me better understand and accept the place after I moved there in 1977. When Elaine gave me the news that Paul Nelson was found dead in his apartment on the Upper East Side in July 2006 (the death was attributed to heart disease), I sagged down in a chair. A cynosure in my life was gone, and could never be replaced.

Here's to the Rolling Stone editors who advised and helped renew me during my cancer seasons. First, Jann Wenner, the magazine's cofounder and longtime editor. After I moved from Portland to Los Angeles to write for the magazine, I'd drink whiskey at night and take Dalmane—a pill used to treat insomnia. My writing was off and I admitted as much to Jann. He said, "I think it's understandable stage fright. You'll be okay." In time I was. The first subject of intense passion I got to write about was Lou Reed, formerly the leader of the Velvet Underground. I never argued about anybody in music more than the Velvets and Reed. After I developed cancer, Jann wrote me a thoughtful letter, telling me to take it seriously and prepare myself for a hard haul. That meant a lot to me. He'd already frequently sent me kind notes about my articles, and still did after I returned to writing in early 2016. No other reactions have meant so much.

Rolling Stone editors Jason Fine, Nathan Brackett, and Christian Hoard were also reassuring and inspiring. They gave me inspired subjects to write about and edited my verbosity in ways that made for better final pieces. Although unintentional, most of the writing I did during and after cancer was about musicians who suffered and died from cancer: The Ramones (three of four original members), Merle Haggard (ravaged), Leonard Cohen, Gregg Allman, and Aretha Franklin. Not all of the articles were written during my cancer period. Except in a way, they were. Once you've had stage-IV cancer you feel you've been transformed and something about the malady remains resident, even after recovery.

Thank you also to Bruce Springsteen for allowing me to compose liner notes for *The Ties That Bind: The River Collection*. And, thank you to Willie Nelson and Kris Kristofferson, who used my notes in *The Highwaymen Live: American Outlaws*. I also supplied a lengthy biographical essay to Kristofferson's sixteen-disc set, *The Complete Monument & Columbia Album Collection*. Months later I woke up one morning and Elaine said,

"Baby, you've been nominated for a Grammy for the Kristofferson liner notes." The moment didn't seem real. I still remain surprised.

To our many friends on Facebook: Elaine elicited and attracted a community for us there, and from that undertaking *Stay With Me* emerged. This book wouldn't be except for their concern and support. It would be foolhardy to single out even several, because I would be negligent to too many good people. I will, however, like Elaine, pay special thanks to Paul Slansky, who helped Elaine assemble chosen contents into manageable digital form—and his wife, Liz Dubelman. They are friends and dinner partners for life. Also, I want to pay gratitude to Michael Sugg and author Steve Erickson.

Once more, I want to acknowledge Elaine. She was the driving force behind my second life and, as I say, the shaper and motivator of this book. We didn't start off with it in mind, yet she was the one who saw the possibility on the day of my first clean scan, and she is the one who constructed it. As Lou Reed once sang, "The glory of love/The glory of love, might see you through . . . I swear I'd give up the whole thing for you."

Mikal

# ABOUT THE AUTHORS

**Mikal Gilmore** is a prolific author and journalist who specializes in the music industry. Since the 1970s, he has written numerous cover stories and musical critiques for *Rolling Stone*, and his books include *Night Beat: A Shadow History of Rock and Roll*, *Stories Done: Writings on the 1960s and its Discontents*, and *Shot in the Heart*, which is a National Book Critics Circle and L.A. Times Book Prize-winning memoir. The book was adapted to film by HBO. He lives in the Los Angeles area with his wife, Elaine Schock.

**Elaine Schock** is president of the Los Angeles-based public relations firm Shock Ink. A few of her past and present clients include Willie Nelson, David Lee Roth, Gabriel Iglesias, Heart, Billy Joel, Sinead O'Connor, Brooks & Dunn, Annie Lennox, Roberta Flack, Genesis, Trisha Yearwood, Rhonda Vincent, DierksBentley, Michael W. Smith, Phil Vassar, Melissa Ethridge, Henry Rollins, Buddy Guy, Harry Connick Jr., Lucinda Williams, and the American Music Awards. She lives in the Los Angeles area with her husband, Mikal Gilmore.

# BOOK CLUB QUESTIONS

1. Do you feel there is a stigma around HPV cancer? If so, what specifically is it?

2. How would you feel if a partner or spouse was diagnosed with HPV-related cancer?

3. Whose love is stronger, Mikal's or Elaine's? Why?

4. How do Mikal and Elaine try to maintain normalcy during his treatment?

5. Before reading this book, had you heard of HPV cancer? If so, was the information you heard correct?

6. How does Mikal's interest in music help him through his treatment?

7. What keeps Elaine focused and strong?

8. If you were diagnosed with HPV cancer, would you tell the world, or keep it more private?

9. What would you have liked to hear more of in their story? Less of?

10. What makes Mikal and Elaine's relationship so connected?

11. Other than music and Elaine, who and what else helped Mikal stay positive during his treatment?

12. Has *Stay With Me* changed your views on cancer, and specifically HPV cancer? If so, how?

## IF YOU ENJOYED THIS BOOK, YOU MAY ALSO ENJOY THESE, AND OTHER, AWARD-WINNING BOOKS FROM COOL TITLES.

Learn more at CoolTitles.com or
fulfillment@cooltitles.com

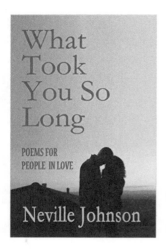

*What Took You So Long*

Here, 167 poems and rhymes honor the magic and mystery of romantic love, and then celebrate what happens when it all goes well. These poems were all written for the author's wife, but they apply to everyone who is in a relationship, and to everyone who is in love. Each of these funny, sweet, quirky, and heartwarming poems were written in love, and about love. Don't be surprised about the impact they make, because love makes life worth living.

From *Midwest Book Review*: If you only have time in your life for just one book of poetry, or as a librarian if you only have the budget to add one more book of poetry to your collection, then make it *What Took You So Long: Poems for People in Love*—and you'll never regret it.

*Dreams*

Emerald McGinty experiences dreams and visions and is diagnosed with schizophrenia. When she stumbles upon a trail of hidden secrets, her father decides to send her away to a special clinic. She flees her home to a safe haven in the Colorado Rockies where she meets a rancher who suggests he recognizes the voice she hears. Battered by a relentless storm of strange encounters, Emerald struggles to discover love, and her true reality.

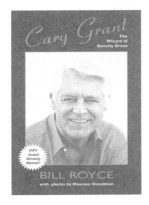

### Cary Grant: the Wizard of Beverly Grove

The most candid portrait of the legendary film actor that fans will ever read, packed with new information about his career and life, and told with the honesty only a true intimate could provide. When Bill Royce met Cary Grant, he was a twenty-five-year-old fan magazine editor and the film star was nearly seventy. As these two men from different generations forged a friendship that lasted until Cary's death, they found both had impoverished, and brutal childhoods. With true frankness, they stripped away the walls each built to survive. To learn the truth about Bill's abusive past, Cary spared no detail about his own painful childhood. By opening up his home, and his heart, Cary revealed facts behind the myths that haunted his life. Glimpses into Cary's life include details of his alcoholic father and mentally disturbed mother; his early years in New York where Cole Porter, Noel Coward, and others groomed an awkward young Englishman into a worldly matinee idol; his secret fears for his daughter, Jennifer; the lowdown on his leading ladies; a day when Cary was attacked by Minnie Mouse; a visit with Elvis Presley where he tells Cary about aliens; and Cary's crush on black movie actress, Pam Grier. This is an honest, compassionate book for fans, for all who have kept secrets, and for survivors of abusive childhoods. Poignant and compelling, this book shows how a difficult childhood can be changed into a loving and rewarding future.

### Woodenisms

John Wooden was arguably the greatest coach, the greatest leader, of all time. These Woodenisms, a collection of his wisdom and sayings, will inspire, motivate, and prepare you for any challenge you face. Woodensims provide good common sense, and will assist you in being a leader and a team player, and will also give you strength to carry on in whatever you do. Excellent gift book, or source of daily motivation.

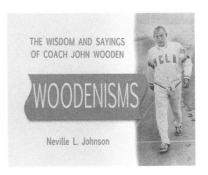